TIANA TEMPLEMAN

ABSOLUTELY Faking IT

BANTAM
SYDNEY • AUCKLAND • TORONTO • NEW YORK • LONDON

Note: All prices referred to are in Australian dollars unless otherwise specified.

ABSOLUTELY FAKING IT
A BANTAM BOOK

First published in Australia and New Zealand in 2006
by Bantam

National Library of Australia
Cataloguing-in-Publication Entry

Templeman, Tiana.
   Absolutely faking it.

   ISBN 1 86325 464 1.
   ISBN 9 78186325 4649.

   1. Templeman, Tiana – Travels. 2. Voyages and travels –
   Anecdotes. I. Title.

910.4

Transworld Publishers,
a division of Random House Australia Pty Ltd
20 Alfred Street, Milsons Point, NSW 2061
http://www.randomhouse.com.au

Random House New Zealand Limited
18 Poland Road, Glenfield, Auckland

Transworld Publishers,
a division of The Random House Group Ltd
61–63 Uxbridge Road, Ealing, London W5 5SA

Random House Inc
1745 Broadway, New York, New York 10036

Cover design by Blue Cork Design
Cover images courtesy Australian Picture Library
Typeset by Midland Typesetters, Australia
Printed and bound by Griffin Press, Netley, South Australia

10 9 8 7 6 5 4 3 2 1

Tiana Templeman was born in Brisbane in 1969. After travelling overseas for the first time in 1988, she returned to Australia and worked as a personal assistant in various organisations to finance further trips.

In between working and gallivanting around the world, Tiana got married in 1993, was named Brisbane Secretary of the Year in 1999 and eventually changed careers. She now works for one of the big four accounting firms as a corporate trainer, specialising in IT.

When not writing or working, Tiana can usually be found continuing her quest for the best cup of coffee in the world.

Absolutely Faking It is her first book.

For trip photos and more information, visit
www.tianatempleman.com

For Trevor and Tex,
with love

CONTENTS

PROLOGUE

'Good afternoon. My name is Ana and I am your butler.'

The woman standing before me in the doorway is stunning. She executes a small formal bow and enters the suite, where she places two delicate crystal champagne flutes on the coffee table. Ana smiles as she expertly rearranges the two dozen crimson roses in the vase beside them and pauses briefly to inhale their sweet scent.

'These are my favourites. They are so lovely, don't you think?' she says in English tinged with a strong Spanish accent.

We nod dumbly. This is not what I expected. Butlers are supposed to be silver-haired gents the same age as my dad, not Argentinean women who look like supermodels. This woman's waistcoat and black tails should look ridiculous, but somehow they don't. I can understand why my husband, Trevor, is watching her with the passionate fascination he usually reserves for rich chocolate desserts.

We've only been in our suite at the five-star Alvear Palace Hotel in Buenos Aires for a few minutes, but one thing is already clear – this is going to be no ordinary holiday. As I settle back against the plump satin cushions on the elegant settee, Trevor squeezes my hand and grins, motioning discreetly for me to look around the room. I haven't taken in any of its details yet, but now I notice the heavy Louis XVI-style furniture, upholstered with soft, rich velvet.

At the sound of ice cubes shifting against the silver ice bucket, I turn back to watch Ana lift out the bottle of French champagne and flick open the neatly folded white cloth hanging over her left arm. She wipes beads of moisture from the bottle's surface in one fluid motion before approaching the couch.

'May I open this for you now?' she asks, presenting the bottle for our approval.

'Only if it's free,' I think, but I don't say it. Trevor nods happily to Ana and, after a brief hesitation, so do I.

She grasps the cork in one hand and the base of the bottle in the other, turning it expertly so the cork eases out with a contented sigh. Ana pours the delicate salmon-pink champagne and, with another small bow, hands us a glass each.

'Welcome to Buenos Aires and the Alvear Palace Hotel. Please don't hesitate to call if I can assist you in any way.'

Like any male with a pulse, I am sure Trevor can think of a few things Ana could do for him already. The fact our butler is a gorgeous woman has come as a complete surprise – almost as much of a surprise as how we've come to be at the Alvear Palace Hotel in the first place.

1
I SHOULD BE SO LUCKY

'LOOK AT THIS,' Trevor says, dumping plastic bags of groceries onto the kitchen bench. He hands me a *Vogue Entertaining and Travel* magazine opened to a page headed 'Win the Trip of a Lifetime'.

A competition invites readers to send in a photograph taken from any hotel room in the world and tell the story behind it for a chance to win three nights' suite accommodation at ten hotels around the world, plus $15,000 worth of travel expenses. The prize is valued at more than $65,000 and the hotels are members of the Leading Hotels of the World group, an exclusive organisation that only admits the best five-star hotels. These places are the *crème de la crème* and just looking at the pictures is enough to make me drool.

I read about the competition and smile. There is no need to ask which photograph Trevor has in mind or which story we should submit for our entry. I still remember clearly the disastrous day we spent travelling to the tiny town of Hallstadt in Austria on our last overseas trip, when one mishap after another had us arriving long after dark, exhausted and with nowhere to stay. When we finally found a hotel with a light on and were shown to a tiny room with a dodgy shared bathroom, the last thing we cared about was whether we had a room with a view. This made the sight that greeted us the next morning even more amazing. We awoke to the sound of nuns singing at a nearby church and Trevor opened our shutters to reveal the sun rising over a shimmering lake ringed by majestic mountains, with Hallstadt silhouetted by its orange glow. He grabbed his camera and captured the image a few seconds before the light changed.

I sit down at the kitchen table and begin drafting our entry, playing around with the words and trying my best to describe what happened on that trip, five years ago.

By the time I've finalised our story and combined the entry form with a print of Trevor's photograph, the entry has taken me hours to prepare, but I think the effort is worth it, even if Trevor isn't convinced.

'You used the enlargement from the back of our photo album!' he cries when I show him my handiwork.

'But it's a huge prize,' I say, 'and someone's got to win it!'

'Probably the Managing Director's daughter,' Trevor grumbles.

Several months later, we are returning from a backpacking trip around Australia when I remember the competition.

While we are waiting to board our flight back home to Brisbane from Uluru, I flick through the latest *Vogue Entertaining and Travel* at an airport newsagency.

'The winner's name is meant to be in this edition,' I say to Trevor, 'but I can't find it.' We agree they must still be judging the entries and forget all about it.

On Monday morning I reluctantly return to the office. Trevor doesn't have to go back to work until Tuesday – something I am very jealous about. I don't hate my job, but I don't want to be a personal assistant anymore, especially since I've started working as a part-time trainer at the large accounting firm I work for. They were keen when I suggested qualifying as a trainer so they didn't have to fly people up from down south, but I am still only doing it part-time along with my secretarial job. Our trip around Australia has given me time to think and I've decided to pour my energy into turning the training role into a full-time position.

But when I walk into the office, the first piece of news I receive doesn't bode well for my plans. Colleen, the secretary who was filling in for me while I was away, has quit, which means I'll have to do two jobs until they find a replacement. I check my computer to see if she has sent me an email about any outstanding work and sigh as the number '217' appears next to my Inbox.

I scan the screen until I find Colleen's message, but when I get to the last few lines I suddenly forget about the urgent things I am supposed to be doing.

'. . . *and a guy from Leading Hotels in Singapore has been trying to get in touch to say you won a competition. I said you were on holidays so he is going to call back this morning to give you the details.'*

I stare at the screen, reading the words over and over as if that will make them seem more real. Have we *really* won? My hands are shaking as I flip through the files on my desk and try to concentrate, but it is hopeless. I can hardly put two thoughts together. There are so many questions spinning around in my head that I feel dizzy and my stomach is churning like a washing machine. On autopilot, I look through the rest of my emails, reading and deleting, reading and deleting. All I think about is the impending phone call from the Leading Hotels of the World.

By the time an international number flashes up on my phone just before lunchtime, it is all I can do not to grab the receiver and scream 'Have we won?' It is lucky I don't as the Vice President himself is on the line.

His name is Mark Greedy, and when he hears I've been backpacking for the last month, he laughs.

'Well, the prize you've won is definitely not back-packing,' he tells me. 'You and one other person will be staying at ten of the best hotels in the world. Breakfast is included at a few of the places and I think there's a dinner in there as well, but what you get at each individual hotel depends on what they were prepared to offer in exchange for being included in the promotion. There are some fabulous properties – you've got the New York Palace, the Peninsula in Hong Kong–'

I'm so excited I interrupt him. 'I don't know what to say except *thank you so much*. You can't imagine what winning a competition like this means to me – my husband and I live to travel.'

I can almost hear Mark smiling through the phone. He tells me his PA will fax a list of exactly what we've won so I can tell Trevor, and I wait in the mailroom and read the name of each hotel as the paper rolls slowly out of the fax machine. By the time I have the whole fax in my hands, they are shaking so much I can hardly dial Trevor's number.

'Hi there,' he says. 'How's your first day back – bad as always?'

Judging by the muzak warbling in the background, I've called while he is in the supermarket.

'Umm – no, not really. Do you remember that competition we entered in *Vogue Entertaining and Travel*?'

'The one with the hotels?'

'Yeah, that's it. Well . . . we won.'

'Won what? One of the consolation prizes?'

'There *were* no consolation prizes.'

'You're kidding!' There is silence, then I hear a gasp followed by lots of thumping.

'Trevor, are you okay?'

He must be because I can hear him laughing.

'I'm fine, but the cereal display has seen better days.'

That night we go out for a celebratory dinner and begin planning our trip. Although the prize originally included

$15,000 for travel expenses, Leading Hotels of the World have since discovered there will be unfavourable tax implications for them if they give us money, so they have instead offered to pay for our around-the-world economy-class airfares and let us use the balance as credit for accommodation at two extra Leading Hotels of our choice. It's not the hard currency we were hoping for, but staying at a couple more five-star hotels isn't exactly a hardship.

We quickly decide it would be a waste not to add some extra destinations along the way, especially as Trevor can take long service leave and I am entitled to a leave of absence from work. This means we'll have jobs to come back to, which is a good thing considering how much the trip is going to cost.

The toughest part of planning the trip is agreeing on destinations. 'Venice? Why would you want to go there?' Trevor says with a derisive snort. 'Venice is full of nothing but tourists. And it smells.'

'Venice does not smell!' I counter.

'Ha! You didn't say it wasn't touristy though, did you?'

He has a point but I still want to visit Venice and am also convinced it is the perfect place to use some of our hotel credit – even when I see the prices of the Venice hotels in the Leading Hotels of the World directory. Most of them don't even give a price – it just says 'rates available on request'.

This battle is one I end up winning, but there are so many others that we have to come up with a way to stop the arguments. In the end we agree that each of us can choose two add-on destinations and one of the extra five-star hotels but the rest of our itinerary has to be mutually agreed. This is the fairest option but when I look at some of the places on Trevor's wish list, I regret agreeing to his final rule: neither of us can veto any destination chosen by the other person.

As usual, Trevor and I have very different opinions on where we should go. He is more adventurous and past trips saw us in places like Hungary and the Czech Republic before they became popular destinations for Australian travellers, whereas I favour more popular countries like France, but like to stay in tucked-away places most tourists have never heard of. Our different approaches to trip planning have made for some memorable holidays and, despite the odd argument, we enjoy the planning almost as much as the holiday itself.

In fact, travel has been a constant topic of conversation every since we met. Our first (blind) date at a coffee shop was spent discussing upcoming trips – Canada for me and Europe for Trevor – but things didn't work out quite as planned. Less than three weeks later Trevor and I were engaged, with his trip savings paying for the engagement ring and my holiday money covering the cost of our wedding. We didn't see any point in waiting to get married and decided to travel together as much as possible once we did. So far we've explored eastern and western Europe, tripped around the South Pacific and seen a large part of Australia.

The list of places we've visited is about to grow considerably thanks to our win, but this trip will be a change from all the others. Trevor and I usually travel as backpackers, which means past holidays have involved one-star hotels in dubious neighbourhoods, not places like the Hôtel Ritz Paris.

'Make sure you polish your thongs,' our friends laugh at the party Trevor and I throw to celebrate our win. They are a huge part of our lives and we'll miss them while we are away.

Over the next three months, Trevor and I scour every travel guide we can find and try to decide where else to visit in addition to the countries where we have prize hotels. The around-the-world airfares mean we are spoilt for choice but now we aren't getting any spending money from the prize, our budget is extremely tight.

I buy a second-hand 1970s *Meals on a Budget* cookbook and at night we pore over hotel brochures filled with chandeliers, champagne buckets and marble bathrooms stocked with Chanel toiletries while we eat bowls of 'Thrifty Pasta Bake'. It is hard to even imagine what staying in such luxury will be like. We aren't cultural Neanderthals, but I start to wonder how we'll cope in accommodation where everything is geared to those with champagne tastes, not a beer budget. In a magazine article I read about one of our prize hotels, the writer orders a hot drink from room service because there are no tea and coffee making facilities in her room. The cup of coffee is delivered by a white-gloved waiter carrying a full silver-service tea tray and costs the equivalent of our daily food budget.

'It must be too taxing for rich people to boil a kettle,' Trevor says.

We are looking forward to the luxury associated with our prize, but are also apprehensive about fitting in with the image these hotels portray. The accommodation will mostly be free, but we'll still be on our usual shoestring budget when it comes to everything else. Will the staff be snobbish and give us poor service because we aren't their usual clientele? Neither of us owns any designer-label clothes and our trusty backpacks are black and battered and nothing like the monogrammed luggage I see in the brochures' photographs.

'How am I expected to pack clothing suitable for both the Hôtel Ritz Paris and backpacking through Syria?' I lament. Glossy magazines make it sound easy to put together a simple, yet stylish, travel wardrobe but in reality it is a struggle. I always feel more at ease knowing I am appropriately dressed, and once spent an evening feeling desperately uncomfortable in jeans and a t-shirt when Trevor surprised me on a trip by booking a table for two at one of Melbourne's best restaurants. The experience isn't one I am keen to repeat, especially not somewhere like the Ritz.

I make it my mission as a well-travelled woman to assemble the perfect wardrobe to cover the five months we'll be away and spend ages poring over our itinerary trying to work out what to pack. I start with a little black dress and work backwards, settling on shorts and a few t-shirts for hiking, a smart pair of jeans, a straight skirt and an assortment of stretch knit tops to wear with an old black work jacket for what I hope will be a casual, yet chic, look. I am confident my cunningly assembled ensemble will look quite dressy with a bit of make-up and be suitable for any occasion.

After six months' planning, our trip is slowly coming together and we are becoming more and more excited, but then something changes the world – September 11. Trevor and I are shocked and saddened by what happens and lots of people think we are crazy to go ahead as planned. Our departure date is less than six months away and even the Leading Hotels of the World are concerned, offering us an alternative hotel if we no longer want to go to New York.

But Trevor and I have already made our decision. We'll proceed as planned unless the Australian Government issues an official warning declaring one of our destinations a no-go zone and even if that happens we'll only modify our itinerary.

'The world's a big place,' we reassure everyone. 'We'd have to be extremely unlucky to be in the wrong spot at the wrong time.'

No one looks convinced, but nothing they say can change our minds.

The itinerary for our trip ends up including every continent except Africa and Antarctica and is a logistical nightmare as the Leading Hotels of the World need all our dates in advance so they can make our bookings. These can't be changed once we are on the road, so it is imperative our ground and air transport is coordinated so we don't miss connections and arrive late. Trevor suggests I do the logistical stuff as I am better at organising things, but it is a huge responsibility and has to be carefully costed. Our budget is much tighter than we'd anticipated – something I hadn't thought possible – but it is too late to cut back our itinerary so this trip will be done on even more of a shoestring than usual.

My secretarial experience comes in handy during the three months before we leave as I prepare budgeting spreadsheets and keep detailed notes about our arrangements. Our 'trip file' grows to two lever-arch folders and contains everything from Croatian ferry timetables to a Paris restaurant review clipped from a local newspaper. The information needs to be pared down to fit in the document wallet that is coming with us, but for now I have enough to think about.

2

UNDER THE SOUTHERN CROSS

'COME ON, OLD GIRL,' the lady beside me yells into the wind, 'you can do it!'

The sky is a brilliant blue and the sun's rays glint off the harbour so brightly I have to squint. It is Australia Day and Trevor and I are standing on the Sydney Harbour Bridge, watching four ferries powering towards the finish line of the traditional Australia Day Ferry Race. Their green and cream paintwork is covered with balloons and streamers and their decks are packed with people yelling and cheering. Hundreds of spectator craft fill the water, jockeying for position. People in boats no bigger than dinghies bob around crazily as the wake from the mighty ferries ripples across the harbour.

The race is nearly over, but the finish is the most exciting part. After leaving Circular Quay, the ferries sped into the harbour and around Shark Island and are now trying to claim line honours by being the first under Sydney Harbour Bridge. All of them churn along at full speed and it is going to be close, but one of the ferries is slowly pulling away. It is covered in red and white bunting and the passengers on its decks are waving to everyone up on the bridge. Plastic Australian flags flutter around our heads as Trevor grabs my arm and we join in the chant of 'Go, go, go!' as the winning ferry charges underneath where we are standing. Her horn gives one long, triumphant blast and the crowd erupts into cheers and whistles as the rest of the boats cross the line a few seconds behind.

'Sydney Harbour has to be the best place in the world to spend Australia Day,' Trevor says as we walk back through the historical Rocks area towards the Observatory Hotel.

Our official departure date is still two months away but we've been forced to take our first prize hotel as a stand-alone trip. Our around-the-world airfares mean we can see the world, but making more than one extra stop in Australia before we do so incurs a huge surcharge. Flights between Brisbane and Sydney are cheap and only take an hour, so we decide to use our three nights at the Observatory Hotel as an introduction to what awaits us on the big trip ahead.

The hotel is named after the nearby Observatory Hill, where some of the first astronomical photographs in the world were taken. Air pollution and city lights saw the Sydney Observatory building converted to a museum in 1982, but the hill's sweeping views of Sydney harbour remain unchanged.

'Perfect for a picnic,' the hotel concierge suggested.

Trevor and I have only been guests here for a day, but we are already impressed. The Observatory Hotel was built in 1993 but, because it is located in the Rocks, it was skilfully designed to blend in with the older surrounding buildings. Its interior, filled with antiques and original artworks, is reminiscent of a 19th-century colonial mansion and the cream marble floor and iron-balustraded staircase in the foyer evoke the elegance of days gone by.

'I'm glad we brought our best clothes,' Trevor whispers as we walk towards the lifts.

And we'd better enjoy them while we can, I think to myself. Each of us will only be taking one dressy outfit on our big trip, not the five or six we've packed for just three days in Sydney.

The first of the Leading Hotels of the World isn't as intimidating as I expected. The staff are professional without being stuffy and we were shown to our room by a guy who grew up in Brisbane. Chatting to him put us instantly at ease and the room is lovely.

'You did well to get this suite,' he said as he showed Trevor and I around before leading us through a set of French doors and out onto a balcony. 'The Australia Day fireworks will look brilliant from here tomorrow night.'

Back inside our room, I admired the etchings of old Sydney buildings on the walls and had a look around. The large sofa and low wooden coffee table must be reproduction antiques, but would look at home in any wealthy colonial's lounge room. As soon as the porter left, we went down to the hotel's famous basement-level pool to see what the guidebooks had been raving about.

'I can't find the Southern Cross yet,' Trevor said as he floated on his back, 'but I know it's there.'

Fibre optic lighting imbedded in the pool area's midnight blue ceiling created a realistic representation of the Southern Hemisphere's night sky and 'stars' twinkled and winked just like the real thing.

'We won't be able to see this for most of our trip,' he mused. 'I wonder what the stars in Syria will look like.'

That night we sit on the balcony sipping celebratory champagne we bought from a bottle shop as the lights of Darling Harbour, a waterside area known for its restaurants, sparkle prettily and boats cruise by on the water. There isn't much between us and the harbour except historical townhouses – and a super freighter berthed at the old wharves right in front of our hotel.

'They didn't show *that* in the brochure,' Trevor says as we watch cars being unloaded under the harsh glare of the wharves' lights. Some guests might be less than pleased when they notice the wharves, but the docks are a long way from the hotel and, anyway, I like watching what is going on down there.

'It says here that the wharves have been there since the 1800s,' Trevor says, reading a brochure on the Rocks that he finds in our room. 'Can you imagine what this area was like back then?'

I can and am glad we weren't around. The Rocks

started as a seedy portside area known for its drunks, whores and bashings and although there were originally some wealthy residents, the majority of them were gone by the late 1800s, driven away by the area's violence and the stench of its streets. Things got so bad that the government was eventually forced to buy the Rocks for more than a million pounds to protect public health. They cleaned it up a bit, but most of their time and money was spent on demolition to make way for projects like the Sydney Harbour Bridge.

When the government decided to clear the area completely, the locals refused to go and were joined by activists and conservationists who demanded the historical area be preserved. Thankfully, the residents prevailed and the government formed the Sydney Cove Authority to oversee the area's management. The once dangerous alleys and cobbled lanes are now filled with charming restored buildings and the closest thing to robbery is the prices being charged in the gift shops.

Trevor unwraps the ham and cheese baguettes we picked up at a sandwich bar earlier this afternoon, hands one to me and refills my glass. Our meal isn't officially room service, but it still feels luxurious sipping champagne and eating dinner while we watch the boats sailing by.

'I know it's only our first night, but how do you feel about the five-star experience so far?' I ask.

'Terrible,' Trevor grins, draining his glass. 'I don't know if I'll be able to take much more of this.'

Neither of us can believe the world we've stumbled into. A maid knocks on the door to ask if we'd like our bed turned down and someone comes by to check if we want fresh towels, even though we only checked in this morning. However, it is the Observatory's doorman who has impressed us the most.

'Have a pleasant day, Mr and Mrs Templeman,' he said as we walked outside this afternoon.

'They even learn your name,' Trevor said in awe.

Despite the fact the Observatory Hotel has 100 rooms, all guests receive similar treatment and the friendly welcome the hotel extends to overseas visitors makes me proud to be Australian.

The next morning we eat the room-service breakfast included in our prize and walk the ten minutes to the Harbour Bridge so we can watch the ferry race. Timing our trip to coincide with Australia Day means there is plenty of free entertainment and after the race we walk back to the hotel to freshen up, then spend the afternoon at a concert in the park before stopping at a sausage sizzle for dinner.

'This five-star stay is hardly costing us a cent,' Trevor says happily, wiping tomato sauce from his chin with a paper napkin.

Trevor is in an unusually quiet mood as we sit out on our balcony waiting for the fireworks to start later that night.

'What's on your mind?' I ask.

'I've been thinking about having a photography exhibition when we get back from our big trip,' he says. 'What do you reckon?' He looks excited and terrified at the same time.

'It's a brilliant idea!' I smile and reach over to hug Trevor as he explains his plans for 'Taking the World', an exhibition of travel photography from around the globe.

As fireworks shoot into the sky, we lean against the balcony, inhaling the sharp smell of gunpowder and staring at the inky black sky. This hotel stay is so different from anything we've done in the past. After years of making do with whatever we could afford, staying somewhere like the Observatory feels like a dream come true.

The next day we have a picnic lunch on top of Observatory Hill, then loll around in the pool all afternoon.

'This makes a change from our usual holidays,' Trevor laughs. 'We're usually desperate to get *out* of our hotel, not stay in it.'

We've been prepared to look at pretty well anything on previous Sydney trips, as long as it doesn't involve spending more time than necessary in our dodgy accommodation.

Our stay at the Observatory makes a wonderful change, although it is over too soon and we return to Brisbane to begin final preparations for what *Vogue* billed as 'The Trip of a Lifetime'.

After we get back from Sydney, the departure date comes around surprisingly quickly. Our flight leaves in the evening and Trevor takes the day off but I'm keen to save my precious annual leave, so I spend my day at the last place anyone would expect – work. It is a strange feeling. Nothing is different from the day before and everyone is doing the same old thing, except me.

'Bet you can't wait to get on that plane,' colleagues say.

'Not long now . . .'

'Are you excited?'

I say yes, but it is the answer they want and expect rather than the truth. Despite our wonderful stay at the Observatory Hotel, some of the anticipation I've been feeling has been replaced by fear of the unknown. We have been planning this trip for so long and have invested so much time in it – not to mention money – what if it is a disappointment?

I spend my morning in the office tidying up loose ends and giving Lynda, my colleague-turned-housesitter, some last-minute tips before handing over our keys. The nine-to-five grind isn't something I'll miss, but it's a different story when it comes to the people I work with. As I go from floor to floor to say goodbye or hand in paperwork, it really hits home how much I am going to miss everyone in Australia.

It is only when I meet Trevor on the train to the airport that I begin getting really excited, although commencing such a grand journey on a domestic flight feels strange. Leaving for previous overseas trips meant browsing in duty-free stores and seeing names like

London, Singapore and Osaka on the departures board – not flying two hours to Melbourne. Trevor and I want our three-night experience at each Leading Hotel of the World to last as long as possible, so we are paying for a night's cheap accommodation and checking into our prize hotel early tomorrow.

Arriving in Melbourne, we take a taxi to the place I booked on the Internet for our first night. The run-down motel squats, toad-like, on its gravel forecourt and fluorescent lights covered in insect droppings flicker over the door leading to reception.

'Have you already paid for this?' Trevor asks tactfully.

'It looked different on the website,' I tell him. 'I'm really sorry.'

It is the truth, but the fact he is being so gracious only makes me feel worse. Trevor is a true romantic and always puts a lot of effort into organising something special. Someone who cooks dinners for two and buys flowers for his wife 'just because' wouldn't have chosen a 1970s airport motel for the first night of our exciting adventure. The unattractive room kills off any thoughts of romance and the roaring traffic on the busy main road outside ensures we get the early start we're after.

'Do you remember what I said about the Windsor last time we were here?' Trevor asks as our taxi stops at some traffic lights on the way to our prize hotel the next morning.

His words come back to me as our taxi pulls up outside

the grand hotel and I look at its five-storey, balcony-draped facade. The downmarket accommodation we stayed at on our last trip was located surprisingly close to the Windsor and we have walked past it many times. 'Why don't we stay there instead?' Trevor would joke.

The Windsor Hotel – sometimes known as 'The Duchess of Spring Street'– is one of Australia's original 'Grand Hotels' and has a fascinating history, not to mention a fine pedigree. It was considered in the same league as the Savoy in London, the Waldorf-Astoria in New York and the Hôtel Ritz Paris when it opened in 1883 and famous visitors included Sir Laurence Olivier, Sir Robert Helpmann, Gregory Peck, Vivien Leigh and Sir Robert Menzies, Australia's longest serving Prime Minister, who virtually lived in Suite 306.

An elderly doorman rushes down the wide stone steps to open the taxi door and summons a porter to take care of our luggage.

'Welcome to the Windsor, sir, madam,' he says, looking at each of us in turn and doffing his top hat. 'Reception is through the doors and to your right.'

I am smiling as we walk into a foyer surrounded by tall arched windows topped with delicate leadlighting. A grand staircase reaches from the ground floor to the upper reaches of the hotel and large vases of fresh flowers decorate the lobby.

The Windsor is formal in an old-fashioned kind of way, but the service is unaffected and courteous and I feel at ease despite the grand surroundings. When the lift doors open and the porter leads us through a rabbit warren of wallpapered corridors, our lengthy ramble takes us back in time.

'This is your room,' the porter says and opens the door to a suite overlooking the roofs of the trams outside. It is atmospheric, albeit a little noisy. The room smells of furniture polish and is painted a soft white with eggshell blue cornices. It is filled with heavy reproduction furniture, which suits the Victorian era of the hotel but makes the suite feel a lot smaller than it is. Even at first glance it's obvious the furnishings have seen better days.

The Windsor is still charming, but I try not to notice the chunk of plaster dangling precariously beside one of the skirting boards, or the wardrobe door that keeps springing open. Instead of exuding opulence and tasteful decadence, our suite looks a little tired and worn.

The longer we remain at the Windsor, the more I warm to the hotel's shabby elegance, but it isn't a patch on our first prize hotel – except for the staff. Everyone from the maids to the managers wears a smile and our expectations are always exceeded. When I ask for an extra blanket, a selection arrives for me to choose from and Trevor is given a whole box of handmade chocolates by the housekeeper turning down the bed, instead of the couple more he requests. 'The Duchess of Spring Street' could do with a facelift, but she is still a classy dame.

Trevor and I spend our time walking beside the Yarra River, picnicking in Fitzroy Gardens and riding around on the trams, which are a novelty as we only have buses and trains in Brisbane.

'And they're convenient,' Trevor jokes as the trams outside clang their bells noisily. There is a busy stop right below our window.

It is coming into autumn and the air is crisp and cold, especially in the morning when Melbourne's streets are filled with bustling commuters on their way to work. Their suits are of the latest cut and most of them have scarves wrapped around their necks. I can't decide whether it is because of the climate or the fashion, but Melbourne always reminds me of Europe.

'It won't feel like we've really started our holiday until you and I leave Australia,' Trevor says on our last night at the Windsor.

He's right but I can imagine how nervous we'd have been starting somewhere like the Dorchester or the Hôtel Ritz Paris first up.

We have dinner at a café before returning to the hotel to finish packing for our early morning flight to New Zealand. We've been there before, but this time we'll be staying at Huka Lodge, a Leading Hotel of the World.

'Did you know the Queen stays at Huka Lodge for a few days R and R whenever she visits New Zealand?' Trevor says.

'Nice of her to test drive it for us.'

3

CATCHING CHOCOLATE TROUT

HUKA LODGE'S VISITORS' book is filled with some of the most well known, rich and powerful people in the world and it became one of our most anticipated prize hotels after Trevor and I read an article about it in a glossy travel magazine. There were stunning photographs of lounge suites arranged around cosy log fires, dining tables groaning with gourmet food and the Lodge's seven hectares of private grounds, but it was something else that caught our eye.

'There's a complimentary cocktail hour every evening where guests can mix and mingle,' Trevor read out excitedly, 'plus breakfast and dinner are included in the room rate.'

This means we'll be able to enjoy the full five-star experience without worrying about our budget and despite the Lodge's world class reputation, it encourages guests to dress down, so we won't have to worry about our lack of fancy clothes either.

* * *

We fly from Melbourne to Auckland and pick up a hire car for the three hour drive to Taupo, the town closest to Huka Lodge. My suggestion to save money by spending our first night at another motel isn't enthusiastically received and Trevor pre-books a B&B from an accommodation guide at Auckland airport.

The 'separate guest wing' promised in the brochure is anything but as we have to walk through our hosts' bathroom to get in and out of our room. The creepy host couple lurk outside it to check we are comfortable (and not wearing our shoes indoors or messing up the room) and they stay up late with the television blaring before taking long and very noisy showers in the shared bathroom.

Any remaining guilt I've been harbouring about my poor choice of accommodation in Melbourne is gone by the following morning as Trevor's choice of B&B makes my horrible motel look good. 'We're saved,' Trevor whispers when our taxi arrives just after 9 o'clock.

After a short drive through the outskirts of Taupo, we arrive at the top of a driveway where a wooden gate with 'No Trespassing – Lodge Guests Only' written on it has been swung open in preparation for our arrival. The taxi drives towards a building surrounded by enormous trees that look as if they've been there forever. I can smell pine needles and a hint of rain in the air as we climb out of the taxi and are shown into the sitting room I saw in the magazine. It is much bigger than it looked in the photograph and attractive coffee table books have been artfully arranged beside each sofa. Trevor and I flick through them while our hostess goes outside to see to our baggage.

At first glance, Huka Lodge feels more like a (very rich) friend's place than a hotel. The furnishings are more cosy than elegant and it is filled with little touches that subconsciously invite you to relax. A half-completed game of chess has been left on a side table and the cushions scattered over the day bed make me want to curl up on it with a book. I walk over to one of the large windows overlooking the Waikato River, which follows the Lodge grounds. A long rolling lawn slopes down to the river's edge, less than 50 metres away, and the water flowing past is a cool ice blue.

'The grass is so green it's almost glowing,' I say to Trevor as he joins me by the window.

We watch the river tumbling over the tiny rapids until our hostess returns with some guest registration forms and helps us fill them out. Then she almost breaks Trevor's heart.

'There's nothing better than a hot breakfast on a morning like this,' she says brightly. 'Come through and I'll get you some menus.'

Trevor and I exchange mournful looks as we follow her into the sunlit dining room. As we weren't officially due to commence our stay until the check-in time of 2 pm this afternoon, the two of us downed rubbery scrambled eggs, watery coffee and cold toast at the B&B. Trevor now squeezes in freshly cooked pancakes with vanilla poached peaches but I can't manage more than a cappuccino.

There are only two other couples at breakfast and both of them are at least 20 years older than us. They smile and nod when we walk in and later one couple stops by to say hello.

'We could have stayed here forever,' the woman says. 'You'll have a wonderful time.'

They are both casually dressed in slacks and polo shirts, but their air of comfortable prosperity is something only plenty of money can buy.

Trevor and I have been worried about fitting in at Huka Lodge, where mixing and mingling is encouraged and everyone is rich. Perhaps naively, we assumed the other guests would be wealthy high fliers who talk about nothing but money and brag about their Ferraris, but it isn't like that at all. Our casual clothes fit right in and, to our amazement, it appears Trevor and I have also gained access to 'the money club'.

'Everyone assumes we're well off just because we're here,' Trevor says.

Unfortunately this won't work at the other five-star hotels, where there is no relaxed dress code. And while we may appear to fit in here, we realise we'll be having a very different stay from many of the others guests when Rob and Debbie suggest we take their favourite Huka Lodge day trip.

'Just spectacular,' they enthuse. 'The helicopter drops you off, then waits for a couple of hours while a guide takes you hiking. We went two days in a row, it was so good.'

Trevor and I say, quite honestly, that it sounds fantastic, but know we won't be going – especially not twice!

'We're due to fly back to the States today,' Rob says, looking out towards the river. 'Our lift is due any second.'

The four of us chat for a few minutes until we hear a low thrumming noise in the distance.

'And here it is now,' he says and they stand up as a bright red helicopter swings around from behind the trees and hovers above the lawn before coming to rest in front of the main Lodge building. We watch in amazement as the couple waits for their luggage to be loaded before climbing aboard the helicopter like it is nothing more than a bus. They wave at us through the window as it lifts off and swings out across the river on its way to Auckland.

We are still staring at the sky when our hostess arrives to escort us down the narrow fern-lined pathway to our room.

'When will breakfast be served tomorrow?' Trevor asks her as we arrive at the door to our suite.

'Whenever you like, sir,' she smiles. 'We'll wait until you're ready.'

She opens the door and steps back so Trevor and I can enter, but we don't get far.

'Look at the river,' he exclaims and stops to stare out

the French doors of our suite where the Waikato River is tumbling over small rapids less than 30 metres away. A lawn so finely groomed it looks like carpet leads to the water's edge where small clumps of reeds sway gently in the breeze and two wooden banana lounges and a low table have been set up.

'It's lovely to enjoy luncheon or drinks down there,' the hostess says, 'and we've got cashmere rugs to wrap up in if you get chilly.'

Trevor gives me a discreet glance and raises an eyebrow as if to say 'not just any old rugs, but *cashmere* ones'. Our suite is half the size of our house back home and has three separate sections – the main bedroom, a dressing room and the bathroom which looks out onto a private fernery. There is no need for a dining area as meals are taken up at the main lodge.

'This controls the heated floor, there's recessed lighting here which is really nice for when you take a bath and this switch turns on the special lights for the make-up mirror,' her hands dance over the electronic controls mounted on the bathroom wall. 'This does the air-conditioning and this button is so you can ring for service. We change the towels three times a day, but if you'd like it done more often just let us know.'

She leaves and we are instantly overcome with indecision. Should we go down to the river's edge with our cashmere blankets and a cup of coffee, flop into one of the easy chairs with a book or spread out on the king-sized bed?

The view outside makes it feel like we're camping in isolated wilderness, yet we are surrounded by every imaginable luxury. Perhaps it is the rushing river, but a feeling of peace settled over me the minute we walked into our suite.

'I'm going to test drive the tub,' I say and disappear into the bathroom. It fills with clouds of fragrant steam as I sink down into a bath so deep I can fill the water high enough to reach my neck.

I look out of the windows at the private fernery and realise the design of each suite ensures guests are shielded from prying eyes. I think about the stars who might have splashed around in this bathtub before me. Perhaps this low-key privacy is exactly what the rich and famous crave. It gives me an illicit thrill knowing we are interlopers in these Leading Hotels of the World, and this atmosphere is perfect for Trevor and me to keep the secret of how we've come to be here.

Whether to tell people about our prize or not is something we discussed in detail after winning, but in the end we've decided to keep it a secret. We aren't sure how paying guests in these hotels will react to our news. Trevor's job has shown us first-hand how quick people can be to pass judgement based on who you are and how much money you earn. I can't count the number of times we've been getting on famously with someone at a function until they ask what Trevor does for a living.

'A storeman? But you don't *seem* like a storeman,' they say in disbelief and make their excuses shortly thereafter.

We can never predict who is going to react like this until it is too late and Trevor and I are anxious about what might happen if the rich folk discover we are lowly budget travellers. We don't want anyone looking down on us and spoiling our wonderful five-star experiences. We've been able to bring along so few good clothes that I've even become paranoid about getting chucked out for not being well-dressed enough.

'They can't do that,' Trevor said, 'we're still guests.'

But he didn't look all that sure.

I climb out of the bathtub at Huka Lodge and dry myself with a fluffy towel from the heated towel rail before climbing into a warm bathrobe and going back to join Trevor. He's made us a cup of coffee and is relaxing in one of the comfortable arm chairs with a book.

'All that's missing is Pistachio,' Trevor says, patting his lap. Our much-loved cat is back in Australia bossing around the housesitter.

I am about to start reading too when I notice a pair of green eyes staring at me from outside the sliding glass door. A large ginger tomcat on the deck outside our suite sits patiently waiting to be let inside.

'Looks like somebody heard you,' I tell Trevor, who almost drops his book.

The cat sashays inside and jumps onto Trevor's lap before turning three times, flopping into position and falling instantly asleep. His ginger tail twitches and a guttural purr fills the room as Trevor shakes his head.

'They really do think of everything.'

After Trevor finishes a few chapters of his book, we dress and go back to the main lodge to enjoy the fire. The cat waits by our feet while we lock the door, then sticks his long ginger tail in the air like a flag and escorts us up to the main building.

'I see you've met Rusty,' says the hostess as we walk in. 'He likes to adopt people.'

I suspect Rusty knows we could use all the help we can get.

'That's not going to be warm enough,' Trevor says later that evening when I emerge from the huge walk-in wardrobe wearing my little black dress and a jacket. 'You'll freeze.'

'It's all I've got,' I shrug.

Trevor hands me his huge hiking sweater.

I am going to refuse, until he points out it is so chilly outside that the windows have fogged up. The sweater's sleeves extend past my hands and its hem sags baggily around my hips. Rusty takes one look and meows to be let outside. The cold air is a shock after the cosiness of our suite and we sprint up to the main building. I manage to whip off the sweater before anyone catches sight of my crime against fashion.

'It's going to be even colder on the way back,' Trevor says as we stand in front of the fire with two glasses of crisp New Zealand sauvignon blanc.

The river has been floodlit and the mist floating just

above its surface makes it look mysterious. A well-stocked bar has been set up on a side table at one end of the room and on the way in we are invited to help ourselves.

'Did you see all the different bottles of gin?' Trevor says in amazement. I look over and notice five different brands lined up in a row, with a similar selection of other spirits. Huka Lodge obviously prides itself on giving guests *exactly* what they want. When I take a bite-sized soufflé from a passing tray of canapés and pop it in my mouth, it is all I can do not to quiver with pleasure.

Two other couples have arrived while we've been talking, but they are obviously friends and more than twice our age. We don't feel comfortable interrupting their conversation and don't have the language skills – or the confidence – to approach the chic European guests.

'They're the same age as us,' I exclaim as another couple walk in and look hesitantly around the room. For once there isn't a staff member to be seen and I can see they are unsure about fixing themselves a drink. Trevor notices their discomfort as well and suggests we go over to say hello. It's a kind gesture, plus, after a week of no one to talk to but each other, we are craving company.

'It's a help-yourself arrangement,' Trevor explains, after we've introduced ourselves. 'If you like wine, the sauvignon blanc is very nice.'

I assume the couple, John and Grainne, are honeymooners as they are obviously very much in love, but I can't see any wedding rings.

'To holidays,' John says, proposing a toast.

The four of us clink glasses and start talking about the different places we've been. John and Grainne are from London and are visiting New Zealand because the exchange rate means they are effectively getting 75 per cent off everything.

'A place like Huka Lodge would normally be out of the question,' John explains, 'but the exchange rate means we can treat ourselves. We're visiting some wineries in Hawkes Bay after we leave here.'

Trevor's eyes light up. 'We did that on our last trip to New Zealand! Would you like some recommendations?'

They nod enthusiastically and we start discussing the cellar doors we visited and the differences between European and Australian wines. John is extremely knowledgeable but he doesn't take himself too seriously.

As he goes to get Grainne another drink, I am struck by how much he reminds me of Trevor. They are both well over six feet tall and are 'gentlemen' in an old-fashioned way, with impeccable manners.

'It's so nice being able to relax and dress down,' John says. 'I thought a place like this would be more formal.'

Trevor and I couldn't agree more, although it's hard not to smile. John has loosened the old school tie at his throat, but only slightly. He really is the quintessential Englishman.

We're getting on so well with John and Grainne that I almost tell them how we've come to be at Huka Lodge, but Trevor gives a small shake of his head just as I am about to launch into the story. He is probably right.

Telling John and Grainne might be okay, but what if the other guests find out the truth? It would be a shame if someone's rudeness spoiled our stay.

'Everyone's gone!' Trevor exclaims as we stop talking and look around.

A young waiter steps forward and approaches us.

'I didn't like to interrupt as you seemed to be having such a good time,' he says, 'but it is time for dinner.'

'Would you like to join us?' Trevor asks.

'Very much,' John says, 'but I've already organised a romantic table for two. What about tomorrow?'

We agree and arrange to meet John and Grainne for dinner the following evening.

We expect to see them at breakfast, but the dining room remains deserted the whole time we are there. Today we're having a fly fishing lesson – the one thing we are able to afford from the list of guest activities.

'You can see the trout swimming around in the water,' Trevor tells me. 'How hard can it be?'

Much harder than we thought, as it turns out, but the lesson is still a lot of fun. I was expecting to walk down to the river and start fishing straight away, but the instructor insists we practice casting our lines on the lawn first. It doesn't take long to get the hang of it and once my technique has improved enough that I can hit the piece of paper he's put on the grass with pinpoint accuracy, our instructor invites me to try my luck in the Waikato River. The fact he hasn't bothered bringing down a net to lift my catch out of the water should tell me something. The fishermen I've seen arcing their flexible rods so their fly only touches the surface make it look easy, but my first attempt at an artful imitation of an insect dancing on the water sees my line snapping back and wrapping itself around Trevor's head.

'At least you caught something,' the instructor laughs.

The feathered fly on the end of it hangs directly in front of Trevor's nose and he struggles to free himself. We can hear the laughter of the guests who are watching us from the Lodge's deck as the instructor and I stop chuckling long enough to help. Trevor swears the fish are smirking.

In the evening we return to the sitting room for the complimentary cocktail hour to find John and Grainne are already there.

'The waiter just stopped by to say they've organised somewhere special for the four of us to have dinner, but he wouldn't tell me anything more,' Grainne says.

We start talking about what we've been doing that day and get so involved in the conversation it feels like only minutes have passed before a waiter announces it is time for dinner.

'When we overheard you talking about wine last night, we thought you might enjoy the opportunity to dine in our private cellar,' he explains.

I am touched they've put so much thought into our evening and we hurry through the cold night air to the separate building that houses the Lodge's stocks for their impressive wine list. The staff have gone to enormous trouble and the setting for our dinner is stunning. In the middle of a whitewashed room, lined with wine racks reaching from floor to ceiling, is a heavy wooden table crowned by a three-tiered candelabra. Its flickering candles make shadows dance on the walls and give our faces a soft glow.

'I'll let you choose the wine,' John says and suggests a price limit that scares me to death.

He passes the list across the table and I scan the pages with shaking hands. I've never had this much to spend on a bottle of wine in my life. What if I mess it up? After choosing a back vintage red from Coonawarra in South Australia, I offer a silent prayer as the waiter pours me a small amount to try, then smile up at him and indicate he can pour us a glass each. Everyone swirls their glasses before taking a small sip.

'Ohhhh,' John says rapturously and grabs the bottle to read the back of the label, 'that's very, very good.'

I breathe a sigh of relief and settle back to enjoy the evening. My choice of wine gets things off to a great start and our three-course meal goes even more quickly than the cocktail hour. We all finish with dessert.

'Once I see the word "chocolate" on the menu,' John says, 'my choice is made.' He and Trevor are even more similar than I'd thought.

Grainne and I swap spoonfuls of dessert with the boys, who declare our fresh berries delicious but far too healthy. When Grainne pretends to reach over and sneak another spoonful, John laughs and gives her an affectionate hug. Their warmth towards each other reminds me very much of Trevor and me, although, unlike us, John and Grainne have only known each other for a few years and are still dating.

'We might get one married one day though,' says Grainne with a small smile.

'Coffee is being served in front of the fire if you'd like to join us inside,' the waiter says when he comes to clear our dessert plates.

'It's your best chance of catching a trout,' Trevor teases and starts telling John and Grainne about my embarrassing moment on the lawn as we run back through the cold night air and into the warmth of the sitting room.

'Much easier than the river,' I say, plucking a tiny chocolate trout petit four off the silver platter.

'So where are you off to after this?' John asks.

We begin reeling off the names of the cities until John and Grainne stop us when we get to London.

'You can come and stay with us!' they say.

Trevor and I thank them for the offer, but explain we've already booked in at the Dorchester.

Both of them murmur how nice it is, and we can see they are intrigued. Why would people on a world trip staying at places like Huka Lodge and the Dorchester have booked two bus tickets to Auckland instead of flying? John and Grainne are too well-mannered to press further, but we are sure they are dying to ask.

The following morning the four of us have breakfast

together and go for a long walk around the grounds before John and Grainne leave Huka Lodge in their hire car. Although we won't be staying with them in London, we arrange to meet up for dinner on our last night there.

'Will we tell John and Grainne the truth next time we see them?' I ask Trevor as their car disappears up the driveway.

'Yes, but not straight away,' says Trevor with a mischievous grin. 'I've thought of a fun way to get John back for all those Steve Irwin jokes.'

That night, as we finish the evening with coffee and chocolate trout by the fire after our last dinner at Huka Lodge, Trevor says, 'I'm really going to miss this. It's been so good to relax and not have to think about how much things cost.'

We love being able to enjoy the full five-star experience without worrying about our budget, although our stay at Huka Lodge has been very different to what we expected. The service and accommodation are five-star all the way, but everything else is low key and relaxed. It is a delightful combination and we can see why Huka Lodge has won so many awards.

'Would you pay to stay here?' I ask Trevor.

It is a long time before he answers.

'Yes,' he says thoughtfully, 'yes, I think I would.' He reaches over for his coffee cup and another chocolate trout. 'It's all a question of value for money. You can pay $40 a night at a hostel and feel ripped off, but I think the

$1000 a night they charge here would be worth it for a special occasion.'

Trevor notices my expression.

'Okay, maybe only for a *very, very, very* special occasion. Do you agree?'

'Absolutely! How about a return visit for our twentieth wedding anniversary?'

'Only if we can start saving now,' he laughs and polishes off his fifth trout.

We say goodbye to the staff after breakfast the next day and one of the receptionists drops us off at the bus station in Taupo.

'I wish we'd been able to take the helicopter instead,' Trevor says wistfully as the bus pulls out.

We haven't been able to get a cheap enough rate on a hire car for the return trip to Auckland, so we are catching the bus, which takes twice as long and makes about 30 stops along the way. The guy sitting behind us has industrial-strength foot odour and the trip is even more boring than we imagined. Trevor cheers when the bus pulls into Auckland where we catch a taxi to the international airport for our late-night flight to Buenos Aires.

'I'm going to be tired of aeroplanes by the time this trip is over,' Trevor says as we board the Boeing 747. He is an aviation freak, so this is really saying something.

'Do you think we'd enjoy the flights more if we were in Business Class?' he asks as a champagne cork pops at the front of the plane.

'Forget I asked,' Trevor sighs as he sits down and twists up his long legs like a pretzel in preparation for the 12-hour flight.

4

THE DEVIL'S THROAT

Despite travel warnings imploring Australians visiting Argentina to 'exercise extreme caution' (whatever that is), we have stuck to our original plans to visit Buenos Aires but when we arrive I wonder if we've made the right decision. To say Argentina is going through a bad patch is an understatement. The country has just defaulted on an $800 million debt repayment to the World Bank, the local currency is worth almost nothing after the government ceased pegging the peso to the US dollar and Buenos Aires is full of rioting locals protesting at the injustice of it all. We like to think we are still visiting Argentina because we are daring and intrepid travellers, but the real reason is slightly less glamorous. The illicit thrill of getting something for nothing is too much for a couple of backpackers to resist – especially when it is three nights at Argentina's best hotel.

But, as Trevor and I enter the chaos of the arrivals hall, we wonder if our decision was a good one. There are a few business travellers and a handful of other tourists, but the rest of the crowd is made up of locals gathered in groups near sturdy crowd control barriers. They are so desperate to earn money that they have resorted to touting for business even though it is illegal.

We can see the game of cat and mouse they are playing with the security guards posted around the arrivals area who are employed to stop them. One of the local men in the crowd looks left and right before leaning out towards me and asking first in Spanish and then in English if we want a room, but a guard moves him on before I have time to reply. Not that we would take him up on the offer. Back home, there were stories in the paper about tourists being lured into dangerous parts of Buenos Aires and robbed. We were full of bravado and joked about 'exercising extreme caution' before we left but, as I look out at the touts behind the barriers, it isn't funny anymore.

'I'll ask a security guard where we catch our connecting flight,' Trevor says with a forced cheeriness I remember all too well. The last time I heard it we'd missed a train in Austria and his upbeat 'Not to worry – there'll be another one soon' was followed by a six-hour wait on a freezing platform. Neither of us is prepared to come right out and admit it, but I know we are thinking the same thing: coming to Argentina was a mistake.

The Alvear Palace, our prize hotel in Buenos Aires, is the main reason we've come here but we won't be going to our five-star digs straight away. First we're spending two nights at a place called Iguazú Falls in the middle of the jungle. Our friends Brett and Katey had raved about the 55,000 hectares of jungle listed by UNESCO as a Natural World Heritage Site, which contains monkeys, iguanas, giant anteaters and a horseshoe-shaped waterfall spanning 2.7 kilometres. Iguazú Falls caused Eleanor Roosevelt to say 'poor Niagara', but it made Trevor and I say 'poor Brett and Katey' when we heard about the bus trip that got them there. Yet despite spending over 24 hours with two families suffering from food poisoning, a screaming baby and a young Argentinean soccer team who got on the bus drunk and managed to stay that way for the entire trip, Brett and Katey insisted seeing Iguazú had made it all worthwhile. We concluded the place must be amazing and decided to go too – but not by bus.

The flight takes less than two hours and the airport servicing Iguazú is a relief after what we experienced in Buenos Aires. There is no extra security and the taxi drivers wait in an orderly line near the baggage area until travellers claim their bags. One of the drivers steps out and approaches us.

'Taxi?'

We nod and after agreeing on a price for the 15-minute journey, he drives us past enormous trees with vines snaking around their trunks like ropy necklaces and into the national park. The one hotel located within the park is the Sheraton Internacional Iguazú Resort, and this is the only time we'll be paying for an expensive hotel out of our own pocket. We're both looking forward to more of the luxurious trappings we've enjoyed earlier in our trip.

'I can't wait to slip into that fluffy bathrobe,' says Trevor with a dreamy look.

But when we are shown to our room on the top floor of the low-rise hotel, we have to hide our dismay. It is perfectly respectable, but the Sheraton's hefty room rate had conjured up visions of silk pillows piled high on the bed and soft bathrobes beckoning seductively from behind the bathroom door, not the standard hotel room we are standing in. The fancy marble bathroom we've been fantasising about is nowhere to be seen and the furniture is drab brown veneer. The porter closes the door behind him with a gentle click and we flop onto the bed.

'It's not exactly Huka Lodge, is it?' Trevor says, with a rueful smile. The room is spotless and far better than anywhere we usually stay, but it is a huge disappointment after what we've been expecting. I try not to think about the $300 per night it is costing us to stay here.

'That air-conditioner is a bit of a worry,' he adds. 'It sounds like a jumbo jet's about to take off out there.'

The muted roar of what sounds like an ancient air-conditioner has been wafting noisily through the closed doors leading onto our balcony even since we walked in. Both of us have raised our voices in an attempt to drown it out but this isn't something we want to do the whole time we are here. I dump my backpack and walk outside to give the air-conditioning unit a thump.

'Can you fix it?' Trevor shouts out after a few minutes have passed.

'Not exactly. I think you'd better come outside.' I grin and tuck myself into the far side of the balcony so I can watch his reaction.

Trevor strides out through the sliding doors and stops dead before wandering over towards the balcony railings to stare into the distance. I step out from where I've been hiding.

'I guess there's not much we can do about the noise, eh?'

Trevor drapes one arm around my shoulder.

'That's amazing,' he says, almost to himself.

There is no air-conditioner outside our room – only the sound generated by tonnes of water tumbling over Iguazú Falls. The falls must be over a kilometre away, but they are so large that they are still clearly visible from our balcony and there is dark green jungle and bright blue sky as far as the eye can see. I start reading the brochure I picked up from the bedside table. It explains that, all up, the falls comprise over 275 separate cascades but when I look at the map on the back of the brochure I realise we are only seeing the 14 falls making up the Devil's Throat, Garganta del Diablo, the most famous and spectacular Iguazú waterfall, which permanently sends 30 metres of spray flying up into the air. The solid curtain of water forming the Devil's Throat undulates like a billowing white sheet and the cloud of moisture hovers above it like a spectre. I look out at the distant plumes of spray and begin to understand why Brett and Katey were so insistent we come here.

Trevor races inside where he scrabbles for his camera bag so frantically that anyone would think the Iguazú Falls were about to disappear. I should be used to it by now, as Trevor has been a keen photographer ever since we met, but I often wish he'd stop looking at the world through his viewfinder and enjoy the moment instead.

I lean out and look along either side of the hotel at the other rooms facing the falls, but we are the only ones enjoying the view. No wonder we've been given such a great room – the hotel is virtually empty.

Soon we head out, walking a few hundred metres to where the small train that ferries tourists around the park departs from. It reminds me of a kid's theme park ride, but the train is surprisingly fast and it takes less than five minutes for us to arrive at the tiny station near the pathway leading to Garganta del Diablo.

After a short walk through the jungle, we arrive at the first of a series of metal walkways leading out over the water. We both hesitate slightly before stepping onto the open mesh. The soupy brown water is only metres away and small trees and logs rush below us like cars on a freeway, occasionally slamming into the thick pylons holding up the catwalk. Logic tells me the walkways are perfectly safe, but I can feel my stomach churning nervously as we walk along.

'You wouldn't want to fall in,' I hear a man behind us say to his wife.

I couldn't agree more. The walkways are taking us right into the centre of the river feeding the Devil's

Throat and the current is so strong it looks like the water is boiling. As another log whacks into the walkway with a resounding thud, Trevor and I exchange anxious looks and lift our pace until we reach the main viewing platform. This is much larger than the narrow walkways, but the ferocity of the torrent falling into the gorge 350 feet below is almost frightening. The water roars, but it isn't the constant sound we heard from our room – this noise rises and falls like the growl of a primitive beast. It is wild and exciting and we have to shout to be heard.

'This is incredible,' Trevor yells, pointing to the falls. 'Look at all that water!'

I start telling him I think it is spectacular too, but he motions that he can't hear me and holds out his hand instead. Trevor points to the edge of the viewing platform as if to say 'shall we go?'. We hold hands as we walk carefully to the edge of the slippery wet metal platform. It looks like the handful of other tourists who were with us on the train have also given up trying to talk and we stand in silence, staring down into the water where hundreds of black swifts dance in and out of the cascades. Of all the places to build a nest, these birds have chosen the basalt cliffs around Garganta del Diablo and court death each time they swoop home. It is like they are participating in an elaborate courtship dance with the falls, but it will only take the slightest miscalculation for them to plummet to a watery end.

We hurry back to catch the last train of the day, and the roar of Garganta del Diablo can be heard in the distance as we arrive at the station near the hotel and walk along the pathway back to the Sheraton. I've always loved waterfalls and have been to quite a few on bush-walks in Australia, but even the big ones have been trickles compared to Iguazú.

The jungle surrounding us looks like it would engulf the walkways, kiosks and other human trappings in a matter of minutes if it weren't for the staff who look after the national park. There is a team of rangers plus gangs of men who hack at the jungle foliage with huge machetes. I see them working in the distance, slicing through thick tree branches like they are butter. The thickest part of the jungle we come across is between the train station and the edge of the hotel grounds. No light filters through the canopy of trees and everything is dark and silent, except for the sound of creatures scuttling through the undergrowth. We stop to look at a yellow sign with a picture of a sleek black cat on it.

'I didn't know they had cats here. I wonder if we'll see one,' Trevor muses.

'Probably best you don't,' says a voice behind us.

Trevor and I turn to see the man and his wife who were on the walkway with us at the Devil's Throat.

'They're wild jaguars,' he explains. 'One of the rangers lost a child to one a few years back – most of the staff carry guns now.'

It's a reminder of how untamed the jungle really is and I find myself constantly searching for glinting eyes in the dense undergrowth.

That evening I watch toucans zoom past our balcony like they are doing fly-bys at an air show and mentally thank Brett and Katey for pushing us to come here. Enjoying the luxury of Huka Lodge was a superb experience but, as I look out across the dense jungle stretching from the edge of the hotel grounds to the distant falls, this appeals to me much more. The sense of awe and excitement I felt seeing Iguazú Falls for the first time could never be matched by the sight of a fancy room.

Tragically, I am almost as excited about the fact that although our accommodation is priced in US dollars, everything else at the hotel is in pesos. This means we are about to enjoy room service for the first time ever and Trevor can't resist teasing me about how thrilled I am about a burger and chips. Having food delivered feels like such a luxury – I could definitely get used to this.

The next morning we get up and go for a hot, sticky hike down the zigzagging concrete pathway leading to the river at the base of Iguazú's many falls. Trevor set our alarm for an early start in an attempt to beat the heat, but I'm not sure it helped much. The jungle is already steaming and the perspiration running in thin rivulets down our backs reminds me of the tiny waterfalls we can see through the trees. The river doesn't look that far below us when we start, but it takes over half an hour to reach the base of the rocky cliff.

'It's going to be a slow trip back,' Trevor says, looking up towards the start of the walkway which is now high above us.

Soon we reach the jetty just a couple of hundred metres across the swirling water from Isla Grande San Martin, a jungle-covered island. As we step onto the small waiting ferry, the driver nods to us and folds up his newspaper before turning on the engine. The bench seats are clammy and the moist air makes it feel like I am breathing through a wet handkerchief.

'I feel like Robinson Crusoe,' Trevor says as we get off the ferry. 'We must be the only people here.'

In silence we follow the path until we reach a viewing platform where myriad separate cascades create rainbows in one huge cloud of spray. I realise each set of falls has its own sound the same way humans have voices which are entirely unique. The noise here is still a roar, but it has a higher pitch than the thundering of *garganta del diablo* and seems somehow lighter. If the waterfalls were people, the Devil's Throat would be a towering nightclub bouncer with jet black hair and a menacing sneer and the waterfalls in front of us could be his pretty girlfriend.

Trevor is more interested in his upcoming photo exhibition than enjoying the view. Instead of admiring the scenery he is hunched over his beloved camera bag, trying to protect its contents from the spray hanging heavily in the air. I can see what he has in mind – the shimmering rainbows *would* make a great photo – but I don't like his chances.

'I don't know who's going to get wetter – you or the camera.'

Trevor pretends he doesn't hear me and sneaks open the bag's zipper, putting his hand inside it to expertly swap lenses before easing the camera's shiny body out. It only makes it halfway before he utters a heartfelt curse and plunges the camera back inside.

'Could you stand there and block the spray while I get out the camera?' he asks me.

'And get absolutely soaked? Sorry – no way.'

For the next ten minutes Trevor tries to devise ingenious ways to protect his precious gear, but it is no use. Even if he manages to keep the camera dry, it only takes a few seconds for the lens to become peppered with water droplets, making it completely useless. When I notice the slump of his shoulders and see him zipping up the camera bag, I know he has admitted defeat.

'I've already got plenty of waterfall shots,' Trevor says philosophically as we walk back to the ferry. Considering how many rolls of film he's gone through since we arrived at Iguazú, I am not surprised.

'Is the rafting trip ready to go?' I ask the ferry driver as we get back on board.

'Si, si,' he says, pointing to another jetty further up the river bank. 'They will sell you a ticket.'

There are a number of boat trips available at the falls, from a leisurely meander through the upper reaches of the Iguazú River to the rather more daring escapade we are about to embark on. Considering we are about to play chicken with the strong currents and churning cauldron of water created by Salto San Martin, the second largest waterfall in the park, I hope our driver knows what he is doing or we won't be around to tell Brett and Katey about our adventure. The rafting trip is the main reason we walked down here, but it sounded like a lot more fun before we saw the whirlpools.

As we climb into a rubber zodiac raft, I notice our driver looks exactly like the tyrannical captain of a pirate ship. Trevor and I are his only passengers.

'What do you think of Captain Crazy?' Trevor asks nervously.

I think he's rather sexy, but I'm not going to tell Trevor that. With his wild black shoulder-length hair, a bare chest slick with moisture and a black leather necklace around his throat, the Captain is intensely masculine. He oozes dangerous sexuality and I blush when he catches me watching him. When Trevor isn't looking the Captain gives me a saucy wink.

Suddenly he lets out a joyous whoop and gives us a jaunty thumbs up while gunning the zodiac's engine and shooting the boat out into the water. The dark rock walls rising vertically on either side of the Iguazú River begin to blur as the raft increases its speed and executes a sweeping right turn to take us into the middle of the fast-flowing water. Captain Crazy raises one bushy black eyebrow and treats us to another grin, before puttering more slowly towards the base of Salto San Martin, where he leaves the engine idling at a slow throb and positions the raft for our first run. Trevor clutches my hand and grins with wild exhilaration.

The Captain's look of concentration reminds me of playing skipping as a child – I would agonise for ages as I tried to gauge the speed, height and arc of the spinning rope before dashing underneath it. As we watch the shifting pattern of the current ebbing and flowing around us, I feel the first twinge of apprehension and we yell with fear and excitement as our raft shoots towards the thundering falls head on. My hair whips back flat against my scalp and the speed of the raft sends water spraying back in two brown flumes. I bite down on an excited scream as I realise water is flying into my mouth. I'm feeling carefree and excited, but not carefree enough to risk a dose of vomiting and diarrhoea from the muddy river. Suddenly Salto San Martin looms directly in front of us, its falling water sounding like the muted roar of a crowd screaming at a rock concert.

'This is fantastic!' I yell over the noise.

The waterfall is so loud that I can't hear what Trevor says back to me, but it doesn't matter. His huge smile says it all. After a few minutes, the Captain reverses smartly and we look up to see him grinning triumphantly and pointing back towards the falls.

'Again, yes?'

'Si, si! Muchas gracias!'

Eager to put a stop to our atrocious Spanish, the Captain speeds forwards once more, getting the raft even closer than on our first attempt. Despite the fact my knuckles are white from clutching the nylon ropes running around the edge of our raft, which bucks wildly in the current, I can't remember the last time I had so much fun. There is just enough time to look up and catch glimpses of the small rainbow dancing in the spray raining down on us before Captain Crazy returns to the opposite bank where a motley looking group of his friends have gathered by the jetty. They amble to the end of it and are full of animated conversation – although we don't speak Spanish, it is obvious they are congratulating him. I think it is for the Captain's daring second run at the falls, until I look down.

Captain Crazy has excelled himself all right: zooming so close to the falls meant we got soaked and the delicate lace of my bra and just about everything else is clearly visible through my sodden white t-shirt. A pair of chilly nipples strain against the thin fabric like two punctuation marks and I slap my arms across my chest and cringe with embarrassment as Trevor laughs uproariously – until he realises everyone is copping a free eyeful of his wife's breasts. He whips a jacket out of his bag and thrusts it towards me with ill-concealed panic. The Argentineans' laughter and good-natured applause follow us as we race up the path, still buzzing on adrenaline and embarrassment.

We spend the evening packing in preparation for our first night at the Alvear Palace Hotel. I am looking forward to it, but we've had such a memorable time at the falls I am almost sad we are moving on. There are plenty of walks we haven't done and Trevor is disappointed he was unable to get a good shot of a toucan.

'They need to stuff one so it doesn't move so damn fast,' he says.

Wherever the toucans are flying to, they always seem to be in a hurry – unlike us. Being surrounded by the primitive beauty of the jungle, Trevor and I have really relaxed and my worries about not fitting in at the Leading Hotels of the World have faded away.

'Are you ready for the Alvear Palace?' Trevor asks.

'Provided I can find something clean to wear, the answer is yes,' I say, digging around in my backpack. 'But, at this point, it's not looking good.'

'Don't worry. As long as it passes the "sniff test", you'll be fine.' Trevor picks up the shirt he was wearing the day we arrived, presses it against his nose and inhales deeply.

'Still good,' he declares.

I doubt many guests staying at the Alvear Palace even know what the 'sniff test' is.

As I look out of the window of our battered taxi on the journey from the airport to the Alvear Palace, I am surprised. I expected to see protest marches and people begging on street corners but at first glance Buenos Aires could be any European city we've visited on past trips.

'It reminds me a bit of Paris,' Trevor says as we zoom along wide tree-lined boulevards.

'I know what you mean,' I agree, looking at the buildings, 'but the traffic reminds me of Italy!'

We make a mad grab for the seats in front of us as our

taxi screeches to avoid yet another near miss. Our driver doesn't give the car that nearly hit us a second glance and I get the impression this drive is business as usual as far as he is concerned – except for our destination. When Trevor said 'Alvear Palace, *por favor*,' the driver turned around and said, 'Alvear Palace Hotel?' just to make sure he'd got it right.

When our ancient taxi pulls up beside an assortment of gleaming Mercedes and luxury Peugeots, we understand why the driver double-checked our destination. The doorman is better dressed than we could ever hope to be, even with access to our full wardrobes at home. The two Australian hotels and Huka Lodge were far more casual. I grab Trevor's hand and wonder if he feels as out of place as I do. As Trevor pays the driver I gaze in through the floor-to-ceiling glass at the front of the hotel lobby. A group of people are standing beside a towering vase of fresh flowers. One woman wears a cream pants suit that fits her like a glove and, when she tips her head back and laughs, I notice what looks like a glittering string of real diamonds fastened around her elegant neck. Everyone in the group looks just as poised and glamorous as she does and, needless to say, there isn't a pair of jeans or hiking boots to be seen.

Perhaps I am being paranoid, but I am sure I detect a look of disbelief when Trevor walks up to reception and says we have a reservation. I hide behind him and curse my last-minute decision not to wear my little black dress. While 3 pm is technically too early for evening wear, my jeans and t-shirt are attracting some very curious glances. I thought that following the rules of formal etiquette would keep me out of trouble at the Leading Hotels of the World, but I should have followed my instincts.

Unlike most of the cheap places we've stayed at in the past, the Alvear Palace Hotel actually looks better than the brochure. The hotel was originally a real palace when it was built here in Recoleta, a wealthy neighbour-hood in the centre of Buenos Aires, in 1932. The lobby we are standing in could once have been the grand ballroom. The walls, the floors, the ornate columns topped with gold filigree – everything is marble and there would be plenty of room for dancing if you took out the furniture.

I notice our luggage being wheeled up to our suite on a padded trolley and smile when I see that even our backpacks are getting the five-star treatment. The group I have been watching gives our bags a bemused glance as they trundle by.

'I don't think they've ever seen a backpack before,' Trevor whispers.

One of the staff from reception escorts us to our suite and shows us around but I can't wait for him to leave so I can make myself more presentable. I dive for my make-up bag straight away but Ana arrives with our champagne before I even have time to put on lipstick. I feel embar-rassed but, by the time we have admired our roses and finished the champagne, I decide it isn't such a big deal.

Besides, we have more practical things to think about. Unlike Huka Lodge, only breakfast is included in our package at the Alvear Palace, which means we are back to standard backpacker fare for lunch and dinner.

Feeling pleasantly tipsy, I venture into the bathroom to prepare dinner and our tin camping mugs clatter on the marble vanity as they are filled with boiling water, courtesy of the trusty heating element which accompanies us on every trip. Neon-yellow chicken noodle soup slops onto the bathroom floor as I walk into the lounge room and present Trevor's mug with a scraping bow.

'Why thank you, Jeeves,' he says in a toffy voice. 'How . . . umm . . .'

'Unusual?'

'Exactly,' Trevor laughs. 'It feels a bit weird sitting in a suite that costs $1,500 a night eating cup-of-soup and stale bread rolls for dinner.'

As we finish our meal with dessert – a squished muesli bar from New Zealand – I notice the empty French champagne bottle sitting incongruously next to our mugs on the coffee table and decide Trevor is right. It is bizarre living like backpackers in a room filled with every possible luxury. Trevor suggests that perhaps the butler can prepare dinner next time, but the thought of Ana finding out we've been eating food prepared in the bathroom makes me feel slightly ill. It is lucky we have one of the shiniest, cleanest ones in Buenos Aires – I certainly wouldn't make dinner in the bathroom of our usual hotels.

We feel a bit sorry for Ana when she returns later that evening. She is trying her best to be of service, but Trevor and I are forced to refuse every offer of assistance. Would we like our clothes pressed? No, they're fine, thank you (and covered in mud from Iguazú Falls). A shoeshine? Thanks, but no (our hiking boots wouldn't recover from the shock). We think that will be the end of it, but Ana knocks on our door a few minutes later.

'Can I bring you a cup of coffee?' she says with a hint of triumph.

We exchange a furtive glance. Ana is right – a cup of freshly brewed coffee is just what we feel like – but is it going to appear on our bill? Both of us are too shy to ask so we end up saying no yet again and poor Ana looks crestfallen.

'There is one thing,' Trevor says.

Ana's eyes light up.

'We are planning to visit Recoleta Cemetery tomorrow. Can you tell us anything about it?'

'Si, si. This I can help you with. Cementerio de la Recoleta is not far from the hotel. Let me get you a map.'

After spending some time with Ana, who is delighted to tell us more about Buenos Aires' famous cemetery, we climb into fluffy bathrobes so thick that we have to turn down the air-conditioning. Not long afterwards, two maids arrive to turn down our king-sized bed and place complimentary bottles of designer mineral water on our bedside tables. They also draw the thick velvet curtains and lay out two pairs of slippers, but nothing can top the Hermès toiletries in our bathroom. They come in little green bottles that magically reappear each time our room is serviced. Considering the maids come a minimum of twice a day, my backpack will be groaning with free French toiletries by the end of our stay at the Alvear Palace. We are already looking forward to enjoying the Hermès shower gel later in the trip. Designer bath products and having to wear thongs in the shower will be a unique combination.

It is more than four days since we arrived in Argentina, but we are still struggling to shake off the last of our jet lag. The ten-hour time difference between New Zealand and Buenos Aires is the largest we've ever had to deal with and neither of us has been able to settle into the local time.

'We'll have to set the alarm tomorrow,' Trevor says, hauling on his clothes. 'Hurry up!'

We've slept in so late that the two of us have nearly missed our first breakfast at the Alvear Palace. Breakfast buffets are a dream come true on this trip as they mean we can fill up on free food and avoid buying lunch. We've done this to save money on earlier trips as well, but the Alvear Palace's buffet includes something a cut above the bacon and eggs we've come to expect.

'Did you see what's in the big silver ice bucket near the fruit platters?' I ask Trevor.

'No, I'm focusing on stage one,' he replies. This means he is still trying all the hot food. Stage two will see a full exploration of the continental selection, followed by stage three, which is seconds of anything he finds particularly good. Trevor perfected his approach to buffet breakfasts a while ago.

'Would you like some of what's in the bucket?'

'Depends what it is.'

'I'm not telling. You'll just have to say yes or no.'

'Yes.'

I go back to the buffet and return with a glass which I put down in front of him. Trevor looks up and stops eating – a sure sign I've got his attention.

'You're kidding. Free champagne?'

'Free *French* champagne', I say, but I'm just as amazed. Along with the platters of exotic tropical fruits, the Alvear Palace has bottles of chilled champagne as a standard buffet item. Trevor and I both have a glass just for the sake of it, but drinking so early in the day makes us feel woozy so we give the champagne a miss for the rest of our stay. If only we could work out how to sneak a bottle into our backpacks along with the bread rolls we take for lunch.

Breakfast may be served by white-gloved waiters in immaculate suits, but the atmosphere is surprisingly relaxed. The other guests appear to be wealthy Europeans who must have stayed at the hotel before because the staff know most of them by name and stop by their tables for a quick chat and a joke. They never overstep by mark by being too familiar, but nothing can hide the Argentines' *joie de vivre* and natural graciousness. I like

Buenos Aires a lot and am sorry we can't extend our time here, but we are restricted by the itinerary we had to lock in before we left Australia. This isn't how we usually travel and I'm already finding it frustrating. I miss the freedom of being able to alter arrangements as we go.

After breakfast we take Ana's map and walk through the local streets on our way to Cementerio de la Recoleta. It occupies prime real estate in the heart of Buenos Aires and apparently it's reminiscent of a small city, with ornate mausoleums instead of skyscrapers. Cementerio de la Recoleta is a 'must see' according to our guidebook and only 15 minutes' walk from the Alvear Palace.

This is the first time we've ventured out of the hotel and, even in such an affluent area, the effects of Argentina's economic woes are evident in the empty windows of fancy stores that have gone out of business and the guards keeping watch outside wealthy residents' apartment blocks. We may be walking down wide streets lined on either side by fine-looking trees and French colonial build-ings, but it is hard to ignore the huge security presence. They even have a guard outside the ice cream store.

'They must be worried about someone stealing the Double Choc,' Trevor says, trying to lighten the moment.

There have been plenty of stories on the news and in the papers back home about Argentina's current economic crisis, especially the government-imposed limit on bank withdrawals. The idea is to keep all the avail-able money in Argentina until the economic situation improves, but this means the locals can't access cash that is rightfully theirs. Argentineans who borrowed in US dollars are in an even worse situation, unable to keep up repayments. However, it isn't until we see a dignified lady sitting on a blanket outside a supermarket that we begin to understand that the reality of the country's situation is far more confronting than a few empty shops and some extra security. Her clothes are fine, but the woman looks exhausted and she is pleading desperately for passers-by to purchase something – anything – from her pile of antiques and *objets d'art*.

The government seems to be sacrificing the lives of its people for the supposed good of the country. It is hard to see the wisdom of it.

We walk on in silence until we reach the entrance of a bank, shielded by metal grilles which have been installed as defence against the riots we saw on the news before we left Australia.

'It's terrible isn't it?' Trevor says, looking at the protest posters papering the bank. 'Imagine knowing your money's in there and not being able to get at it. No wonder there are riots.'

'At least we came to Argentina when everyone else was staying away.' It isn't much, but it's a start.

As we approach the entrance to Cementerio de la Recoleta, I notice a welcoming committee just inside the neo-classical gates, but the small group of stray cats scuttles warily away at our approach. It reminds me of a moody scene from a horror flick and I grab Trevor's arm and hurry him through the gates.

The pungent odour of the cats' droppings hangs in the air, mixing with the cloying smell of dying flowers as we walk along the cemetery's paved streets and squeeze past the crowd huddled around the black marble mausoleum where Eva Perón is buried. Argentina loves Evita, the beautiful actress who married the country's President, Juan Domingo Perón, in 1945 and campaigned relentlessly for the country's poor, developing social programs and supporting the women's suffrage movement. When she died of cancer at the age of 33, the country grieved and Eva became a martyr.

It doesn't surprise me that the locals outside Evita's mausoleum are equal in number to the tourists. Argentineans revere their dead – so much so that the plaque on the outside of each mausoleum states each inhabitant's date of death, but not the year they were born. I peer inside one of the crypts to see coffins stacked neatly on either side and a small urn of flowers sitting in the centre of a marble pedestal. A painting of Jesus Christ hangs above the coffins, staring down benevolently at the weathered wooden containers. I don't want to think too hard about what is inside them. Our guidebook describes the cemetery as 'a peaceful haven away from the rush of Buenos Aires' streets', but it is giving me the creeps. The stone and marble mausoleums may be stunning, but they are built so close together that many of them touch, making the narrow walkways appear dark and mysterious. Trevor seems happy to keep looking around but, as far as I am concerned, the sooner we get out of here the better.

'They look like real people,' Trevor says, pointing to one of the many angels perched above the entrances to the crypts. We are on our way out of the cemetery now, but looking at the angels provides a welcome distraction. The statues appear in so many different guises they could almost be spiritual representations of the people inside each crypt – some sit casually on the edge of the roof and many wear sweet smiles, while others are imposing creatures, with powerful wings and stern expressions. They are all beautiful in their own way, but the lifelike shadows they cast make me feel like we are being watched. Cementerio de la Recoleta is a fascinating place, but I am relieved when we re-emerge through its ornate iron gates onto the streets outside. The tooting car horns and locals rushing past the cemetery are a relief after the eerie silence of where we've just been.

We take our time walking back to the hotel, peering into leafy gardens almost completely concealed by high stone walls and admiring the façades of wealthy residents' apartment blocks. The guards at their front doors nod courteously and we are greeted with a friendly *'buenas tardes'* by nearly everyone we pass.

I enjoy our walk, but a sense of unease creeps over me as we get closer to the hotel. I glance down and use my hand to try and wipe the dust from the graveyard's narrow walkways off my boots.

'I don't know why you're worrying,' Trevor says. 'Nobody's going to say anything.'

I know he is probably right, but the fancy cars pulling

up in front of the Alvear Palace, filled with guests who look so at home in their lavish surroundings, make me feel even worse. I watch a limousine drive in and my feet start to drag.

'Do you think there's a side entrance?' I suggest.

For all his talk about not worrying, Trevor isn't feeling that brave either, so we skirt around the hotel's grand entrance and into the shopping arcade next door instead. Tucked in beside the boutiques offering glamorous evening wear, jewelled handbags and stylish suits, there is a small side door leading into the hotel lobby. We slip through it and escape to the sanctuary of our room.

'We still look out of place,' Trevor says, switching on the two chandeliers in our suite's living room, 'but at least in here we can do it in private.'

I laugh and walk over to open the wardrobe, where I find our two backpacks stacked neatly on the wardrobe's floor. Our butler has done up the straps to make our bags look neat, but the clips are connected in all sorts of weird ways.

'I don't think Ana's seen a backpack before either,' Trevor says.

We were so ashamed of our luggage that we pushed the backpacks under the bed before we left this morning, so no one would find them, but we didn't count on Ana's thoroughness. I cringe as I imagine her dainty foot catching on our stinky luggage, which is still covered in Iguazú mud. I worry that I won't be able to look her in the eye next time we see her, but when Ana stops by to ask if we enjoyed our day, I get so involved in our conversation that my embarrassment is forgotten.

I am feeling proud of myself the next morning as we drag our backpacks onto the bed. The smell emanating from them – even while still zipped up – is proof that I have overcome my obsessive urge to hand wash in the bathroom sink every night while travelling. It's something that annoys me even more than it does Trevor. After getting out of the shower each night at Iguazú Falls, I hovered over the basin in the bathroom – dirty clothes in one hand and a bar of soap in the other – but I didn't wash a thing. On past trips, having a backpack full of fresh, clean outfits became the equivalent of a security blanket: even if everything else went to hell, at least I had something to wear. But I am determined things will be different on this trip, and so far my resolution has remained strong.

As Trevor slowly unzips his backpack full of dirty clothes, the reek of stale sweat mixed with a damp jungle funk rises into the air. I gingerly pluck a piece of clothing from my bag. My white t-shirt, since dubbed 'the porno top' – is streaked with mud and still damp. Probably with perspiration, judging by the smell. The contents of our backpacks are ripe and desperately in need of a wash, but first we have to smuggle them out of the hotel and to the laundromat we passed on our way back from the cemetery. We are tempted to give the clothes to Ana for washing at the hotel, but one glance at the hotel's laundry price list confirms it would be cheaper for me to buy a new bra than to have them wash one of mine.

Trevor hands me two plastic laundry sacks embossed with the hotel's fancy gold logo and we cram them full of clothes before stuffing them into our small day-packs. While we attempt to saunter casually through the lobby with our bulging bags, I notice an elderly man standing stiffly by his wife, who is making a big show of relaxing on one of the baroque settees. Her ruffled cream blouse is about 20 years too young for her and is accented with a single strand of black pearls the size of marbles. I would think they were fake if her clothes weren't screaming 'designer label' so loudly. Her husband gives us a courteous nod, but she is less polite. She says something to him in Italian and stares at us so disdainfully I want to run over and point out that she looks just as awful as we do. This is the first time we have been subjected to such open disapproval.

'Money obviously doesn't buy good manners,' I say to Trevor indignantly.

He gives my arm a reassuring squeeze.

'Don't worry about it. If you had that sort of cash to spend on clothes, you'd look a million times better than her anyway.'

There are several people waiting near reception plus a few other couples sitting on either side of the lobby, but the hotel is noticeably quieter than when we arrived.

'Damn!' Trevor exclaims, pointing to the large cases blocking our side exit. 'We'll have to go out the main entrance.'

We pass the large flower arrangements near reception and nod to the concierge as we cross the main lobby, which is so large that velvet lounge suites have been placed around its perimeter for people to sit on. Aside from a maid dusting the already spotless coffee tables, there is no one else nearby.

'So far, so good,' Trevor says as we get closer to the main doors. I am about to agree when I notice the zipper on Trevor's pack has crept open. I lunge towards it, but the bag pops open and my knickers explode onto the red carpet. I grab Trevor by the strap on his bag to haul him backwards.

'Stand there and pretend you're looking at the paintings or something,' I whisper urgently.

'Huh?'

There is no time to explain – I am too busy scrabbling under the velvet chairs trying to retrieve my g-strings. A businessman in a pinstriped suit smirks as I stand up and shove everything back into the bag. Trevor looks around hastily to see if anyone else noticed but it looks like we got away with it.

'Go, go, go!' I link my arm through Trevor's in a feeble attempt at nonchalance as the doorman swings open the door.

'Do you remember dreaming about the glamorous life we'd get to experience at these hotels?' I ask Trevor.

'The style,' he begins, 'the elegance, the cultured refinement of . . .'

'. . . two backpackers flinging dirty undies all over the red carpet!' I finish.

The laundromat seems much further away now we have bags full of dirty clothes on our backs, but we finally make it. Unlike coin-operated laundries in Australia, this laundromat has an elderly woman standing behind a scarred wooden counter. The smell of bleach is overpowering as Trevor holds up the bags in each hand like dead chickens and I thumb through our Spanish phrase book and ask 'how much?'. The woman brushes a lock of faded blond hair off her lined face and writes the amount on a piece of paper as Trevor hands over the bags which are emptied into a raw calico laundry sack. As she is folding our bags, the woman notices the Alvear Palace logo on the front. Her gaze travels from the gold emblem to Trevor and me, and with a look of disbelief she points to the logo and then at us.

'No entiendo,' she says, pointing to the logo and our sack of dirty washing.

I'm not surprised she doesn't understand. Why would guests from the Alvear Palace traipse downtown to drop off their laundry? We don't know enough Spanish to explain, so I start trying to describe our situation in mime. Trevor starts to laugh.

'Pretend to draw out the winning entry,' I tell him, really getting into it. We amass a substantial audience as the rest of the staff come out to see what is going on. We jump up and down in mock delight as we accept our prize and I point at the Alvear Palace logo on the bag, hold up three fingers and mime going to sleep three times.

'*Si, si.*' The woman smiles as though she now understands and says something else in Spanish, before shaking her head in amazement.

The laundry will take a few hours, so we have afternoon tea at a café while we wait.

'This probably sounds crazy, but it's quite nice to get away from the hotel for a while,' Trevor says as our coffees arrive. 'It's not that I don't love it, but . . .'

'. . . it's good to go back to being our daggy old selves?'

'Exactly!'

Having to make an effort to look well dressed every time we leave our room feels too much like hard work and is the complete opposite of our usual holiday objective: one hundred per cent relaxation. Past overseas trips provided the perfect excuse to dress down and take it easy, but we can't bring ourselves to do this at hotels like the Alvear Palace. Make-up for me, shaving every day for Trevor and trying to look our best every time we go outside is a drag.

The staff at the laundromat are extra friendly when we return and collecting all that clean washing makes my day. I am in a great mood as we walk back through Recoleta and into the shopping arcade where we slip through our usual side door to the hotel. But as we emerge at the edge of the lobby and walk towards the lift, I notice one of the security guys watching us intently and mumbling into his cuff. His wrist mike is coupled with a flesh-coloured speaker tucked discreetly into his ear and a tightly coiled wire disappears under the collar of his shirt. We keep moving, but when a couple of his black-suited associates begin striding in our direction, I realise to my horror that we are about to get chucked out. Trevor makes a grab for my arm and drags me towards the lift – probably not the wisest move. In a flurry of rapidly spoken Spanish, the three men half run towards us as one of them calls an urgent 'Excuse me please – sir, madam!'

When a bellboy scoots across the lobby and slides to a dramatic stop between us and the men in black, I think we're in for even more trouble until I recognise him: he was working when we checked in. I could kiss him when he offers a curt explanation to the three security men and sends them on their way. He probably says something like 'I know it's hard to believe, but yes, they *are* guests here', but it gets us out of trouble. The guards give us courteous nods and return to the main lobby while the bellboy escorts us to the lifts and pushes the button.

'Such a superb day to be out in Buenos Aires,' he says pleasantly, as if nothing happened.

I want to thank him, but referring to the fiasco will probably embarrass all of us, so we end up making small talk until the lift arrives. My nightmare about being thrown out of a Leading Hotel of the World nearly became a reality and the whole experience has left me shaken. I console myself that perhaps we were only challenged because the civil unrest is making security staff extra cautious, but when I catch sight of our reflection, I realise I am wrong – I would have thrown us out too.

'We can't let this spoil our last night in Buenos Aires,' Trevor says, and he is right. We've planned to treat ourselves to dinner at a restaurant recommended by Brett and Katey and I've been looking forward to it all day. By the time we get ready and take a taxi to the steakhouse near the centre of town it is nearly 8.30, but the restaurants and bars are deserted. Though it feels late to us, we are dining very early compared to the Argentineans, who eat dinner between 9.30 and midnight. The waiters are still setting up, but one of them stops what he is doing and shows us to a streetside table where we gratefully accept the English menu he offers, even though it feels like cheating. The waiter lights the small candle on our table and asks what we'd like to drink.

'A bottle of Cab Sav would be good,' says Trevor, 'but we aren't sure whether to have one from Chile or Argentina.'

The waiter clutches his heart in mock horror.

'But of course you must choose Argentina!' he says. 'Let me show you.'

He disappears and brings back two small glasses of wine for us to try. When he asks which one is the best, I point to the glass on the left.

'*Si*. Did I not tell you?' he says smugly.

Our waiter is also the restaurant's sommelier and we have an animated discussion about Argentinean wine. Dining so early may be unfashionable, but it means the staff have plenty of time to make our experience special. When our bottle of red arrives, it is accompanied by two glasses of white wine.

'I think our red is better, but while you are in Argentina I think you must try some white wine also,' our waiter explains. 'No charge,' he adds, just in case we misunderstand. The restaurant isn't fancy, especially not compared to the opulent Alvear Palace, but our evening is one of the highlights of our stay in Buenos Aires. Trevor and I sip our wine and watch locals strolling by as the streets outside the restaurant gradually start to fill. Everyone has done their best to dress up, even though some of their outfits look well worn.

'Kind of like us at the Alvear Palace,' Trevor muses.

By the time our steaks arrive, the bar is packed with people enjoying a pre-dinner drink and the restaurant is buzzing, but our waiter still gives us his full attention.

'I used to think Australian beef was the best,' Trevor tells the waiter, as our plates are cleared, 'but that was the best steak I've ever had.'

'Thank you,' he says, looking genuinely pleased. 'I'll tell the kitchen.'

A few minutes later the large chef comes out for a chat. The apron straining across his belly is splattered with food, but he walks between the tables like royalty, stopping to say hello to other diners along the way. He is delighted we enjoyed the meal and curious about the trends developing in Australian restaurants. Our waiter hangs around to do some interpreting, but the language barrier doesn't hamper our conversation. By the time we've had dessert and coffee, there isn't a spare table to be seen and we thank our waiter and wave goodbye to the chef before catching a taxi back to the hotel.

The next morning Ana knocks on our door and asks if she can pack our bags.

'Please,' she adds. 'It is my job but I would also like to do this for you.'

We are so used to packing our own bags that the concept feels strange, but we don't want to say no to Ana yet again. Trevor and I sit in the lounge room of our suite enjoying our last hour of luxury as Ana wraps our clothes in tissue paper and places them carefully into our backpacks. I don't feel uncomfortable around Ana anymore and will miss her when we leave the hotel.

When she is finished, she offers her hand first to Trevor and then to me. 'It is sad to say goodbye,' she says. 'I will miss you.'

'And we'll miss you too,' I say truthfully.

'Here's something for you to remember us by,' Trevor says, pressing a small object into Ana's hand.

She looks at it and laughs with delight.

'Thank you, that is so cute. It is, how do you say it, a ko-a-la?'

Trevor and I nod, pleased she is happy with the gift.

We were worried that the clip-on koalas we bought from a tourist store in Brisbane were a bit tacky, but it appears they are going to be a hit. When Ana squeezes its shoulders, the koala's paws open and the bundle of tightly folded pesos it is holding falls to the floor. Ana picks them up with a frown and tries to give them back, but we refuse to accept them.

'They're for you,' we insist. Ana deserves something more than a koala, especially in light of Argentina's economic woes, but getting her to accept the money is easier said than done. She keeps trying to give it back and we keep insisting she keep it until it gets so ridiculous Ana starts to laugh.

'Okay. Let us say that this is for you,' she says, putting our money firmly on the coffee table, 'and this is for me.' She clips the koala onto the lapel of her jacket and smiles. 'Thank you. He is perfect.'

With that Ana slips out the door but we leave the money for her in an envelope at reception on our way to the airport. Ana put so much effort into ensuring we felt at home in our opulent surroundings that she has more than earned her tip.

5
CALLING ELVIS

'HERE'S YA KEY. Don't break nothin' or you'll have to pay for it.'

'Welcome to America,' I think, smiling weakly at the flinty-eyed check-in clerk. A musty smell I can't quite identify is rising up out of the carpet, which is a lurid pastiche of red and purple swirls.

'At least the hotel's cheap,' I say as we trudge through the lobby towards the lifts.

'And popular,' Trevor marvels, staring into the gaming room where middle-aged punters are jammed against each other. There are no spare vinyl stools at any of the poker machines. The jingling melodies of the pokies are soothing in a mind-numbing way.

'Woo-hoo!'

A man wearing a stained white polo shirt jumps up and down in excitement as money pours out of his poker machine near the entrance. His trousers are creased from sitting in the one spot for a long time.

'See that guy?' Trevor says. 'That's what I'm going to

feel like when we finally have a shower.'

As we wait for the lift I am digging around in my bag, putting away travel documents, when a nickel escapes my purse and drops onto the grimy floor, where it spins for a second. A foot in a scuffed brown sandal slams it to the ground. I am touched someone has come to my aid until I look up at the hard-bitten woman with trowelled on make-up. She glares at me with her jaw set and I realise she has no intention of handing it over. Her creased green eye shadow glows brighter than the flashing signs outside and I'm certainly not going to take her on over five cents. The haughty woman in the foyer at the Alvear Palace was intimidating, but this nickel-hag is truly scary.

We've never been to the United States before, so this trip will be our first real introduction to a culture we've always had trouble understanding. Looking at the red, white and blue circus from the laid-back land Down Under, America seems a very strange place indeed – where carrying a weapon is fine, but glimpsing a naked breast on television is to be avoided at all costs. Everything I know about America and its people has come from the media, so I'm looking forward to seeing the place for myself.

A crazy town like Las Vegas might not be the wisest place to get our first taste of authentic Americana, but we've wanted to come here since our wedding day. The around-the-world airfares meant we could add Las Vegas as a free side trip and the timing is perfect: we'll celebrate our tenth anniversary while we are here and a wish I made on our wedding day is about to come true.

There is no prize hotel for us here, so our Las Vegas accommodation is a huge contrast to the luxurious Alvear Palace and anything but five-star. Our cheap hotel's sludge-coloured façade is covered in flashing billboards advertising 'all you can eat buffets' and 'the cheapest gambling in town', but after our long and exhausting journey from Buenos Aires, all I am after is a cheap sleep.

But inside the room I realise we've got something more: the threadbare brocade curtains, the gold braid running rampant over every soft furnishing and the view of the strip outside provide a fleeting glimpse of what Las Vegas used to be.

The room is a throwback to the time in the forties, fifties and sixties when Las Vegas was *the* place to come and live it up, with Hollywood's glitterati – people like Frank Sinatra, Dean Martin, Sammy Davis Jr and Marlene Dietrich – flocking to the fancy hotels and elaborate shows. Back then Vegas had underworld connections, and in 1946 Benjamin 'Bugsy' Siegel and Charles 'Lucky' Luciano built and opened the luxurious Flamingo Hotel, funded with mob money. It came complete with pink flamingo statues on the lawn and Bugsy worked in its specially constructed bulletproof office.

Vegas isn't quite the classy destination it once was, but this doesn't stop images of elegant women and men wearing dinner jackets and dangerous smiles filling my head as I drift into a deep sleep.

More than six hours have passed and day has turned to night by the time we awake. Light shimmers through a gap in the heavy curtains that Trevor flings aside to reveal a very different Las Vegas to the one we saw before going to bed. The slightly tawdry main street we drove down on arrival has been replaced by a neon extravaganza that is completely over the top. This is the Las Vegas I've come to see and we race outside to experience the fun and excitement promised by the bright lights

Most people come here to gamble but Las Vegas itself has been touched by Lady Luck over the years, especially in the late 1920s when work commenced on the Hoover Dam less than 50 kilometres away. Thousands of dam workers came to town to spend their money and once the dam was finished, a continuous stream of tourists came to see the dam. As if that wasn't enough, in 1931 gambling was legalised for the first time since 1909. Las Vegas had been an underground gaming haven for years, so it wasn't surprising that the first Nevada gaming licence was issued to a local club.

The crowds of holidaymakers make it appear Las Vegas is filled with no one but tourists, but it is the fastest growing city in America. Considering there is always plenty of work and a large amount of the gambling revenue is spent on things like schools and community facilities, it isn't surprising.

'It's Disneyland on drugs,' Trevor says, pointing to an illuminated building in the distance. The full-size castle is spotlit from so many directions that its red, blue and gold turrets glow like magic mushrooms. 'They've got a dinner show with live horses and jousting,' he adds, reading aloud from our guidebook, 'plus 100,000 square feet of gaming. Talk about something for everyone.'

Las Vegas' mega-resorts are designed to provide exactly that. They are destinations in themselves with thousands of hotel rooms, multiple restaurants, huge gaming areas and lots of on-site entertainment. And each hotel has a theme. There is the Luxor, with its pyramid-shaped hotel and full scale reproduction of King Tut's tomb; the New York New York Hotel, with a half-scale Statue of Liberty framed by a miniature Manhattan skyline; and Treasure Island has a large pirate ship floating out the front.

'I think something's about the start,' Trevor says as we squeeze past the crowds outside Treasure Island's lagoon. 'Look, there are people on the ship!'

As actors dressed as pirates emerge slowly from the decks and begin unloading their cargo onto the dock beside the ship, we stop walking and find a spot where we can stand and watch. Not long afterwards a British frigate emerges from behind the hotel and sails into the lagoon.

'Can you believe that?' Trevor laughs as the *Britannia* comes to a stop in front of the pirate ship and begins firing mock cannonballs. Fireworks make barrels of gunpowder look like they are exploding and crew members fly into the water.

'Aaarrrrggggh, me hearties,' one pirate cries as he leaps off the rigging and splashes into the lagoon.

The actors are hamming it up shamelessly and the audience claps and laughs like children at a pantomime. It appears the pirates have met their match until their captain grabs a rope and swings across his ship to light the fuse on its final cannon.

'The Brits are finished!' the old guy next to me cheers as the *Britannia* sinks slowly into the lagoon and the show comes to an end.

'How often do they do that?' Trevor wonders aloud.

'Every 90 minutes,' a tourist behind us answers. 'There's a volcano down the road that's pretty good too.'

We go to see the 18-metre-high cone-shaped waterfall at the Mirage Resort morph into a volcano. Flames shoot out of its centre and lighting effects turn the water into molten lava.

Once it finishes, we squeeze around the people waiting for the next eruption and continue down the crowded footpaths. Both sides of the street are so packed that it is almost impossible to move and everyone is bathed in sweat – including us. There isn't much humidity in the desert air but we probably don't smell much better than when we first arrived after our gruelling trip from Argentina.

I was expecting lots of overseas visitors but when

I overhear the conversations going on around us, it sounds like everyone is from the United States.

'It's the last-minute deals,' Trevor explains.

Las Vegas used to be a playground for the rich and famous but now it is the home of the package deal. These are heavily discounted if you are prepared to take them up at short notice and include flights, accommodation and food. We have a longstanding joke that the only thing better than a holiday is a cheap holiday and it looks like everyone here agrees.

Back at the hotel, Trevor steps gingerly into our ancient shower for the second time that day and fiddles hopefully with the taps. 'So, what do you think of Vegas?' he asks.

'It's a fun place, but once you've seen the strip and the shops that's about all there is to it unless you're into gambling.'

'Or Elvis weddings. Ready for tomorrow?'

Am I ready? I can't wait! When Trevor asked on our wedding day how I wanted to celebrate our tenth anniversary, I told him I wanted a trip to Vegas to renew our vows with Elvis. It became a bit of a joke as we've never been huge Elvis fans, but tomorrow morning we'll be doing exactly that.

Before leaving Australia we did a lot of research on Vegas weddings and decided we were 'going to Graceland'. The Graceland Wedding Chapel is over 50 years old and was the first chapel to offer Elvis weddings. As we wait at the bus stop outside our hotel, I blot my face with a tissue in an attempt to stop my make-up running in the dry desert heat. It is just after 10 am, but the temperature is already soaring.

'A bit different from the first time, isn't it?' Trevor says with a smile and I think back to our wedding on Lord Howe Island, a World Heritage-listed spot two hours by plane off the east coast of Australia. Our parents flew over for the ceremony on a headland overlooking a beach known as Lovers' Bay, where Trevor and I spent our wedding day snorkelling and relaxing until it was time to get dressed.

'You must be the most relaxed bride I've ever seen,' Trevor said, as we walked down the hill to meet the celebrant. A magnificent sunset turned the sky bright pink while we exchanged our vows and Trevor and I sipped champagne with our families as the sun disappeared below the horizon.

My wedding day was so memorable that I was surprised this morning when I caught myself taking as much time getting ready for our 'Elvis wedding' as I had for the real one. Originally I suggested renewing our vows in Las Vegas as a bit of fun but I feel differently about it now we are here. I want our ceremony at the Graceland Wedding Chapel to be special and when I was dressing I found myself wishing I'd brought along something more suitable. Trevor assumed I'd be wearing my little black dress, so my protests that black is an inappropriate colour to get married in were met with long-suffering looks.

'You must be the only person who reads those books on modern manners from cover to cover and actually enjoys them,' Trevor grumbled, looking at his watch.

It's true, I do love books on etiquette and have quite a collection, but I have none with me. Even if I did, I'm sure none has a chapter on what you should wear to an Elvis wedding.

The bus trip only takes 15 minutes, but the area around the wedding chapel looks different from where we've just come from. We are still on the same main street, but the fancy neon and dancing lights have been replaced by rundown buildings and appliance repair stores and the neighbourhood feels like a place fallen on hard times.

'Well, you certainly can't miss it,' Trevor says, pointing to the Graceland Wedding Chapel.

The tiny white chapel, with its miniature bell tower and brightly painted trim, is the exact opposite of the buildings surrounding it. Someone must put in a lot of time and effort to keep it looking so smart. Trevor and I hold hands as we approach the white picket fence, which only comes up to my knees, and walk onto the porch and through the front door.

The tiny reception area is dominated by a wood-panelled reception desk and the walls are papered with glossy photographs of happy couples. In the pictures, couples of all ages are wearing everything from traditional bridal wear to jeans and t-shirts and there is even a wedding party dressed as Elvis.

'Isn't that some heavy metal singer?' I ask, pointing to a guy with long hair and a very young bride. Trevor peers at the photo but he isn't sure.

I hear someone clearing their throat and turn around to see a woman in her mid fifties standing behind the desk, clasping her hands together and looking extremely uncomfortable.

'Oh dear,' she says, fingering her 'Peggy' name tag anxiously after we tell her who we are. 'I guess you didn't get my message about Elvis. I left a message on his answerphone reminding him about your booking, but he's only just got back to me which means he'll be about an hour late. I called your hotel, but you must have already left.'

Peggy's floral cotton blouse is buttoned neatly at the neck and I can smell the spray starch she used on the collar. The needlework cushions on the seats in reception look like Peggy's own work and her ample curves hold the promise of hearty servings and home-cooked meals. She reminds me so much of a quintessential 1950s sitcom mom that when she bustles out from behind the counter, I half expect her to give us milk and cookies, but what she offers is even better. Peggy feels so bad about the mix-up she promises to make it up to us with complimentary photos and a free video of our ceremony. After sitting us down, she gets us glasses of water and chats about what it is like living in Las Vegas.

'Do you ever go to the strip?' Trevor asks.

'Sometimes if there's a good show in town, but we

find it a bit tacky. Oh no, I hope I haven't offended you!' Peggy exclaims hurriedly. 'I mean, you two have come a long way to see it and . . .'

'No, no, it's okay,' Trevor laughs. 'We think it's tacky too.'

She smiles with relief. Peggy's tales of raising her children and socialising with friendly neighbours seem a world away from the neon craziness of the strip and show us a very different side of Las Vegas. Trevor and I are so involved in our conversation, we almost forget why we are here until Elvis comes bounding through the door.

'Hi guys,' he booms, holding out an enormous hand for us to shake. 'I hope this turns out to be worth waiting for. I'll try to do something a bit special for you.'

When it comes to Elvis, we've been hoping for 'big Vegas' rather than 'skinny *Blue Hawaii*' and the man inside the tiny chapel couldn't be more perfect. Elvis' shiny black rhinestone-encrusted jumpsuit strains at the seams and glittering rings adorn each of his chubby fingers. It is even his own black hair that has been combed and lacquered into an elaborate quiff.

Elvis and Peggy disappear out the back and we take our places in front of the closed doors leading from reception into the chapel. As the opening bars of 'I Can't Help Falling in Love With You' float out, Peggy returns and throws open the arched doors with a flourish, then steps aside so we can begin our slow walk up the aisle.

Trevor and I look at each other and exchange smiles as we step onto the deep purple carpet and walk between the miniature pews lining either side of the tiny church, which comes complete with pretty stained-glass windows. The man who only looked like a person dressed as Elvis when we saw him five minutes ago has been transformed; even the way he moves has changed. As he croons tenderly into a microphone set up in front of the pulpit, our Elvis is remarkably like the real thing.

We come to a halt in front of him as he finishes singing and begins to speak in a soft Tennessee drawl.

'Dearly beloveds – that's you guys,' he adds with a wink, 'we're gathered here in the Graceland Wedding Chapel . . .'

He talks about love, togetherness and the significance of making a sacred commitment to another person for the rest of your life. As an instrumental version of 'Love Me Tender' plays softly in the background, I glance at Trevor and am not surprised to see his soft, serious expression. I was expecting laughs and crazy fun, not heartfelt sentiments that sound sincere and meaningful, even in the tacky confines of a fake wedding chapel on the highway to LA. It takes both of us by surprise and I am kicking myself for leaving my tissues out in reception. Trevor's attempt to wipe a tear from the corner of his eye is disguised as a scratch of his cheek, but I notice even if Elvis doesn't and squeeze Trevor's hand lovingly.

'It's such a busy world out there,' Elvis says, 'that sometimes it's easy to forget what matters most. But love, tenderness and making time for one another really is the most important thing of all.'

'True love is a precious gift that not everyone receives,' he continues, looking at us both in turn, 'but judging by those smiles, I'd say you're two of the lucky ones.'

Peggy is doing a masterful job of operating the video recorder set up on a tripod and moves around the room with her camera, snapping off photos with the practised ease of someone who's done it a million times before.

Once he's finished the formal part of the ceremony, Elvis drapes a narrow pink scarf embossed with the words *'With Love From Elvis'* around my shoulders and turns Trevor and me to face each other. With strict instructions to stare passionately into each other's eyes, it is time for us to exchange our 'solemn vows', promising again to love and cherish each other.

'And "I promise to never leave you at heartbreak hotel." Or any other hotel,' Elvis adds with a grin, 'unless it's one of those fancy ones you guys have been staying at.'

Trevor and I laugh. Peggy must have told Elvis about our prize before the ceremony. Right now, I am more grateful than ever that we won the competition, as Las Vegas is a long way to come just to renew your vows. We probably wouldn't have made it here if it weren't for our prize.

'"... because I'll always be your hunka hunka burnin' love."'

Trevor is finding it so hard not to laugh that his face turns red.

'Nearly finished,' Elvis chuckles. I can tell he is

enjoying himself. '". . . and you'll always be my little good luck charm."'

Trevor finishes his vows and then it is my turn. I have to promise Trevor I'll love him tender and never return him to sender before agreeing not to step on his blue suede shoes.

This is more like what I was expecting. Elvis leans casually on the pulpit and plays up to the video camera as we repeat each tacky line after him, before he segues effortlessly into another song. He hams up the lyrics with meaningful glances while urging us to keep gazing passionately into each other's eyes. We eventually give up trying to be romantic and start dancing instead.

The practised way Elvis delivers certain lines makes me realise he's said these things countless times before, but there is no hiding how much he enjoys his work. His well-padded hips gyrate with unbridled enthusiasm and the long suede tassels running down either side of his ample belly flick around like spaghetti.

'This is brilliant,' Trevor whispers. 'He's great, isn't he?'

Even though Elvis is only playing to an audience of two, not counting Peggy who's undoubtedly seen it all before, he works the tiny chapel like a superstar playing in front of thousands of adoring fans. Perhaps it's because we are so obviously enjoying ourselves, but I feel that Elvis is keeping his promise to do something a bit special.

At the end of his energetic performance, Elvis mops his brow with a white handkerchief and shakes our hands before turning towards the video camera with a mischievous grin. He directs us to walk back down the aisle towards the chapel doors. 'But you're not allowed to go outside just yet,' he calls after us.

Trevor and I hold hands and whisper excitedly as we walk back down the purple carpet.

Elvis pushes a button on his sound system and the backing track for 'Viva Las Vegas' fills the chapel as he grooves down the aisle towards us, shaking his butt from side to side. He comes to a stop beside me and brings the microphone to his lips then links arms with me. As I take Trevor's arm, Elvis sings and we all high-kick our way up the aisle. We stop at the end to boogie on the spot as Elvis thrusts the microphone towards us for a couple of enthusiastic choruses to wind up the song.

After Peggy turns off the video camera, Elvis excuses himself and ducks out the back, returning with two extra sets of dark glasses which he hands to us.

'I know I've said it before, but I really am sorry about being late. I thought these would make for some good photos, so if you guys come and stand over here . . .'

Peggy arranges the three of us in front of the stained-glass window behind the pulpit and we clown around for the camera. It isn't exactly a spiritual experience, but as I look over at Trevor and Elvis leaning against each other in fits of laughter, I feel an overwhelming love for my husband and an intense gratitude that we've managed to find each other.

Over the past ten years, Trevor and I have done things we never would have dreamed possible before we met.

I've gone from being a secretary to a corporate trainer and Trevor's first photographic exhibition is less than six months away. The promise we've just made to 'share our triumphs and our disappointments' has certainly reminded me of our wonderful life together so far. Even when things aren't so great, we can always rely on each other no matter what. I hadn't expected our ceremony's emotional impact but it turns out to be the perfect way for us to renew our commitment. The wacky sentimentality of our vows with Elvis has combined the emotional power and sense of fun that is the essence of our union.

After the photo session, we talk to Elvis about his life as an impersonator and as the man inside the sequinned jump suit slowly begins to emerge, we discover Dale is very different from his alter ego. When Trevor asks Dale if he enjoys doing the Elvis weddings, he answers without hesitation.

'Oh yes, very much so.'

Out of character Dale is quietly spoken and his showy brashness is replaced by a thoughtful intelligence. His responses to our questions are so considered it often seems like a long time before he answers. 'This may seem strange, but I take my job very seriously,' he tells us. 'Being asked to play a part in people's lives is a real privilege and it means a lot to me.'

Dale is one of the 'Vegas Elvis originals' – he has been doing Elvis weddings for more than 20 years – but we are surprised to discover he is also an ordained minister.

'Have you married many couples as Elvis?' I ask.

'Nope, not one,' says Dale. 'I won't actually *marry* anyone dressed as Elvis. I nip off for a quick change after I've pronounced them man and wife and we do the fun stuff after the ceremony.'

He must realise that we are confused.

'Exchanging vows and making a life-long commitment is a serious business,' he explains. 'I don't think it's right to make light of something like that.'

'Does anyone do a full Elvis ceremony?'

'Probably,' Dale says with a shrug. 'But that's their choice.'

Initially Las Vegas gave me the impression that everything here is fake and outlandish, but Dale and Peggy's genuine warmth makes me realise this isn't the case.

Trevor and I head back uptown for a celebratory lunch at Mandalay Bay, one of the more upmarket casinos. I've read on several websites that the casino likes to think of itself as 'one of the classiest on the strip' but considering it is up against fake Eiffel towers and hotels themed around children's stories like *Treasure Island*, Mandalay Bay doesn't exactly have stiff competition.

'It's like a cut-price version of a Leading Hotel of the World,' Trevor observes, as we walk through the casino's air-conditioned corridors.

There is plenty of gold and marble, but none of it is genuine and the large pot plants in the foyer look suspiciously plastic. We take the lift down to the Border

Grill, a restaurant we have heard is great, and are shown to a table for two.

'Hi, my name's Melanie and I'm your waitress for today.'

Trevor knows I always have to fight the urge to politely introduce myself back when this happens, and he gives me a knowing smile. After ordering, we sit back to look around the restaurant. The crowd is more up-market than I expected and most people look like they've dressed up for lunch. The couples chat amiably, sipping margaritas and glasses of wine that we eye enviously. Alcohol is out of the question for us – we simply can't afford it here – so we raise our water high instead, in a toast to Las Vegas and to us.

When Melanie returns with two towering plates of food, I am sure she's mixed up our order.

'I think that might be somebody else's,' I tell her. 'We only ordered one meal to share.'

Melanie gives me a weird look. 'No, ma'am, this is definitely yours.'

She is holding a plate so large it is almost a platter – sharing one meal to save money isn't going to be a problem. A mountain of spicy pork is accompanied by guacamole, there are greens on the side plus there is a second plate stacked with fresh flour tortillas. It is delicious and we can't believe our luck.

After lunch and a walk up the strip, Trevor and I dart into the nearest casino to escape the heat. All we want is somewhere air-conditioned so the miniature version of

Venice we discover on the ground floor of the hotel is a bonus, albeit a bizarre one. I can't decide which is tackier – the hotel's white plaster statues depicting Venetian artworks or the junk inside its souvenir shops. Trevor puts down the miniature gondola he's been looking at and walks out of the store so we can peer over the balcony.

'Look at all that romance,' he says, as we stand on the top level of the shopping mall and look down at the Grand Canal. The people in the gondolas are more interested in gazing into the shop windows than each other's eyes. I've always thought the gondola rides in Venice are a bit tacky, but they are nothing compared to this. This heavily chlorinated Grand Canal winds through a shopping boulevard while gondoliers with American accents steer boats that are the gondola equivalent of sawn-off shotguns. They are at least nine feet shorter than the real thing, but this hasn't deterred the long queue of people waiting to pay their US$15 for a ten-minute ride. Nearly all the gondoliers are singing 'O Sole Mio', but unfortunately not at the same time.

'Would the new bride like to honeymoon in Venice?' Trevor teases.

Some of the singing is excellent and the set-up is certainly a novelty – it's not every day you can float down a canal in the middle of the Nevada desert – but this Venice is as far removed from romantic as you can get.

'Do you realise the real Venice is less than a month away for us?' Trevor says.

It's still hard to believe we are visiting so many different places in the space of five months. *Vogue* advertised the competition as 'the trip of a lifetime' and it is – even before we added the extra destinations. Las Vegas is the first extra stop I suggested we include and, by strange coincidence, the second one was Venice. I didn't plan to see them both on the same day but Las Vegas is just that kind of place.

Renewing our vows with Elvis saw one of my long-held wishes come true, but as we fly out of Las Vegas the next morning, I feel a twinge of guilt that Trevor won't get to experience one of his: a scenic flight over the Grand Canyon.

I clearly remember how disappointed he was during the planning stages of our trip when I broke the news that our funds weren't going to stretch to accommodate his longed-for flight. Watching Trevor make a paper aeroplane out of the brochure and throw it despondently into the air made me feel awful.

But our Las Vegas luck is still with us, for not long after takeoff, the pilot makes an announcement. 'If you look down to the left,' he says casually, 'you'll see we're flying directly over the Grand Canyon.'

Before I even have time to register what the pilot said, Trevor's seatbelt is undone and he is leaping into my lap. At six foot three, he resembles a Great Dane trying to scramble out the window of a Mini, and I start laughing before volunteering to swap seats. It appears Trevor is going to get his scenic flight after all.

We hold hands as I lean towards the window to catch glimpses of the Colorado River snaking through the canyon like a thin blue ribbon and the rocky red canyon walls glowing in the harsh Arizona sun. The minerals in the rock strata give the canyon its unique colour and its rim seems incredibly close to the plane, compared with the canyon bottom, which is over 1,500 metres away at its shallowest point. The majesty of the landscape below us seems even more spectacular after our previous flights, which felt like nothing more than a way of getting from one place to another.

When I look over at Trevor fogging up the window with his hot breath, I can't bring myself to take up his honourable offer to return to his own seat and content myself with watching his expression change as he gives me a blow-by-blow description of what lies below. As I listen to his excited voice, I begin to understand Trevor's concession not to take the scenic flight obviously meant much more than he'd let on and, when I see his un-disguised delight, I feel guilty that he came so close to missing out. We both made sacrifices during the planning stages of the trip, but being in charge of our budget meant I ended up having more of a say when it came to what we could and couldn't afford.

Although, unfortunately, not even this can save me when it comes to our next destination. Trevor is deter-mined to go to Washington DC and there isn't a damn thing I can do about it.

6

THE MOST BORING
TOURIST SITE AWARD

'I'VE WANTED TO SEE this place since I was a kid,' Trevor says, pressing his face so hard against the fence around the White House that its metal bars leave long, thick indents on his cheeks.

I'm finding it hard to get excited about the White House. It wasn't originally even white. It was only after the War of 1812, when British troops set fire to the building and it had to be rebuilt, that a decision was made to paint the sandstone exterior to cover the fire damage. I think the building has too many curves and colonnades to be taken seriously, but then I would think that: there's not much I like about Washington. The White House has become my scapegoat and I've been picking on it since we arrived. I'm almost beginning to enjoy it.

Even before we won the trip, Washington DC was at the top of Trevor's list of dream destinations and right down the bottom of mine. Whenever Trevor has a book in his hand – which is often – it is a political thriller and since most of these are set in Washington, his fascination with the city has only grown. I have no patience with anything even vaguely political, so the prospect of visiting Washington DC – the national capital – held zero appeal and I've been dreading coming here ever since it appeared (at Trevor's insistence) on our itinerary.

The bright side is our accommodation. It isn't five-star, but I get the feeling our stay is going to be fun as we got on famously with our Washington hosts, Sid and Lisa, when we met at a friend's barbecue just after we won our prize.

'That's fantastic,' Sid said when we told him about our win. 'Imagine a couple of backpackers getting to stay at all those five-star hotels! Bet you didn't tell *Vogue* you got their mag from the library.'

'And don't you tell them *either*, Sid, you stirrer,' our mutual friend warned. Sid was a journalist for one of Australia's major newspapers and he seemed to know everyone.

As the night progressed, Lisa explained she was re-locating to Washington for work and, in a rush of drunken bonhomie, she and Sid insisted we come and stay with them on our way to New York. I still have no interest in Washington's monuments, but I'm looking forward to spending more time with Sid and Lisa.

Our flight from Las Vegas was followed by a bus trip from the airport, so Trevor and I are weary by the time we arrive in downtown Washington. But nevertheless,

Trevor is so keen to see the White House that we stop off for a look on the way to Sid and Lisa's place. After what seems like hours of staring at the building, we set off on the 20-minute walk to our hosts' house. It feels like much longer, carrying our backpacks.

'Are we there yet?' Trevor whines, flashing me a cheeky smile.

After our arduous journey getting to Las Vegas, this phrase has become a running joke. I laugh and shake my head, then try to distract myself from my bulging backpack and blistered feet by looking at the narrow brick apartment buildings lining both sides of the street. Each has a small paved garden out the front, with either small beds of bright spring flowers or a tangle of weeds, depending on how houseproud the owner is. A guy dressed like a rapper walks down the street towards us, pausing briefly to slip off his headphones as he gets closer.

'Hey, where yo' goin'?' he teases, pointing to our backpacks. 'There ain't no campgrounds 'round here.'

I can hear music pumping out of the headphones in his hand.

'You want directions or somethin'?'

We smile and shake our heads. Trevor already has a map so there is nothing for it but to keep walking. By the time we arrive at Sid and Lisa's rented apartment, we are drenched in perspiration and have to lean against the wrought-iron gate to catch our breath. I finally summon enough energy to bang the heavy iron knocker and Sid opens the door, pausing to lean casually against its edge.

'You two look buggered – come on in,' he says, hitching up the waistband of his faded pants and walking up the stairs in front of us. With his ancient t-shirt and hair sticking up crazily at the back, Sid doesn't look much like the high-powered political journalist he was before leaving Australia with Lisa, who accepted a top job in Washington. Sid jokes about his new life as 'a kept man', but I suspect that underneath the laughter he is wondering how he'll cope with the change in lifestyle.

Trevor and I look at the stairs in front of us and groan theatrically before lifting our legs onto the first tread. We've hardly bought anything on our travels to date, but our backpacks still seem to get heavier every time we put them on. I feel like a sweaty snail as I bend myself double and lug my black canvas 'home' up to the top of the stairs where Sid is standing. He waits patiently until we both make it, then points silently up another flight of stairs to our room, laughing when he sees the looks on our faces.

Our bed for the next two nights is a double mattress that has been made up on the floor with crisp royal blue sheets and, as Sid and Lisa's bedroom has a large en suite, we effectively have our own bathroom. I am the first one in there and climb gratefully into the shower. The curtain is covered with a full size map of the world and I stand with hot water cascading down my back and trace our journey so far on the wet plastic.

I don't think either of us understood the scale of our trip before we left Australia but, as I look at the map and listen to the water's pitter patter on the shower curtain, it starts to dawn on me how much we have experienced and how much adventure is still to come. It is strange to think that home is still months away. When people asked if we'd miss our modest little house in Brisbane while we were overseas, we assumed they were kidding.

'When we're staying in all those five-star hotels? Not likely,' Trevor laughed.

But now I am feeling perhaps they were wiser than we thought. It isn't the house itself I am missing, but the comfort and familiarity of somewhere Trevor and I have lived for years. Every corner of it has become a point of reference for all the good times we've shared and seeing the comfortable clutter of Sid and Lisa's apartment makes me lonesome for our own homey muddle back in Australia.

When Trevor knocks on the bathroom door with another reminder to hurry up, I turn off the water, push aside the world and step onto the bath mat. After changing into some fresh clothes, I trot downstairs where Sid pours me a glass of Australian chardonnay and asks if I want to put on a load of washing before dinner.

'You're better than Ana,' I laugh and tell him about our glamorous butler at the Alvear Palace.

It looks like the 'life of leisure', as Sid ironically refers to it, is agreeing with him. He's lost quite a bit of weight and, as he talks enthusiastically about Washington's great jogging tracks and bike paths, I notice how relaxed he is. Sid is in demand as a freelance journalist and various publications keep him busy with requests for articles. It looks like he's stumbled upon a pleasant alternative to the high-powered life he was living in Brisbane. After Sid hands Trevor a beer with a cheery 'Here ya go, mate', the three of us sit back on the lounge to await Lisa's arrival. By the time she flies in the door just before seven o'clock, Trevor and I are onto our second drink and talking to Sid about our prize hotels.

'Does it feel weird going from a fancy hotel to a budget one?' he asks.

'Not exactly weird, but it really makes you appreciate the five-star places,' Trevor says. 'Then again, we've only stayed at one dodgy hotel on this trip.'

'The only dodgy one *so far*,' Sid reminds us with a grin.

Lisa stops for a quick chat before dashing upstairs to change out of her suit and re-emerges in a pair of ancient fleecy track pants and fluffy socks.

'Sorry to rush away,' she says, 'but that feels so much better.'

As Lisa pads into the kitchen to get herself a glass of wine, the pilled red fabric around her bum sags like she is wearing a full nappy. Trevor looks over at me and smirks. Considering Lisa is the Australian Broadcasting Commission's highly respected Washington correspondent, whom we see on the news each night updating us on world events, her current look will take a bit of getting used to.

Lisa flops dramatically onto the couch, but not so dramatically that she spills her glass of wine, and grabs a handful of chips. I've forgotten how her face, which appears so professional and composed on television, can contort into such crazy exaggerated expressions. As she regales us with self-deprecating tales about standing in front of the White House in the snow and attempting to deliver a bulletin through chattering teeth, I am reminded why Trevor and I liked Lisa so much the first time we met. Despite her high profile, Lisa is charmingly unaffected and her keen intelligence is tempered by a wicked sense of humour. The spicy aroma of Sid's chicken curry fills the apartment as the four of us talk about how Sid and Lisa have settled in to life in America.

'Did you find it scary moving to Washington less than three months after September 11?' Trevor asks Lisa, who's propped her feet on the coffee table the same way I do back home.

'Not really,' Lisa says. 'I was so flat out at work that I didn't have much time to think about it.'

'What was the hardest thing about coming here?' asks Trevor.

'Tipping!' Sid and Lisa cry out in unison.

They explain it is common to tip for just about every-thing in America and that they were hopeless at this when they first arrived.

'At the hairdresser, you don't just add a tip when you

pay at the register,' Lisa says. 'You're supposed to go around and personally hand cash to each and every person who touched your hair.'

I mentally go through the process of having my hair done.

'Wash, colour, cut, blow dry – that could be up to four people.'

'Five actually,' Sid interjects. 'You forgot the woman at the counter.'

'And the girl who made your coffee,' Lisa says, 'which makes six.'

Aside from the odd tipping faux pas, things have been going well but Sid and Lisa are still missing something they previously took for granted: Australians.

'We're so glad you guys came,' says Lisa happily. 'Washington's great but we've missed having some Aussies around.'

'How come?'

'It's hard to explain. I suppose Australians don't seem to need people like Oprah to help them analyse the meaning of life. They just roll up their sleeves and get on with it.'

We try to work out exactly what it is that makes Australians unique, but it isn't easy. It seems so much about us is a contradiction. Our reputation for being easygoing is well deserved, but the laid-back attitude only goes so far – Aussies don't like to be pushed around and aren't afraid to say so – and for a nation affectionately dubbed as lazy, our inherently strong work ethic makes no sense at all. Using humour to deflect the pain of life's bitter blows is the norm and our easygoing exterior frequently hides an iron will.

'You are so typical,' Sid explains, pointing emphatically at the two of us. 'Instead of the latest terrorist rumours scaring you off, they made you even more determined to go on your trip.'

We don't tell Sid, but our supposedly brave move has seen us travelling at the safest time for years. Security is so pumped up, especially at the world's airports, that the bad guys don't stand a chance.

When we get up the next morning, our hosts are eating breakfast and grappling good-naturedly with the newspaper, having what sounds like a familiar squabble over who gets which bit first. The two journos are only interested in the bits of the newspaper I usually toss in the bin, so I am still able to settle down with the weekend colour magazine. I beat Trevor to the jar of Vegemite in the centre of the table, slather it on my toast and bite down on the slightly burnt bread with a satisfied crunch.

'This is really nice,' I say, looking around as I cradle my cup of coffee.

'You guys have been away for a while now,' Sid says. Trevor and I nod. 'No wonder you're desperate for a Vegemite hit.'

The toast isn't what I was talking about, but I smile. After such a long time living out of a suitcase, it feels good to settle back into a more normal routine, even if it is only for a while. We didn't realise how mentally and physically exhausting continually moving from one place to another would be. Sid and Lisa's feels like a haven where we can rest and recharge our batteries.

I've barely had time to slurp down the last of my coffee when Trevor drags me off to see the White House again, even though I would give anything to stay curled up with the newspaper instead. I am not interested in the sights outside, but Trevor is thrilled to be here so I try to summon some enthusiasm.

'There's not as much security as I thought there'd be,' Trevor says as we get closer.

Or as many tourists, I think to myself. There are only a handful of other people around and most of them wear suits and hurry past us on their way to work.

I find it hard to comprehend what the attraction is for Trevor: all I see is a boring building that looks much smaller and less impressive than on television, but Trevor is in raptures. I am sure it isn't just seeing the White House that is making him so happy. While his first choice of add-on destination was always going to be Washington DC, coming here was out of the question until we met Sid and Lisa. We could have stretched our budget to cover living expenses or accommodation in Washington, but not both. When Sid and Lisa invited us to stay, Trevor joked that his prayers had been answered. It also meant my nightmare had come true, but I kept that to myself. I watch my husband staring at the White House and can almost hear the dialogue from all those action novels running through his head.

He is, and has always been, a contradiction. My first

Christmas gift from him was a subscription to the theatre so we could see plays together and one of our early dates was a visit to an art gallery. Not to impress me, but because there was an exhibition he wanted to see. My girl-friends, who have to drag their partners along to anything even mildly cultural, are incredulous enough without me explaining that Trevor's love of the arts is combined with a passion for movies with explosions, car chases and ridiculously rugged heroes saving the day. It is an unusual combination, but even though the books and movies are largely to blame for our Washington visit, these disparate parts of Trevor's personality still delight me.

Trevor sets up his camera gear and I sit on a nearby bench, watching people standing in front of the White House's high fence having their photo taken. The friend holding the camera directs their subject 'a little to the right, a little to the left' until it looks like the tourists are square dancing. Across the street, a group of anti-war protesters sits peacefully under some trees, sipping soft drinks and chatting amiably with passers-by. One of their placards reads 'What part of "thou shalt not kill" don't we understand? Change all armies into Peace Corps.'

It sounds like a good idea to me. No one has gone to war yet, but a lot of people want to after what happened on September 11. I am contemplating walking over to see the protesters when Trevor returns and drags me to the train station for a ten-minute ride to the Pentagon – one of the largest office buildings in the world and the proud winner of my 'Most Boring Tourist Site' award.

'There isn't anything to see,' I say, scowling at the high security fences. The White House is finally off the hook: I have found a more worthy victim.

The Pentagon is surrounded by a sea of car parks for the thousands of employees who work there and looks exactly like what it is – a huge office block constructed in 1943. It is grey and ugly and populated by officious military personnel who stride past without giving us a second glance. There are a few security guards wandering around so Trevor asks one of them about tours, but they've been cancelled since September 11.

'You can go around the corner and see the hole where the plane went in though,' the guard offers, referring to the aircraft that crashed into the Pentagon 30 minutes after the two planes hit the World Trade Center.

'It was going over 300 miles an hour but some of the workers here didn't know we'd been hit. The Pentagon's made up of these five wedge-shaped sections,' he says, arranging his hands to show us how they fit together, 'so a lot of people were protected.'

I look up at the Pentagon and try to imagine an aeroplane ploughing into the side of it. The building looks so solid from where we are standing, with its sheer concrete wall and evenly spaced windows, but it couldn't withstand the aeroplane's impact. The smoking hole it left in the side of the Pentagon horrified me when I first saw it on the news. Of the thousands of people who went to work at the Pentagon that day expecting just another day at the office, 125 never made it home.

'Do you want to go and see the crash site?' Trevor asks.

'No. I wouldn't have minded touring the building, but I don't want to relive September 11. It was bad enough the first time.'

I know many people feel the need to see where the events of that day took place, either to provide a sense of closure or simply out of morbid curiosity, but I'm not one of them. Trevor decides to give it a miss as well, even though I suspect he would like to go and have a look. Our visit to the Pentagon has been a non-event until a loudhailer booms across the grounds.

'Ma'am, excuse me, ma'am. Yes *you*, ma'am – with the camera. Please put your hands in front of you and approach the vehicle.'

The green jeep that screeches to a dramatic stop holds the promise of some much-needed excitement, but I can't see what the fuss is about until I notice a middle-aged couple staring at it like deer caught in the glare of a semi-trailer's headlights. The woman's small instamatic camera has frozen halfway through its journey up to her eye.

'Lower the camera please, ma'am.'

The woman snaps her hand down to her side and almost stands to attention, her soldier-like pose contrasting sharply with her pink singlet top and red hibiscus-print pants. The poor woman needs a visit from the fashion police – not two guys in a military jeep.

'Thank you, ma'am. Now, please approach the vehicle.'

The hapless tourist looks helplessly towards her male companion for guidance. As the soldiers' loud-hailer booms '*Now*, please, ma'am', he slips an arm deftly around her waist and propels her towards the jeep.

'I told you not to,' he hisses.

The bored soldiers lean out the window like they are ordering fries at the drive-through and give the woman a stern dressing-down while she nods earnestly and shoves the camera back into her bag like she's been burned. I thought it was common knowledge that you shouldn't photograph any military buildings, not just the Pentagon, but perhaps it is something that Trevor told me. Aside from the fact there are signs everywhere showing a camera with a big red line through it, I can't understand why anyone would want to take photographs of something as boring as the Pentagon in the first place.

Once we realise the show is over, Trevor and I follow the camera-happy tourists to the train station and spend the next few hours exploring the Museum of American History, which houses everything from the flag 'Old Glory' to some props from 'M*A*S*H', before stopping in a nearby park to eat our cut lunch.

'Washington is a bit like Canberra,' I say, as we walk towards the Lincoln Memorial, our last stop of the day. Australia's national capital has a similar mix of office buildings, monuments and memorials and most of the people who live there work for the government.

Washington is nicely laid out and the people are friendly but, like Canberra, it feels a bit soulless.

The Lincoln Memorial reminds me of a Greek temple and I touch one of its white columns as we walk inside the cool building and pause in front of Abraham Lincoln's feet. Unlike the White House, this building is bigger than I expected and the 19-foot-high statue of Lincoln inside it looks both imposing and benevolent.

'Are you enjoying Washington more than you thought you would?' Trevor asks.

Strangely enough, I am: though the buildings are as underwhelming to me as I'd expected, I love watching Trevor enjoy himself and Washington has also provided me with an unexpected trip highlight – staying with Sid and Lisa. They are excellent company and not having to worry about fitting in or what other people are thinking is a tremendous relief.

Staying with Sid and Lisa means we are able to revel in being our less-than-glamorous selves – the complete opposite of our stays at the Leading Hotels of the World. The toughest part of starting the day at Sid and Lisa's is battling over the Vegemite, whereas at the fancy hotels my mornings begin with a despondent flick through the wardrobe. Most of my outfits look due for the rag bag already and my good poloneck sweaters have been reduced to a raw woolly tangle where my backpack straps rub against them. Looking at them makes me acutely aware of how out of place they look surrounded by the opulence of whichever hotel we are staying in.

On the morning of our departure, Sid and Lisa catch the subway with us to Washington's Union Station so they can see us off. It was the largest station in the world when it was built in the early 1900s and still receives over 25 million visitors a year, but I would give anything to be back at the apartment instead. Sid and Lisa's cheerful chatter does little to hide the way we are feeling and we all stand to one side, shuffling awkwardly on the spot as people stream past us.

'I wish we didn't have to go.' I blurt it out before I even realise what I am going to say. We are reluctant to leave the little patch of Australia we've stumbled across and the four of us throw our arms around each other's shoulders as the final call to board burbles through an overhead speaker. As the train pulls away from the station, I look forlornly into the crowd and wave madly at Sid and Lisa's rapidly disappearing figures. I should be excited but the main emotion I feel is sadness. I don't want to stop travelling or go home to Australia, but the small taste of it I got at Sid and Lisa's leaves me longing for more.

'What's wrong with me?' I wonder, as I settle back for the three-hour journey to New York. I've been overseas plenty of times before and homesickness has never been a problem, but there is no denying the melancholy I am feeling.

'You're quiet,' Trevor says. 'What are you thinking about?'

I make up something about wondering what our next

hotel will be like, but it isn't true. All I can think about is how much I miss our home, our family and our friends. As the train speeds towards New York, I find myself thinking about them, but then I remember something that makes me smile.

'You'd better enjoy yourselves at these hotels or I'm coming over there to do it for you!' my friend Tammy threatened before we left.

Considering our next prize hotel, the New York Palace, is in Tammy's favourite city, I'd better cheer up fast.

7

THE RECESSION SPECIAL

ARRIVING IN NEW YORK is like walking onto a movie set. Everything I've seen on the big screen over the years – the Empire State Building, the Chrysler Building and the busy sidewalks crowded with New Yorkers – whizzes past the window as we speed along in a canary-yellow taxi from Penn Station. When Trevor calls out 'We're on Madison Avenue', I realise we are approaching the New York Palace Hotel.

Located in the Villard Houses, a cluster of brownstone townhouses built in 1882 for New York's elite by a prominent American financier, the hotel fronts onto Madison Avenue and is topped by a modern 55-storey highrise. The Houses' original carriage entrance provides a grand approach but, as our room is in the most exclusive section of the hotel, we will enter through a small modern doorway around the corner. The discreet entrance must be a blessing for the singers and movie stars who usually inhabit the 'hotel within a hotel' called The Towers, but it isn't what we are expecting.

I make a mental note to pay more attention to what is going on around us when I notice a bellboy has picked up our bags from the sidewalk. One thing we don't want is people helping us to do things we can easily do for ourselves because, every time somebody does, we feel obliged to tip them. Although we've been in the United States for a few weeks already, this is the first time we've had to worry about tipping since our trip began. Trevor and I bought most of our food at the supermarket in Washington and Las Vegas, so the only times we have been expected to tip was after lunch at Mandalay Bay and when we caught taxis. We've been able to add an extra ten per cent to the bill and put the whole amount on our credit card up until now, so we have avoided the need to hand over cold, hard cash.

Australians have no idea how to tip and we've been suffering from a bad case of Tipping Anxiety that has been getting worse the closer we've come to New York. We don't know what to do: should you slip money discreetly into someone's hand or pass it over with a big smile and a 'thank you'? What if you get terrible service – do you still have to tip? And then there is the biggest question of all: what do you do if you're penniless back-packers staying in the most private, exclusive section of one of New York's premier hotels?

I give the bellboy a few dollars and try to ignore his surprised look as we are escorted through to The Towers' modern private check-in. What I've given him is nowhere near enough at a flash hotel like this, but it is all we can afford. The New York Palace is attractive but the gilded flourishes that have been added to fit in with the Villard Houses' design features look faintly ridiculous and everything is too shiny and new to evoke the old world ambience I imagine the designers were trying to create. I prefer the old-fashioned, almost European charm of the Alvear Palace Hotel in Buenos Aires, even if we never did work out what to do with our butler.

There isn't another guest to be seen, probably due to the exclusive nature of our accommodation, and we walk straight over to reception where the staff act so happy to see us that I think they're about to leap over the counter and give us a hug.

'Welcome to the New York Palace Hotel,' the receptionist gushes, 'we are *so* pleased you're here, Mr and Mrs . . .' – there is a slight hesitation while she checks our name on her guest register – 'Templeman.'

Down-to-earth Australian service is very different from this American approach, which is so over the top that, rightly or wrongly, it comes across as fake. Trevor shoots me a wry glance as if to say 'Is she for real?' and begins filling out our paperwork.

As a staff member escorts us to the discreet bank of elevators exclusively for Towers guests, I can see Trevor fingering the crisp bills in his pocket nervously, already wondering how to go about handing them over. The rush of Madison Avenue seems miles away by the time we reach the silence of the plushly carpeted forty-first floor and a door is thrown back dramatically to reveal a huge corner suite furnished in an Art Deco style. The curves of the furniture remind me of the Chrysler Building, which I can see from our bedroom window, and the framed 1930s advertising posters on the walls blend in beautifully with the colours and theme of our suite. We walk around it slowly, wide-eyed at the separate dining room with a table for eight, a loungeroom flanked on three sides by chocolate-brown velvet couches, and a bedroom dominated by the biggest bed we've ever seen.

Huge windows wrap around the main part of the suite, revealing stunning views of the New York skyline and the green cupolas of St Patrick's Cathedral directly below. I stare down at the road with its continuous stream of taxis, finally understanding Trevor's excitement when he stood in front of the White House. I can't believe we are actually in New York and as Trevor puts his arms around me we press our faces against the window, trying to see all the way up and down the street. I have forgotten we aren't alone until a voice brings me back to reality with a jolt.

'If there's anything I can do, please call me anytime.'

The bellboy who has shown us to the suite is hovering in an expectant fashion near the front door, effectively answering one of our other questions – 'How do you know when to tip?'. The answer is 'Right about now!'. Trevor walks over and produces a number of bills before thrusting them forward awkwardly with a sincere 'Thanks very much.' They are met with a bemused chuckle, but are slipped out of sight all the same.

After the door closes, Trevor sags against it and groans. It appears none of the service staff know we aren't paying for the room, so they expect us to tip like their usual guests. Trevor has just doled out our equivalent of a small fortune, but this amount was obviously so inadequate I wonder if there is any point in us tipping at all. I do feel a bit sorry for the bellboy – we are in one of the hotel's top suites so he would be expecting something generous – but having to hand over all that money is painful enough without our humble offerings being mocked.

At least one of our other worries has been alleviated: the suite is stunning in so many ways, but our favourite feature has to be the kitchen. While we would love to dine at New York's famous restaurants, we know it is impossible on our budget and had already resigned ourselves to three nights of cup-of-soup dinners. The chance to enjoy home-cooked meals with a view of New York for company is almost as exciting as the opulence of our suite. As we leave the hotel to buy groceries, the industrial smell of the city fills our nostrils and the strange yet familiar New York accent ebbs and flows around us. New York feels alive and we are glad our win has given us the opportunity to experience it.

When we return to discover a staff member filling our fridge with bottles of Evian and soft drink, which, she tells us, are complimentary, it seems things can't get any better. We make a strategic disappearance into the bedroom, hoping she'll just go away before we have to tip but it is wishful thinking on our part.

'I've finished stocking your fridge,' she calls pointedly.

'That's great – thanks very much,' we shout out, but it's not going to be that easy.

'Can I get you anything else, Mr and Mrs Templeman?'

I feel like asking for a big bag of money so we can keep up with the constant badgering for tips. I know the culture of tipping is a normal part of life in the US because the standard wage is so low, but it feels like no one will do anything for anyone unless there is something in it for them. It seems mercenary and grasping to me, but perhaps it is just my frame of mind. I am feeling homesick and ill at ease and embarrassed about our lack of money.

That night we cook pasta in our state-of-the-art kitchen and the next morning we have toast and Vegemite and strong black coffee while we read our complimentary copy of *The New York Times*. Not much of the news in it is welcome. It is over seven months since the events of September 11 and the paper is filled with speculation about further terrorist attacks rumoured to be taking place over the next three days, during the May Day long weekend. Monuments like the Statue of Liberty have been closed due to perceived security risks and celebrations have either been scaled down or cancelled. But we refuse to allow ourselves to be scared by what we read or speculate about the reports. We've been so excited about seeing New York that staying inside because of something that might or might not happen would feel cowardly. Despite the dire predictions, we decide to carry on as planned and sit in the lobby waiting expectantly for someone called Jo.

When Trevor and I discovered we'd be visiting New York, I remembered reading about a free service called the Big Apple Greeter Program, which was launched a few years ago to try to make New York friendlier and more accessible for tourists. New Yorkers were invited to volunteer their time to show visitors around and the response was overwhelming, with locals practically falling over themselves to offer assistance. They were proud of their city and welcomed the chance to share it with the world. It was simple to book a Greeter over the internet and seemed like a fantastic deal – a free tour and free public transport for the day – but as the hands of the lobby clock make their way closer to 9.30 am, Trevor and I are sure we've been forgotten. Our guide is nearly half an hour late and we've all but given up when someone flops onto the settee beside us and begins speaking so quickly we can hardly keep up.

'Sorry guys! I left home at 8.15, yes, *8.15* – anyway, there was this train, I don't know what happened, but I was waiting at the platform and then . . . oh, hey – I'm Jo.'

She sticks out a small chubby hand and shakes ours enthusiastically before continuing her story without pausing for breath. Trevor shoots me an amused glance before returning his attention to Jo. The Chinese-American is not only our own age, she is also a quintessential New York – or at least our idea of one. Her strident accent suits the edgy pace of the city and she waves her hands around emphatically to illustrate whatever she is saying. Jo is brash, straightforward and exuberant and we find ourselves hanging on her every word as she finishes her story and asks us what we'd like to do.

'Nothing really touristy,' Trevor explains. 'We'd like you to show us New York through the eyes of someone who lives here.'

'Plus walk across the Brooklyn Bridge,' I add. I've read it has spectacular views of Manhattan and I've always wanted to walk from one end of it to the other.

'Okay,' Jo says thoughtfully. 'I love Grand Central, so we'll start there, then I'll take you through my old stomping grounds on the way to Brooklyn Bridge. How does that sound?'

'Great,' Trevor and I say together. 'But first there's something we have to tell you.'

Trevor leans towards Jo and whispers conspiratorially, 'We're backpackers. The only reason we're staying here is because we won a competition.'

'No way!' Jo stares as we nod silently. 'Oh my gosh!' she shrieks so loudly that everyone stares.

'So, despite our grand surroundings,' Trevor explains apologetically, 'we can't afford to take you anywhere fancy for lunch.'

'Don't worry about that,' Jo says, with a dismissive wave of her hand. 'I'll dine out on this story for weeks.'

After she hears more about our prize, Jo sets off at a rapid pace towards our first stop of the day and begins telling us about its history. I've seen plenty of pictures of Grand Central's Beaux-Arts-style arches and Corinthian columns in the guidebooks I've read, but hadn't realised it ended up costing $80 million to complete – a staggering amount of money now, let alone in the early 1900s. Jo explains its correct name is actually Grand Central Terminal and the whole complex is so big, with its office buildings and apartments, it's often referred to as 'Terminal City'. A lot of the money for its construction was raised by selling 'air rights' to the developers who wanted to build on top of it. As we approach the station entrance, Jo points out the 50-foot-high sculpture towering above it.

'Mercury and Minerva,' she says, gesturing to the two figures. 'They stand for mental and moral strength, which are good things to have during rush hour.'

The main concourse is swarming with bustling commuters and filled with the buzz of myriad different conversations. I can't believe nobody is stopping to look around: the railway announcements seem at odds with the spectacular building which looks more like a museum than a train station. Three huge windows, over 20 metres high, dominate the far end of the marble concourse and the sunshine streaming through them bathes the station in a soft glow. When Jo tells us to look up, the last thing I expect to see is a painted ceiling similar to that of the Sistine Chapel. The subject matter is different – Jo explains the zodiac constellations have been taken from a medieval manuscript – but I think it is equally as beautiful. When she notices another commuter walking around us impatiently, Jo moves us towards one of the halls branching off the main concourse and stops to point out a dark black patch in the corner of the ceiling.

'The place was so filthy, that's what the whole ceiling looked like before the 1996 renovations. They left that little bit to remind people how it used to be.'

I would never have noticed it if Jo hadn't pointed out the tiny spot. As she brushes a lock of floppy black hair out of her eyes and gazes around the station fondly, it's easy to see why she works as a volunteer. Jo loves her city with a fierce passion and it is impossible not to get caught up in her enthusiasm. I am glad as I've felt a bit homesick since we arrived in New York and the prospect of yet more new experiences had filled me with dread rather than excitement. I usually love seeing new things and different places, but right now all I crave is the comfortable familiarity of my friends and family. It feels like so long since we've seen them that just thinking about it is making me blue.

As we stand in the middle of the floor, Trevor comments on the high ceilings and soaring arches and Jo claps her hands before leading us bossily to opposite corners of the cavernous space. She turns Trevor in to face the wall and tells him to whisper something to me. I feel like an idiot waiting for the bricks to talk – until Trevor's voice floats out of the wall in front of me.

'Hey babe, I've got a suite at the New York Palace,' he says. 'Wanna come back to my place?'

There is no need for Jo to ask if it worked because I start laughing. She grins and waves me over to where she and Trevor are standing.

'Amazing, isn't it, but please don't ask me how it works – I have no idea,' Jo says breezily as she ushers us through swirling crowds of people and towards one of the exits.

We are swept along in the flow until Trevor stops by a bulletin board in the middle of the concourse. Every available space is covered with notices, letters and photographs.

'Have you seen John?'

'Please, if you have any news at all about our daughter . . .'

'Chris was last seen entering the World Trade Center . . .'

Jo has walked ahead, but retraces her steps once she realises we've stopped. 'That's been left here as a kind of memorial,' she explains. 'There's no chance of these people being found now.'

'Did you know anyone who was killed?' Trevor asks.

Jo stops smiling for the first time since we met her.

'Yes,' she says simply, 'but I think everyone did. That's what made it so tough.'

I look at the tattered, handwritten notices and the glossy photographs – many obviously pulled out of family albums – and realise I haven't really understood the enormity of September 11 until now. Pain and desperation ooze out of the notes, but the prevailing sense of hope is even worse. At the time the notices were pinned up, the people who put them there still believed there was a chance they would see their loved ones again – but they were wrong. Being in Australia, on the other side of the world, enabled me to distance myself emotionally from what happened on September 11. That is no longer possible. The messages on the board are so personal and full of love I feel like crying.

'You'll have to go to Ground Zero by yourself,' I mumble.

Trevor turns to me in surprise.

'Why's that? You said you'd come with me.'

'I'm sorry, but I can't,' I say, turning away from the notices. 'Not after seeing that.'

'But Ground Zero's nothing more than a hole.'

'It doesn't feel right going along to see it like it's the Statue of Liberty or something. All those people died there,' I say, pointing to the bulletin board.

He is still thinking about what I said when we look up to see Jo waiting for us to follow her. Trevor takes my hand and the three of us return to the bustling street outside.

After leaving the station, Jo takes us to the Brooklyn Bridge via Chinatown, pointing out the different shops and describing how the city has changed and grown around the area that originally developed in the 1800s as a protection against racial discrimination. There was safety in numbers, she explains, and New York's Chinatown operated with its own internal governing structure, providing jobs, economic aid and protection to the people who lived there. The two square miles are still home to the majority of Chinese New Yorkers, but the thriving district's restaurants, shops and markets have now been embraced by everyone.

New York's version of Chinatown is very different from the handful of restaurants and Asian supermarkets back home. Here the sidewalks are crammed with stalls and I inhale the tangy spiciness of things I've never smelled before. Trevor and I squeeze past newsstands manned by ancient Chinese men chewing tobacco and stumble along behind Jo, who navigates the crowded sidewalks with casual familiarity. Roasted ducks hang limply beside scrawny chickens' feet in restaurant windows, fresh vegetables sit in large wicker baskets and rapidly spoken Chinese rings out all around us. I can imagine Jo as a child, clutching her mother's hand as they wound their way through the crowded streets, buying exotic items from the shops jammed one on top of each other. It isn't long after we leave Chinatown that we emerge at the start of the Brooklyn Bridge.

'Are you sure you want to do this?' Jo asks seriously, referring to the fact that the bridge is rumoured to be one of the long weekend's prime terrorist targets.

We look at each other, hesitating only slightly before giving her a firm nod. Jo whoops like she is cheering her favourite baseball team and we set off across the bridge. I hope the run of bad luck that plagued its start in life won't be returning to haunt us today. The engineer in charge of the Brooklyn Bridge's construction was killed when a ferry ran into a pylon he was standing on. His son took over, only to succumb to decompression sickness while working below the surface of New York's East River. This left him paralysed, partly blind, deaf and mute, but he continued to supervise the construction from his sick bed, using a telescope to check the progress of works and his wife, Emily, to relay instructions to the work crews. The undoubtedly long-suffering Emily became the unofficial Chief Engineer for the bridge between 1872 and 1883, but there was still more bad luck to come. Twelve people were killed on opening day when word that the bridge was about to collapse spread like wildfire through the crowd and, despite the fact the rumour was completely untrue, caused a stampede.

It doesn't look like there is any danger of that happening today as the 1.5-kilometre-long pedestrian walkway is deserted. I do wonder if we are doing the right thing when everyone else is staying away, but only briefly. We are unlikely to get to New York again, at least in the near future, and are determined to see as much of it as possible. Trevor and I intend to carry on unless we hear something more definite than rumours. As we walk across the bridge towards Brooklyn, fog cloaks the city and buildings peek through it briefly before disappearing again into the gloom. The three of us keep stopping to turn around and admire the brooding Manhattan skyline, where the gunmetal-grey buildings reflect scudding clouds each time they emerge defiantly from the fog.

Jo leads us down to a promenade beside the river

that has a spectacular view of lower Manhattan and a playground with a sign reading 'All Adults Must be Accompanied by a Child'. Laughter and excited squeals fill the air as the children playing on the swings breathe life into the eerie scene in front of us. Someone has tied a bunch of flowers and a large framed photograph to the metal railing. The twin towers of the World Trade Center dominate the shot, making the large hole where they once stood gape like an open wound in the morning's fog-shrouded skyline. I think about what happened and feel incredibly sad. All the people who were killed when the Twin Towers collapsed are gone and their loss will have left a similar hole in the lives of their loved ones. New York City will eventually fill the gap in the skyline, but no one can repair the emotional damage. I stare at the Manhattan skyline until Jo walks over and touches my arm gently, suggesting we take the subway to the Lower East Side.

I am grateful for the distraction, but not looking forward to what we are about to do. Earlier today, Trevor insisted he wanted an authentic New York hot dog for lunch and I am filled with sickly trepidation as we traipse up the subway's litter-strewn stairs. Eating anything made from processed meat is perilous when you've got an active imagination, and visions of unidentifiable offal dance merrily in my head as Jo takes us to a place she insists has 'great dawgs'. I am desperate not to go but for the first time since we've arrived in America there isn't another food store to be seen.

The rundown hot-dog shop isn't much more than a hole in the wall. Plastic bottles of sauce with peeling labels are lined up on the scratched Formica counter, but this hasn't stopped people joining the queue snaking out the door and back along the grimy pavement. I catch a few snatches of conversation and realise nearly everyone is a local. Perhaps this won't be so bad after all. On Jo's advice, we each order the 'Recession Special' – two small hot dogs and a fruit drink for US$2.25. There are no tables and chairs, so we walk over to one of the counters and stand elbow to elbow with the other customers, who are virtually inhaling their hot dogs. I know I am being a starry-eyed tourist, but I love being surrounded by all the 'real New Yorkers', although I am less than enthusiastic about my lunch. Jo and Trevor have already started devouring theirs, but I eye my hot dog warily, watching brownish-red sauce mixed with grease drip onto the white paper plate as I try not to squash the soft white roll. It seems fresh enough, but the frankfurter poking out the end of it is an unnatural shade of pink and wobbles in excitement as I sniff the hot dog apprehensively before taking a tentative bite. The bread feels like a warm pillow and more juices ooze onto the paper plate as I struggle to contain my surprise. The hot spicy frankfurter, combined with sauerkraut and the sauce Jo recommended, tastes fantastic. Then again, perhaps it's only because I am eating this hot dog in the middle of New York City. So many of the special moments on this trip are steeped in time and place and this is definitely one of them.

By the time we finish lunch and take the subway back to the New York Palace, we've spent over five hours with Jo, although it doesn't seem that long. She hasn't stopped talking since we met, but it isn't idle chatter as Jo has spent her life in the city learning about its history. I can see how it could mean different things to different people, but it is impossible to visit New York and not be touched by it in some way.

As we approach the New York Palace, we invite Jo back to our suite for coffee. It is the first time we've been able to share our prize and watching Jo's reaction when she walks in the door reminds me how lucky we are to be here. Enraptured by the luxurious furnishings and fine artwork on the walls, she prowls around our suite. The New York Palace is only our fifth prize hotel, but I've already begun to get used to the opulence of our five-star surroundings. Jo helps me see it with fresh eyes and I wonder if it is going to become more difficult to endure our usual budget accommodation as the trip progresses.

'How do you handle tipping in this place?' Jo asks. 'They'd be expecting a 50-buck minimum if you could afford a room like this.'

Trevor and I exchange a horrified look – the biggest tip we've given out was $10. We grin sheepishly and reveal our new strategy. The two of us get ready to go out, telephone for whatever we need, then tear out the door before anyone can arrive with their hand out. Jo thinks it is hilarious, but we aren't cheapskates by nature and the subterfuge doesn't sit well with either of us. I long to put a big sign on the door of our suite saying 'Nice People – No Money', but suspect it won't get us anything except strange looks.

It is hard coming to a big city like New York after the cosy companionship of Sid and Lisa's apartment. The rushing traffic and frenetic pace of life on the streets outside our hotel feels more intimidating than exciting and my homesickness seems determined to stick around. I am glad we've met Jo as her warmth is just what I needed and, even though I don't know how, I am determined to banish my homesickness. After I see Jo out, I join Trevor in the kitchen to tell him so, but he is busy grumbling about the fact our fridge hasn't been refilled.

'At the rates they charge for a room, you'd think they could at least check it,' he says, doing a remarkable impersonation of a man who is actually paying for his room.

So far we've consumed eight bottles of Evian, six Cokes, a few lemonades and I've just given Jo a couple of cans of soft drink to take with her for the trip home. It is embarrassing to admit, but the drinks tasted especially good because they were free. Trevor calls room service and asks politely for our fridge to be refilled, but no one arrives so he calls again and speaks to someone different. After half an hour, still no one has turned up. Our disappointment and indignation is so acute by this stage, anyone watching would be convinced we are paying for the room ourselves. Simon, the room service manager, is brought to the phone when I call a third time and he proceeds to turn on the charm, apologising profusely and assuring us it won't happen again. When he says the situation will be dealt with immediately, I feel awful, imagining him getting off the phone and whacking some poor employee on the nose with a rolled-up newspaper. Less than two minutes later a guy arrives to restock our fridge, but things must be serious because he doesn't hint for a tip.

Not long after the drinks arrive, there is another knock on the door. Trevor opens it to reveal an enormous gift basket with legs and Simon, who is standing beside it wearing a gold name tag and a smarmy smile. When the basket is put on the dining table, Simon introduces the assistant room service manager who's been hiding behind it and they both apologise again for our expectations not being met, expressing their deepest sympathies that our drinks were not replenished. Simon is practically wringing his hands and weeping at the horror of it all.

'It was an inexcusable oversight on our part,' he says.

When the young assistant manager nods vigorously, I wonder if he was the recipient of Simon's dressing-down and feel even guiltier than before for stirring up trouble. As Simon chuckles at his own jokes and makes inquiries about our day, I feel like rolling my eyes. He is leaning on one of our dining-room chairs with an air of contrived nonchalance and is trying so hard it hurts.

'We do hope this small token will make up for it,' he

says, patting the enormous gift basket and handing over his card. 'Please don't hesitate to call me any time.'

We thank Simon, assuring him the basket really isn't necessary, and stare in disbelief at the gourmet chocolates, nuts, biscuits and bottles of Evian. All this just because our free drinks weren't restocked! The experience has been a real eye-opener and we can't believe the whims of the wealthy are catered to in such an ingratiating fashion – just sending someone to refill our fridge would have been enough. A lot of five-star hotel guests must expect this sort of fawning behaviour, but it feels weird to me.

As soon as Simon has left, our 'sophisticated traveller' demeanour drops like the façade it is and Trevor and I let out joyous screeches before diving into the basket and taking out each item one by one so we can line them up on the table. I can't believe we've just scored over $300 worth of room service goodies for nothing. Trevor opens a packet of handmade biscuits and bites down on one with a contented sigh.

The next day we think about going out to do some more sightseeing, but never quite make it. Although we've been talking about checking out Wall Street and Radio City Music Hall, we can't seem to muster any enthusiasm. I know we should be out on the streets experiencing everything the city has to offer, but my heart just isn't in it. This is the longest we've been away from home and the nature of our prize means we aren't just in other countries, but in completely foreign environments as well. As much as we enjoy our luxurious five-star hotels, Trevor and I often feel uncomfortable and out of place in them – especially at the New York Palace Hotel. We are missing the comfortable routine of our life back in Brisbane so much that even everyday tasks like hanging out the washing have taken on a rosy domestic glow. A bout of homesickness was bound to strike sometime, but it is compounded by how ill at ease we are in our opulent surroundings. Our time in New York is slipping away and we are becoming more and more frustrated by how we are feeling, especially as it makes minor problems take on a ridiculous significance. Like the fact our fridge hasn't been refilled – again.

Trevor stomps around the suite before reaching for Simon's card and picking up the phone, but his voice takes on an ominous tone of false cheeriness as the call progresses.

'There's been a bit of a misunderstanding,' Trevor explains slowly as he puts down the phone. 'Only the first lot were free.'

I do a quick calculation using the Palace's gasp-inducing mini-bar rates and come to the horrible realisation that we've skolled over $180 worth of Evian alone. No wonder Simon gave us the gift basket – he must think we have money to burn. Trevor and I launch into a frenzied search of every piece of guest literature in our suite, hoping fervently none of them outlines the rules regarding the fridge (they don't), before sitting in the lounge room to discuss exactly what was said by whom. Then Trevor flips a coin and I lose.

Simon's business card trembles in my hand as I pick up the phone to dial his direct line. I don't know what I am going to say, but I know it has to be good or the two of us will be washing dishes at the hotel's famous restaurant, Le Cirque 2000, for the rest of our stay. It is one of the most celebrated restaurants in the world and has been frequented by the likes of Princess Grace, Richard Nixon, Bill Clinton and Frank Sinatra, and we'll be scrubbing the dessert bowls if I don't come up with something plausible. Simon doesn't sound happy when I explain politely but firmly that we were informed the beverages were complimentary when the fridge was first filled and, in view of this, we won't be paying for anything consumed since then.

Simon apologises for the misunderstanding and goes off to investigate. He must also stop off to undergo a personality transplant because the man who rings back is nothing like the cheery chap who dropped off the gift basket. Simon's cordiality and jolly demeanour have been replaced by a businesslike frostiness and we are sure he is cursing his misguided generosity.

'But Mrs Templeman, the beverages have been consumed.'

'And if we hadn't been led to believe they were complimentary,' I say with a hint of desperation, 'they wouldn't have been.'

At least I am telling the truth. This time there are no

inquiries from Simon about how we've spent our day – just a very civilised argument until he reluctantly agrees to have the charges removed from our bill. Sorting things out takes the better part of the afternoon and sends our stress levels soaring, but there is an upside to all the drama – with something else to focus on, my homesickness has vanished.

Filled with fresh enthusiasm, Trevor and I are keen to enjoy our last night in New York and can't wait to get out and see the city. Our bad case of the blues has led to a very different New York experience from the one we were dreaming of back in Australia. I wish we could turn back time and start our three nights in New York all over again.

After packing our bags full of Simon's snacks, we catch the subway to the Empire State Building, which was the highest building in the world from the time it was completed in 1931 until 1972. It still towers over Manhattan and the building's façade with its three distinct parts – the base, the tower and the cluster of antennas on the top – is completely flat, except for a series of deep, evenly-spaced grooves that look like they've been cut using a giant's router. The building's Art Deco design reminds me of something out of Gotham City, Batman's home town. We stroll into a lobby lined with sandy-coloured marble and approach the permanent barricades that form a kind of cattle run for the 3.5 million tourists who visit the Empire State Building each year.

'There's no one else here,' Trevor says in amazement.

We ignore the railed corrals and walk straight to the front of the queue where we buy tickets before taking a series of lifts up to the eighty-sixth floor. While Trevor and I are looking forward to enjoying the view, it appears no one else has the same idea. We walk into the spring air to join the smattering of people outside – a very different scene from the one I've heard about from friends, who described a controlled chaos where only a handful of people are let out onto the viewing platform at a time. The first thing Trevor does is start digging around in his camera bag.

'Can't you enjoy it for a few moments first?'

Trevor looks up at my angry face in surprise.

'You're so busy trying to take photographs, it's like you're not even here half the time.'

Trevor has become so obsessed with taking shots for his exhibition that I am beginning to feel more like a glorified photographer's assistant than his wife. I can understand him wanting to whip out his camera to capture something special – that's how he got the photo that won us the trip in the first place – but the view from the top of the Empire State Building isn't going to change anytime soon.

Trevor puts away his camera and gives me a sheepish grin.

'Sorry,' he says and drapes one arm around my shoulders as we lean on the chest-high scalloped sandstone wall surrounding the platform and admire the view together. I love the soft curves of the Empire State Building and the way it has been constructed not simply as office space, but to be aesthetically pleasing as well. Everything about it is graceful and elegant and devoid of the brash architectural arrogance of the more modern buildings surrounding it. As a small boy clambers eagerly into his dad's arms for a better view, I imagine a 1930s family – with mother dressed like Grace Kelly and father in his best suit and tie – travelling across town for a grand day out. Even the antennas on top of the Empire State Building have been here since the thirties, although their number has grown a lot since then.

I step back from the edge of the viewing platform and walk slowly around its perimeter. On a clear day you can see all the way to New Jersey, Connecticut, Pennsylvania and Massachusetts, but I am content just to look out at New York City. The buildings have taken on a golden brown glow in the late afternoon sunshine and we wait until stars begin twinkling and the harsh edges of the skyline soften in the velvet darkness of the clear night. Building interiors are lit with bright spots of light that pierce the surrounding darkness and create a hazy electric halo above the city.

'It's so beautiful,' I say to Trevor, looking out across the city. 'I'm glad we ignored the newspaper reports.'

I wrap my hands around the cold stainless-steel safety bars and press my face up against them so my head almost squeezes through the diamond-shaped gap. Lights on the surrounding buildings start to come on, one here and one there, until the skyline is filled with brilliant twinkles. I notice the Chrysler Building glowing in the distance and smile when I remember we can see it from our bedroom window. Trevor and I may not feel entirely comfortable at the New York Palace Hotel, but we love our wonderful room.

New York pulses with a nervous energy that is still palpable from the top of the Empire State Building. Trevor slips behind me and wraps his arms around my waist, pressing his body against mine so he can rest his chin on top of my head and enjoy the same view. I've always thought Paris was the city for lovers, but standing on top of the Empire State Building and gazing out at the lights of New York with Trevor's arms around me feels incredibly romantic.

It is interesting to see the city like this. The people on the streets breathe life into it, but New York seems to be a living thing in itself. The constant stream of cars is like the blood rushing through its veins, high rise buildings clothe it in showy finery and the city is growing every day. Being so high above New York makes me feel removed from the city and connected to it at the same time.

I am sorry we are leaving tomorrow as our homesickness blinded us to New York's charms. Both of us are keen to return and give it another try. When Jo took us to areas like Chinatown and the Lower East Side, we felt a connection with the city that was lacking in the shiny surroundings of our hotel. I much preferred the guy who slapped my hot dog lunch down on the counter and took my money with a brusque 'Thanks' to the New York Palace's obsequious staff. Next time we'll rent an apartment in one of the neighbourhoods and just wander around, soaking up the city and watching life go on around us. I decide New York City is a place to immerse yourself in, not hide from in the cosseted surroundings of a five-star hotel.

Trevor and I spend the next morning packing our bags and enjoying our last few hours at the New York Palace. I'll never tire of the view and our suite is the most spectacular so far, but we've discovered that a wonderful hotel experience hinges on much more than opulent surroundings, no matter how breathtaking they are. Trevor and I have enjoyed our stay at the New York Palace, but we've never felt comfortable or genuinely welcome here, like we did at Huka Lodge.

'Did you notice the staff have stopped asking us for tips?' Trevor chuckles. By the time we pop down to ask the concierge about getting to the airport that evening, we've given up on keeping up appearances: we are wearing our most casual clothes and approach the desk without a hint of our usual trepidation. It is liberating to ask for exactly what we want without feeling the need to pretend we are like the hotel's other guests. Rather than being disdainful, the concierge goes out of his way to help and we agree with his suggestion to use a pre-paid car with a driver. The concierge is so genuinely helpful that, for one of the first times ever, I feel like spontaneously handing over some cash. We thank him and go outside for one final walk around the streets of New York.

'We'll get back to New York one day,' Trevor says reassuringly, taking my hand. I feel the heartbeat of the city and promise myself the same thing.

8

THE TRAGIC CROISSANT

OUR NEXT DESTINATION features prominently in the imagination and dreams of many travellers and before we left home it came up constantly in discussions about our upcoming trip.

'Are you ready?' Trevor asks me now, as the plane banks away from New York and soars into the night.

I nod and think back to the well-thumbed Hôtel Ritz Paris brochure sitting in our study at home. Our next five-star hotel is the ultimate in glamorous sophistication and the complete opposite of where we usually stay in Paris. This visit will be very different from the ones we've had in the past and while we are excited, we're also extremely nervous.

'The "city of love" awaits,' Trevor says in an appalling French accent and pretends to plant sloppy kisses up my arm.

Paris is our favourite city and I can't wait for the French capital to weave its magic once again. Even the flight – New York to Paris – seems to have a romantic ring to it.

* * *

Paris reminds me of an older woman with laughter lines and a wicked glint in her eye – she doesn't have the chocolate-box prettiness of places like Austria and Switzerland, but the promise of sensual pleasures yet to be discovered lurks around every corner. We fell for the city like two lovestruck adolescents on an earlier trip when we stayed at a hotel in one of the outer *arrondissements* (districts) called Plaisance that was recommended by a friend. The area isn't usually frequented by tourists and by the end of that week, locals greeted us with nods and smiles and the bakery was putting aside a chocolate croissant for Trevor's breakfast, just in case they sold out before he arrived. When other travellers talked about streets covered in dog poo and locals who were impossibly rude, Trevor and I wondered if we'd visited the same city.

We hold hands and peer out the window as the plane descends into Paris, curious to see if we recognise anything from our previous arrival, five years ago.

'We're so far from Australia,' Trevor muses, 'yet this almost feels like coming home.'

Despite the fact we can't speak French, we both felt uncommonly comfortable in Paris when we were here before. Our valiant attempts at the language were rewarded with smiles and willing offers of assistance and our time in Plaisance took on a comfortable domestic routine. After feeling so out of sorts in New York, we are looking forward to returning to the hotel and area we know so well. My homesickness is completely gone as we pass through customs, catch a shuttle bus to the outskirts of Paris and find a metro station with no trouble at all.

'*Un carnet, s'il vous plaît*,' Trevor says with a smile, handing over enough euros for his book of ten metro tickets.

On previous overseas trips we've discovered that people find it much harder to be rude to someone of the opposite sex, so as there is a woman behind the counter Trevor has volunteered to buy our tickets. I shift my backpack to a more comfortable position and we walk through the metro's labyrinth of corridors.

'One thing hasn't changed,' Trevor says, wrinkling up his nose. 'The metro still smells like a urinal.'

It looks like one too. The corridors are lined with off-white tiles similar to the ones in our bathroom at home and footfalls echo around us. Luckily, we've arrived just before peak hour and are able to board a train easily. We squeeze our backpacks into a corner and sway from side to side as the train rattles from one station to the next. After changing train lines twice, we stagger off at Plaisance and head towards the hotel we stayed at on our last trip.

It seems that nothing has changed. The small café on the corner is crowded, the butcher's store still has its faded striped awning and the man who put aside Trevor's croissant every morning is standing at the counter as usual – although his ample belly is even bigger.

We turn right into a side street and there it is – our

old hotel. If you don't include the street level, which contains a tiny reception and dining room, it is only four storeys high and the 16 large windows evenly spaced across the hotel's façade are actually French doors. Each one has wrought iron railings stretched across a platform too tiny to be called a balcony – unless you're the cat who lives in the apartment across the street – but they give the rooms a distinctly Parisian feel.

We are delighted to discover we'll be staying in the same room as before and beam at each other before climbing the narrow flights of stairs to the third floor. Trevor unlocks the door with an old fashioned metal key and pushes it open to reveal that while nothing much may have changed on the streets outside, things certainly look different from what I remember in here. Was it always this small?

The modest double bed in the centre of the room is covered with a shiny brown bedspread and the emerald green carpet must have been bought at a tremendous discount – no one would buy carpet that colour unless it was cheap. There are two mismatched side tables but we can't unpack because there is no wardrobe or chest of drawers – probably because there isn't any space to put them. I squeeze past Trevor and dump my backpack on the floor. It is hard to believe the small ensuite, with its cracked tiles and cheap plastic towel rails, once seemed the height of luxury. After weeks of hotels where we had to traipse down the hall to go to the bathroom, just having a room with its own facilities was a cause for celebration on our last trip, but that isn't the case anymore.

Neither of us says it, but I know what we are both thinking: the room we've been so looking forward to looks like a dive. I know it is unfair to compare this modest, family-run hotel with our luxurious accommodation of last night, but it is impossible not to. Trevor puts his backpack down in the corner and begins silently cleaning out his camera bag as our creeping sense of dissatisfaction settles over the room. Neither of us slept on the overnight flight from New York and we are tired and irritable, but it is too early to go to bed. In an attempt to stay awake I fling open the windows, letting the sounds of the street – and the construction site across the road – fill our room.

Trevor leans back against the pillows on the bed and opens a novel but his head begins nodding almost immediately. I'm sure that if he sleeps now, three o'clock in the morning will see him well rested, wide awake and prowling around the room like a caged animal, so I reach over and give him a gentle prod.

'You've got to try to stay awake.'

'I know, I know – I'm just resting,' his muffled voice says from the mound of pillows. 'Leave me alone.'

'Do you want to go for a walk to help you wake up?'

'No.'

'Come on . . .'

'Will you just *shut up*!' he shouts. 'I'm tired and if I want to go to sleep I will!'

I hate being yelled at and usually look hurt before firing back a withering retort, but I am too tired and fed up to bother. The lump forming in the back of my throat gets bigger as I look around our dingy room and wonder where the romantic Paris I've been so looking forward to has gone. I bite down on a hiccuping sob as tears blur my vision.

'What are you crying for?' Trevor asks wearily.

'You yelled at me for trying to help.' I am crying so hard I can hardly get the words out, and I desperately need a tissue.

Trevor reaches into his backpack and hands me a crumpled Kleenex. 'I'm sorry for yelling, but I'm exhausted. You've got to let me get some rest.'

He reaches over and gives me a lopsided hug from where he is lying.

'But what if you wake up in the middle of the night?'

When Trevor doesn't answer, I look down to see that he's already gone back to sleep. I sit on the ugly bedspread, snuffling into a tissue and feeling sorry for myself.

We usually get on well, but being together 24 hours a day for weeks on end without fighting is impossible and, although there's only been the odd disagreement up until now, it might be good for us each to spend some time alone. Trevor must be thinking the same thing because when he comes back from the bakery with our breakfast croissants the next day he suggests we spend the morning exploring separately and meet up for lunch. The good night's sleep has left us feeling much more cheerful, but I still like the idea.

We visited most of the traditional tourist spots last time we were in Paris, so we're keen to spend our morning alone doing something different. Trevor announces he is going to visit the area known as La Défense, an 80-hectare site of architecturally stunning modern buildings that's also the biggest working quarter in Europe. I know he's always wanted to see the famous La Grande Arche that is located there – also known as 'the one with the square hole in the middle'. It houses government offices and an exhibition centre and was designed as a 20th-century version of the Arc de Triomphe. I am glad Trevor is visiting La Défense alone as going to see 60 office blocks isn't my idea of fun.

I'm not sure what I want to do, but eventually settle on the tour of Montmartre set out in my guidebook. Ever since I saw the film *Amélie*, I have been fascinated by this area in the 18th *arrondissement* that is home to the Moulin Rouge. The movie's street scenes made Montmartre appear so bohemian and romantic that I want to experience it for myself, although I'm so hopeless at reading maps that attempting a self-guided walking tour is going to be a challenge. Trevor still teases me about our driving holiday in New Zealand when I was navigating and insisted I knew where we were going. It turned out I wasn't even using the right map.

It feels strange stepping out onto the street without Trevor. It has never been a conscious decision, but it's always seemed natural for us to do things together. Ever since we got married, I've wondered if we might slowly morph into one of those couples who turn up to parties in matching sweaters and can't do anything without the other person there. Just the fact it feels weird without Trevor beside me makes me realise what a good idea it is for us to split up for the morning. I slip my daypack over my shoulder and bounce off towards the local metro station, determined to prove I can have a great morning by myself.

I greet the man at the Plaisance metro station's ticket office with a cheery *'Bonjour, monsieur. Comment allez-vous?'*, praying he will only respond with the French equivalent of 'good, thanks', and I push a handwritten note across the counter with some change. I did a crash course in German before one of our previous trips, but I've always hated trying to speak French. I can never get the pronunciation right and since I've learned German, my delicate Gallic inflections have to fight it out with heavy Teutonic vowels. The ticket seller reads what I've copied out of my phrase book and hands over a ticket, smiling at the tiny can-can dancer I've sketched next to the word 'Blanche' – the Montmartre metro station where my walk begins.

I grab my ticket off the shiny metal counter and descend into the metro. It is the end of peak hour, so the train I catch is relatively crowded, but I still manage to get a seat near the centre of the carriage. The woman sitting across from me hands over her newspaper when she gets off at the next stop, which I accept with a smile because I don't know how to explain that I can't read it. This is the third time I've been to Paris and I still can't understand why people complain about the locals being rude and unfriendly. I can hardly speak a word of French, but I've never had a bad experience.

I am still holding my copy of *Le Monde* when a man carrying a tiny amplifier and a sports bag gets into our carriage and walks purposefully down to one end. After a quick look around to check there are no *gendarmes*, he reaches into the bag and pulls out a makeshift curtain, which he loops between two vertical poles, before pressing 'play' on the walkman hooked up to his amplifier. An old fashioned wooden puppet holding a trumpet appears above the curtain and, as the first bars of a jazz tune burst out of the amplifier, the trumpeter begins to play. The puppet's tiny eyelids close as he tilts his head back and blows on the trumpet, and his body sways in time to the music. I notice the businessmen across the aisle are tapping their feet.

Suddenly, the trumpeter puppet, which looks a bit like Louis Armstrong, pauses and looks down as a female singer emerges slowly from behind curtain to join him. The trumpeter shrugs his wooden shoulders and continues to play as the sultry chanteuse puppet wriggles her hips and launches into 'Fever'. The song is in English, but I can hear the woman beside me singing it under her breath with a strong French accent. The young puppeteer is so skilful that the jazz duo work the carriage like real performers and I could swear the female puppet is winking saucily only at the men. When the song finishes, most of the commuters applaud as the puppeteer whips away the curtain and takes a small bow before moving through the carriage with his hat held out. I put in two euros and realise I've been so engrossed in the performance that I have no idea where the train is. I wait until the next station, Champs Elysées Clemenceau, appears outside the window and look at my metro map. Luckily, there are two more stops to go before I have to get off and change to another line.

After I arrive at Blanche, I stand on a busy street corner studying my map as people who aren't on holiday hurry past, probably on their way to work. This part of Montmartre, with its busy intersection and rushing commuters, looks nothing like the quaint local neighbourhood I've seen in *Amélie*. I get my bearings and walk up a street called rue Lepic, stopping to look at the nondescript apartment block where Vincent Van Gogh once lived. When Vincent moved into his brother Theo's third floor apartment in 1886, after quitting a beginners' painting class at the Antwerp Academy, he began studying the works of Impressionist painters like Monet, Renoir and Degas and socialising with Toulouse-Lautrec and Gauguin. Montmartre was a thriving artists' community and Van Gogh was greatly influenced by the two years he spent here.

Further up the street, a steady stream of Parisians dart in and out of a patisserie, exchanging banter with the women behind the counter who wear shapeless smocks but still manage to look stylish. I think briefly about buying something to eat, but my stomach is still too full of breakfast croissant, so I inhale the yeasty aromas wafting out the bakery's front door and instead watch the customers come and go. Rich buttery pastries leave translucent stains on the white paper bags everyone emerges clutching like precious trophies. It is too much for one businessman to resist and as he hurries out of the shop, he pauses to extract his pastry and take an enthusiastic bite. His eyes close with pleasure as the chocolate croissant takes revenge for being eaten and drops a gooey brown dollop onto his tie. I hope he isn't on his way to a meeting.

After another quick look at the map, I climb a steep hill towards Moulin de la Galette, one of the few surviving windmills from the 1600s. It is one of 30 that were used by Montmartre's millers, but growing industrialisation and a decrease in agriculture eventually saw the majority of the mills demolished – except for the Moulin de la Galette, which was converted into a tavern and dance hall and became a popular haunt for Montmartre's artists, including Van Gogh. As I look at the windmill's wooden sails tilting defiantly towards the blue sky, I wish I could step back into the past and share Montmartre with the people who lived there in the 19th century.

Vineyards covered the hills and the area was populated by artists, bohemians and performers who took delight in tantalising Paris' bourgeoisie with risqué cabaret acts like the *chahut*, which eventually became known as the can-can. Despite the cars, noise and crush of modern Paris closing in around it, Montmartre retains an air of mystery and its tiny cobblestone alleyways can still lure pedestrians away from the main thoroughfares. Many of the tiny side streets I look down have bars and bistros that look exactly like the place where the character Amélie worked, but I am too shy to walk into them by myself.

Just down from where I am standing, four people are struggling to get an enormous armoire into a small apartment. They stand in a huddle, looking at the stairs, the antique, then back at the stairs again as a man hangs out the top floor window and offers advice. One of the girls sees me watching and gives a theatrical sigh while her friends continue debating how to get the huge piece of furniture upstairs.

I get lost after that but instead of trying to return to the designated route in my guidebook I wander down an unmarked street. The tall apartments on either side of it shut out the noise of the traffic and all I can hear is the sound of my footsteps bouncing off the pale stone walls. I end up at the entrance to a small fenced square, which doesn't appear on my map, although the trees planted around its edge are so large it must have been there a long time. An elderly man sitting on a bench looks up at the sound of my boots crunching on the gravel path. He is dressed in a dark brown suit that would have been the height of fashion 40 years ago and he sits motionless, with his eyes half-closed and his head tilted back towards the sun. The air here beneath the trees is cool, but the sun is warm on my skin. I sit down on the opposite side of the square and feel my eyes closing too.

Birds twitter softly and the rustling trees sound like the swish of petticoats as a feeling of peace settles over me. My senses adjust slowly to the gentle noises in the park, which seem out of place in central Paris, and I am unsure how much time has passed when the old man shuffles slowly past me, pausing to cast a look of understanding and a small smile in my direction. As his stooped back disappears into the distance, I stand up and begin climbing the hill to Sacré Coeur. It certainly provides a change of pace after the solitude and simple beauty of the park. As I pass tacky souvenir stalls selling magnets, mugs and postcards, I think I must be nearly there, but am sure of it when I have to slip into a doorway to avoid a group of name-tagged tourists. As I round the corner, Sacré Coeur looms ahead of me, along with what seems like every other tourist in Paris. This is the one part of my guidebook tour that I haven't been looking forward to: the area around Sacré Coeur is notorious for huge crowds and pickpockets. I've always avoided it in the past and now only give the white onion domes of the basilica a cursory glance before escaping down a set of stairs to the metro, which is what I've really come to see.

Way back when the city's Métropolitain was being built, the architects decided something was needed to entice Parisians to use this new form of public transport.

Rather than resorting to gimmicks or advertising, Hector Guimard, an artist famous for his Art-Nouveau style, was commissioned to design attractive metro entrances. The idea to create something of beauty to entice the population to use the metro is typically French and was enormously successful. The station at Place des Abbesses has one of the two remaining Guimard-designed metro entrances in Paris. I bought an expensive framed photograph of it when I was a teenager because the moody black and white print reminded me of something from an arthouse movie. The metal and cast iron sculpture dominating the metro entrance seemed so sophisticated and exotic to a young girl growing up in Brisbane. I look up at it and realise I have finally kept the promise I made to myself all those years ago. Here I am in Paris, standing right in front of the entrance to the Place des Abbesses station, which is still encouraging commuters to use the metro over 100 years later. I walk underneath the sign and descend 30 metres to the station – the deepest in Paris – and take the train to Pont Neuf, where La Samaritaine department store is located.

Although I love Paris, there is one thing I've never been able to enjoy doing here: shopping for clothes. It always makes me feel hopelessly inadequate. French women put on a simple pair of slacks and a plain top, throw a scarf around their shoulders and look dazzling, whereas I can buy something dazzling and still manage to look plain. I wander over to one of La Samaritaine's racks of clothing for a quick flick through but, at five foot five I am far too short to look glamorous in the flowing, ankle-length skirts that are currently in fashion. I can just imagine my hem dragging along the ground all over Paris so I take the lift up to the rooftop café instead.

The store opened in 1869 and takes its name from a nearby water pump decorated with the Woman of Samaria giving water to Jesus. These days La Samaritaine occupies four separate buildings and is the French equivalent of Harrod's in London – not bad considering it was originally opened as a small boutique by a local street peddler. La Samaritaine is also famous for its café on the roof of store number two, which offers a 360-degree view of Paris. I spend an exorbitant amount on a spectacularly bad cup of coffee while I enjoy the view, positive that cafés with stunning outlooks deliberately choose the most uncomfortable furniture so customers aren't tempted to linger. After watching the spring sunshine dancing on the rooftops and the glittering Seine snaking through the city like a liquid ribbon for over an hour, I discreetly massage my sore behind and return to the streets below. I'm not due to meet Trevor for a while yet, but I don't want to be late. He's already teased me about getting lost when we were deciding on our meeting place.

'How about the carousel at Marais?' he said with a grin. 'We've been there before, remember?' I do remember, mainly because I got us lost on the way there.

I have crammed so much into my morning alone that I can't wait to tell Trevor all about it over lunch and am going to suggest that we do it again. It isn't that I don't want Trevor around, but I love the idea of sharing our experiences when we meet up afterwards. Exploring Paris alone has shown me a different side of the city and I've enjoyed having the freedom to do my own thing.

As I stride towards Marais, I start feeling something isn't quite right: every road I pass is going in a different direction to the one on the page in front of me. According to the scale on my map, I am less than 1000 metres from my destination but it might as well be 1000 miles. I have no idea where I'm going and my confident strides slow to hesitant steps as I turn my map upside down, then right way up, trying to work out where I am. Realising it is time to put my dreadful French to the test, I pluck up the courage to ask for directions – or at least my equivalent of asking for directions, which involves pointing at the map and saying *'Marais, s'il vous plaît?'* with a hopeful expression. Parisians stop to pore over my guidebook, trying to make out street names and direct me to where I am supposed to be meeting Trevor, but they either don't know the area or can't read the map's tiny writing. For once, it appears the map itself is even worse than my sense of direction, although this small consolation isn't helping me get to Marais. Feeling more and more panicky, I flick to the metro map in the back of my guidebook. I know the carousel at Marais is near St-Paul station but when I see I would have to change trains I give up on the idea. I have less than ten minutes and the metro trip would take far too long.

I hop from one foot to the other and clutch my guidebook like a talisman as I wait for the next person to emerge from the Pont Neuf metro station but, when they do, I almost don't bother approaching. Whoever invented the phrase 'tall, dark and handsome' must have had this man in mind. His casual swagger hints at arrogance and it looks like he's in a hurry, but I am so frantic that I take a deep breath and gasp out a heavily accented *'Pardon, monsieur'* before I lose my nerve. When he pauses and walks towards me, I regret my decision immediately. He is very, very French and even more beautiful than the glamorous women I saw shopping at La Samaritaine.

'Oui?'

When he utters that one little word in a deep, velvety purr, I feel like throwing myself at his feet and saying the same thing, until I remember I am supposed to be asking him for directions so I can meet my husband. With a combination of pointing at the map, my wedding ring and then my watch, I explain I have to meet Trevor near the St-Paul metro at 12.30 pm. My knight in shining armour starts to explain how to get there, but it is no use. He can't speak English, I can't speak French and my tiny map is useless, but the handsome Frenchman gallantly refuses to abandon a damsel in distress. After looking briefly at his watch, he beckons for me to follow and sets off at a cracking pace in the direction I came from.

He takes long, loping strides, ignoring every Don't

Walk sign and dismissing the cars' angry toots with a nonchalant wave as I half-run along beside him. He is taking me there, I think in amazement. I'm just beginning to recognise familiar Marais landmarks when my knight comes to a sudden halt and puts his hand on my shoulder, turning my body gently in the same direction as his pointing finger. There is Trevor, standing at the carousel and staring hopefully up the street. I feel like giving the man a grateful hug, but settle for a sincere *'merci'* instead. He says something in French that I expect means 'you're welcome' (although it's possible he was expressing his deep distress that I am already married) and saunters casually back the way we came.

After lunch bought from a patisserie with a crowd three-deep at the counter, Trevor and I head back to Plaisance to recap on our adventures at a café near our hotel. It always looks inviting whenever we walk past and we dive onto the last available seats at a small table facing the street, order two glasses of house wine and watch life unfold around us. Locals pass each other on the footpath, stopping briefly to exchange a few words before moving on, and French voices from other tables rise and fall, mingling with the sound of the traffic. A young waiter moves between the tables, clearing glasses, taking orders and chatting amiably with the regulars.

I love being here in Paris. The streets make me feel like an extra in some arty French film and there is always something to look at. As the waiter returns with our

glasses of wine, Trevor smiles and is about to say something when a very pregnant woman storms dramatically
past the café, followed closely by her boyfriend. The customers' heads turn in unison to watch them. The woman
stops and shakes a packet from our favourite bakery in
front of her boyfriend's pleading face as he attempts
unsuccessfully to mollify her. I have no idea what he's
said to make her so enraged, but suspect a seemingly
innocent question like 'Do you really need that?' might
have had something to do with it. When the lights
change, the woman issues a parting volley of abuse,
snatches the croissant out of its bag and hurls it angrily
at her boyfriend's feet. He stares down at it helplessly
before ambling after her rapidly disappearing figure. A
surreptitious look at the other tables reveals sympathetic
glances from the men, but Trevor only has eyes for the
plump, golden pastry sitting in the middle of the road.

'Oh, that poor croissant – what a tragedy.'

We order another glass of wine and watch the croissant play a one-sided game of chicken until a white
Peugeot speeds through the intersection and transforms
it into a brown smear. We down the last of our wine and
return to the hotel to pack in preparation for our next
five-star experience: the Hôtel Ritz Paris.

When we awake the next morning, blue sky cups Paris
like a huge upturned bowl and I hum 'Puttin' on the
Ritz' while I cram the last few items into my backpack,
choosing to ignore the fact that Irving Berlin was writing

about the hotel in London, not Paris. We are about to check into our most anticipated hotel of the trip, but the Ritz has provoked more trepidation than excitement over the past 18 months. The hotel has played host to guests like Rudolph Valentino, Winston Churchill, Audrey Hepburn, Simone de Beauvoir and the Prince of Wales, and Coco Chanel thought the Hôtel Ritz Paris was so stylish she became a permanent resident there for over 30 years. Just mentioning its name conjures up images of wealth and elegance that have little in common with two backpackers from Australia.

Not many past guests would have travelled to the Hôtel Ritz Paris the way we do today. Our trip on the crowded metro is followed by a sweaty hike from the station, staggering under the weight of our backpacks. We stop walking and peer around the side of a building on the corner of rue de la Paix, staring fixedly at the Ritz's red carpet, which glows richly against the cobblestones of the Place Vendôme. The hotel's façade was listed as a national monument in the 1930s and it is as beautiful as it is imposing. Entry is via a portico flanked by tall stone columns and when I look up, I can see two rows of French doors, with matching shutters and tiny wrought-iron balconies, running from one end of the hotel to the other. I clutch Trevor's hand nervously.

'Do I look okay?' we ask each other anxiously, both desperate for reassurance. Our starched cotton shirts, carefully ironed last night, and our newest trousers would look fine if we were checking into a normal hotel.

Which, of course, we aren't. As a group of stylish women sashay up the red carpet, I look down at my clothes, think back to the security guards at the Alvear Palace and feel physically ill. Tour buses cruise past, slowing so those inside can take photos of the Ritz and, inadvertently, its incongruous new guests who are striding bravely across the Place Vendôme. Everyone else swans towards the hotel and sails under the famous awning like they belong there, but we are so focused on managing our heavy bags we tromp towards the entrance like a pair of Godzilla monsters. Despite our best efforts, we are so underdressed that we might as well be wearing thongs and t-shirts.

The wide red carpet, held down by highly polished brass bars, is smooth and flat against the pristine cream marble steps and a topiary hedge sits in a marble planter box beside a wooden revolving door. This is a change from the highly polished glass and gold entrances of the other five-star hotels but, for some reason, it looks even more fancy. I half-expect the red carpet to whisk itself out from under our hiking boots before we can make it inside, but no such thing happens. Trevor and I keep our heads down and dash past the liveried doormen and up to the front desk, expecting we'll have to convince them that we have a reservation. But if the impeccably groomed staff member is surprised he doesn't show it.

'Welcome to the Ritz,' he intones in English with a strong French accent. 'I'm sure you'll be very comfortable here.'

Trevor shoots me a sideways glance as if to say 'He's got to be kidding'. I fill out the paperwork and try not to notice the haute couture dripping off the other guests as Trevor chats politely to the check-in staff. I am only half-listening to the conversation, until I hear a phrase that fills me with dread.

'May I suggest you enjoy your complimentary break-fast at L'Espadon while your suite is being prepared?'

'No!' I feel like screaming. Our carefully planned arrival is supposed to be followed by a much-needed spruce up in our suite. We are hot and dishevelled and in no fit state to dine in any restaurant, let alone one awarded two Michelin stars and frequented by movie stars and princesses. I am desperate to say as much, but instead we smile inanely and trot obediently off to L'Espadon like lambs to the slaughter.

It stings when we are led to a secluded table near the kitchen, probably so our humble attire won't offend the other guests. The table's location is dreadful – we can hear every little thing going on in the kitchen – but it is still presented like a precious gift and starched linen napkins are draped reverently over our laps. Our waiter gives a small bow before scuttling away to fetch someone in a fancier jacket, whose job it is to present the menu with a flourish. Out of curiosity we open it to see what is on offer, but the fanciest option is the Hôtel Ritz Paris breakfast – the same as the continental one included in our package with an additional cooked dish and a glass of Ritz champagne. It would also cost us about $100 each – twice as much as the continental breakfast.

'Only one glass of champagne?' Trevor jokes. 'You can have a whole bottle at the Alvear Palace.'

The other diners are a mixture of wealthy-looking Europeans and French businessmen, plus a few Americans who are wearing jeans and polo shirts. They have also been seated at the back of the restaurant. At least Trevor and I have company, although they make me realise how truly out of place we all appear. And the Americans look much better than we do.

'They've got the little guy playing polo,' Trevor says wistfully, pointing to the conspicuously empty spot on his shirt where the designer label should be.

The clothes we put on this morning looked quite dressy in the shabby surroundings of our one-star hotel in Plaisance, but they don't look much better than rags now we are at the Ritz. It seems impossible to switch from backpacking back to five-star-hotel mode without coming undone along the way.

People-watching may be one of my favourite pastimes, but you can only do it for so long, especially if you're hungry. We are well and truly ready to order, but the junior waiters are so busy running around, while attempting to look like they aren't, that it isn't going to be easy. The waiters' bowing and scraping makes everything take much longer than it should. As we wait for someone worthy enough to whip out a pencil, it becomes evident that each waiter is allocated a specific task depending on their seniority. For instance, all our first waiter seems to do is show people to their table – the L'Espadon equivalent of wearing an L-plate – and junior waiters can take an order and bring it from the kitchen, but not all the way to the table. The meals are placed tantalisingly out of reach on a holding table where they are collected by a senior waiter and delivered with suitable aplomb.

'Drum roll please,' Trevor says under his breath as one of them delivers bacon and eggs to the next table.

'Do you think rich people really enjoy all this fussing?'

'Not if they're hungry,' Trevor says.

Our three nights at the Ritz includes a continental breakfast each morning, so we order pastries and cereal and sit back in eager anticipation – for a very long time. Our basket of croissants and freshly baked danishes taunts us from the other side of the room, daring us to sneak over and whisk it back to our table. The pastries – which certainly are worth waiting for – finally make it, but they are long gone by the time the cereal makes its grand entrance. We are onto our third cup of coffee when a trolley with three large silver tureens is wheeled to our table. Our waiter looks down his long, patrician nose and pauses to flick an imaginary bit of fluff from his immaculate uniform before he speaks.

'Sir, madam – this morning we are pleased to offer bran, muesli and "cornieflakes",' he tells us, with a seriousness usually reserved for state occasions.

It's hard to keep a straight face. I have the greatest admiration for anyone who can speak a second language, but the waiter's haughtiness makes his mispronunciation hilarious. I am still feeling intimidated, but I'm starting to see the ridiculous side of what's going on. I put down my menu and smile at the waiter in what I hope is a beguiling fashion.

'I'll have "cornieflakes" please. What would you like, Trevor?'

He is struggling not to laugh, but manages to splutter 'Muesli, please'. We grin conspiratorially as the waiter sombrely ladles the cereal into fine porcelain bowls. Just as I am wondering if any other patrons also feel the urge to skip the fancy service circus, a Frenchman in an expensive-looking suit summons a senior waiter and answers my unspoken question. He releases a barrage of French, while pointing to the holding table on the other side of the room and the empty place between his knife and fork. Addressing his irate customer by name, the waiter tries to smooth over the situation, but to no avail. The man looks at his watch, throws his napkin onto the table and storms out of the restaurant. I can almost see the smoke curling out of his ears.

'Something tells me he's not on holidays,' Trevor says.

We aren't the only people who have ever stayed at the Ritz free of charge. In 1915, part of the hotel was used as a military hospital, but I am not sure what a battle-weary soldier would make of the room we are shown to. It is very pink and very feminine, right down to the his and hers bathrobes hanging next to the baby pink bathtub. The gold chandelier over the bed matches the filigree on the elaborately carved cornices and the white furniture has gold handles. Even the carpet is a dusty pink. Our suite is a cross between a rococo boudoir and a little girl's bedroom.

I peer through the French doors that open onto a small wrought-iron balcony and look out over the Place Vendôme, the octagonal square where Napoleon married Josephine. The boutiques around its edges, with names like Cartier, Armani, Bulgari and Chanel, are surrounded by casually dressed tourists. I notice some of the travellers taking photographs of our hotel and I smile.

'Look,' Trevor says, pointing to a woman walking a chihuahua on a skinny red lead. She is wearing a tailored suit with matching navy pumps and walks through the square like she owns the place. A few of the tourists discreetly take her photograph as she approaches one of the high-end boutiques and dis-appears inside. Trevor grins and gives my arm a playful squeeze as it feels like the passing parade is for us alone.

The room really is something special and not just because it is so pink. Suites overlooking the Place Vendôme are some of the most expensive at the hotel and we've been given one for free. Trevor and I stand in front of the French doors and gaze outside. I feel excited and nervous at the same time, but I'm determined to enjoy our stay, even if we do look appalling compared to the other guests.

I am once again reminded what a state my clothes are in when I begin slipping them into our wardrobe's lined drawers. They are so worn they'll need more than a brief lie-down on rose-scented tissue paper to help them recover. I take my two woollen polonecks into the bathroom, hoping that a careful rinse might help them look a bit brighter, and fill the pink handbasin with water. As I squirt in some bath gel, I grin at the irony of using Chanel products to scrub the armpits of my sweaters. I've been doing well with my resolution not to hand wash in the bathroom sink, but it is obvious that desperate measures are called for. Trevor sees what I am doing and doesn't say a word.

In the evening, we pick up takeaway from a local pizzeria and a bottle of cheap red wine and return to the hotel, boldly brandishing our pizza box, which is too big to squeeze into our daypacks. It is the hardest thing we've had to do on the trip so far.

'Just pretend you're the woman with the dog,' Trevor says encouragingly.

I do my best, but it is difficult to swan around like a chic Parisian when you're wearing a backpack and carrying a pizza. We stroll through the foyer while I juggle the hot box from one hand to the other and try to appear relaxed. Then we almost run headlong into the man who showed us to our room.

'Bonsoir, monsieur, madame,' he says formally, looking

at each of us in turn. The box tilts and I gasp as Trevor grabs the corner just before its contents plop onto the floor. I am positive I catch the hint of a smile when the guy notices what I am carrying.

We exchange a few pleasantries then dash the last few metres to the lifts. As soon as the doors close, Trevor exhales.

'I can't believe we just did that,' he says and we both start laughing.

After gorging ourselves on pizza the night before, we decide a visit to the Ritz health club is in order, especially as we can use the facilities for free. The club has been designed to resemble a Roman bathhouse and the area is long and narrow with intricate mosaics on the floor and elegant frescoes of Grecian women standing in the middle of charming rural scenes. The water slaps softly against the sides of the pool as Trevor hands me his towel and slips into the water.

I am walking over to a deck chair to lay out our things when an attendant approaches and presents me with a bathing cap, explaining that everyone has to wear one. Then he notices Trevor, who is already swimming laps. I watch the attendant wrestling with his dilemma: the rules may state that patrons must wear a cap but my husband's skull is clean-shaven. The attendant returns to his desk to collect another cap, but stands there passing it from one hand to the other as Trevor continues swimming. I can hear the rubber cap making flapping noises as I approach the edge of the pool and watch Trevor perform a neat tumble turn. The attendant stands there for a while longer until, with a small decisive nod, he puts the cap back into a drawer and walks into the change rooms. Trevor stands up in the shallow end, takes one look at me in my bathing cap and starts laughing

'Very sexy,' he chortles, blissfully unaware of how close he came to wearing one himself.

After splashing around for a while, we return to our room where Trevor walks straight over to the phone.

'I can't believe it! You're really going to do it?'

'Sure,' he says nonchalantly. 'Why not?'

Trevor calls the concierge and asks if they can organise a Vespa ride around Paris for him. It is something he's always wanted to do but, as neither of us has a bike licence, Trevor needs someone with a scooter who'll take him as a pillion passenger.

'No, a motorbike's not the same,' he explains patiently. 'It has to be a Vespa.'

'He's going to call me back,' Trevor tells me, putting down the phone.

It turns out no one can help with the Vespa ride, but it doesn't really matter. Making the call was the first step in our plan to survive our stay at the Ritz: instead of allowing ourselves to feel uncomfortable, we decide to embrace the opportunity to be seen as the hotel's quirkiest guests.

This works to a point, but little things still creep in to point out how gauche we are. My attempts to be polite by asking if the staff speak English each time I ask for anything elicit a response that makes me cringe.

'And yes, we still speak English,' follows the standard French greeting when I telephone reception.

I am mortified, but continue the conversation as if nothing has happened even though my face is so red it lights up our room.

That evening, we organise a wine bucket ('Yes, that's right – no wine, only the bucket') and chilled champagne flutes so Trevor can do what he's been looking forward to for the past 18 months. After we don our pink bathrobes, Trevor drags two white chairs upholstered in dusky pink velvet over to the window and groans with the effort of moving the solid marble coffee table over to join them. He undoes the clasps securing the French doors and pulls them back to let the soft twilight pour into our suite.

Conversations in every language float up from the street and we can hear the doorman greeting people entering the hotel. Groups of tourists in the Place Vendôme admire the hotel's façade and I wonder if they are dreaming of what it would be like to stay here. Trevor removes the champagne from its ice bucket and pops the cork with a satisfied smile. As sun shines through our fine crystal glasses, the bubbles race to the surface in twirling streams and I inhale the strong, yeasty aroma. I look over at Trevor, who is sipping champagne with a faraway look in his eye. He turns to me and smiles before raising his glass towards the Place Vendôme.

'Here's to Bollinger at the Ritz.'

Trevor has found a way to make his dream come true, even if it did involve buying the champagne at a liquor store and smuggling the bottle up to our room. As I look down at the tourists staring longingly at the hotel, I realise how stupid we've been. What does it matter what people think of us? Embroidered slippers are laid out every night on a fine linen mat for everyone and no matter what I ask for, the staff always do their best to accommodate my wishes simply because it is their job. The sole reason these hotels exist is to make their guests feel pampered and indulged. Every guest receives excellent service – whoever they are or, in our case, aren't. I sip my champagne and think about the fancy hotels we've been to so far. Life inside their walls is a million miles away from reality – probably even for many of their usual clientele – but that is the whole idea. Trevor and I don't have money, but we can still enjoy ourselves as much as any other guests – perhaps even more so.

We aren't rich, famous or clinging desperately to our privacy, like poor Princess Diana who on 30 August 1997 dined at the restaurant downstairs just moments before she and her lover Dodi Al Fayed (the son of the hotel's current owner) were killed when their car slammed into the wall of a tunnel beneath the nearby Place de l'Alma. Unlike many of the other guests at these five-star hotels, we are two of the few who have the complete freedom to enjoy every moment. Trevor and I are the last people who should be worrying about what anyone thinks because, I realise for the first time, what does it really matter? I am sure many of the guests here would be envious of our anonymity.

Hiding behind the glass would be nothing short of sacrilege on such a gorgeous evening, yet the stiffness of the catches and Trevor's struggle with the French doors suggest they haven't been opened for years. I wonder how many rich guests toy with the idea of flinging them open, but shy away from it at the last minute, deeming it inappropriate behaviour. Or perhaps they don't think to do it at all. I look over at Trevor and smile. For the first time since we started our trip, we have done exactly what we want to without worrying about the consequences or what people might think. I am sure it is no coincidence that this is the most relaxed I've been since we began staying at our prize hotels.

Tourists who come to see the Ritz this evening witness yet another unique moment in the history of the hotel. Two backpackers wearing pink bathrobes sit at the window of one of its finest suites, sipping champagne and waving to anyone who notices them. It is fun watching the different reactions. A glamorous couple in a red Ferrari start watching but then feel embarrassed to be caught staring and quickly look away, but others smile and wave back. One man is so discomfited that Trevor can't stop laughing, especially when we catch him watching a second time, and a couple of fellow back-packers mime 'Can we come up?' with such enthusiastic good humour that we almost say yes.

Before we left home, people suggested we might get tired of the fancy hotels and that the luxury would turn into a blur of marble bathrooms and fluffy pillows, but it hasn't happened so far. They may all be Leading Hotels of the World, but each of our prize hotels has provided a completely different experience. We relaxed in understated elegance at the Observatory, were charmed by the staff at the historical Windsor in Melbourne and Huka Lodge is still my favourite so far. Everything about it was casual perfection and the natural setting took our breath away. The Alvear Palace in Buenos Aires, with its chandeliers and Louis XVI furniture, was made even more special by Ana and now there is the Hôtel Ritz Paris.

When we walk through the hotel's common areas, we see the odd person who doesn't appear to be revelling in their five-star experience, but they are few and far between. Harried businesspeople on their way to yet another meeting aside, everyone else looks to be having a great time. We certainly haven't tired of it, but it is the little things I enjoy the most. The complimentary toiletries in our bathrooms are exotic brands that smell divine, things arrive in record time whenever we ring with a request and no one ever disturbs us with something as crass as a knock on the door accompanied by the cry of 'housekeeping!'. I don't know how they do it, but the cleaning staff always seem to know when we've left the hotel and service our room before we return. Not having to clean or tidy is a luxury I'll really miss when we get home.

* * *

Trevor and I spend most of our time at the Hôtel Ritz Paris either revelling in the luxury of our suite or exploring the nearby Louvre. Walking around the huge art museum proves so exhausting we have to return to see works like the Mona Lisa and Venus de Milo that we miss on our first day. We don't go out in the evenings, choosing to enjoy our fabulous accommodation instead, except on our final night when we climb the 284 steps to the top of the Arc de Triomphe at the end of the Champs Elysées. When we reach the viewing platform of the arch commissioned by Napoleon in 1806 to commemorate his victories, Trevor and I are treated to a breathtaking view of Paris and the aural assault of a heavyset American pacing from side to side as he gestures wildly and hollers into his mobile phone.

'Hi! Hi? You still there? Uh huh, uh huh – yeah, I'm just great. Guess what? I'm on top of the Arch de Tromp.'

Trevor sniggers.

'No, not that one – that's the Eiffel Tower.' The guy's voice is ruining the romance of the perfect spring evening and we are becoming more and more annoyed with each mispronunciation and inane comment.

'The Arch de Tromp – yeah, the Arch de Tromp.'

We are about to move as far away as possible when he lets out an anguished cry. 'Oh no, my battery's about to die!'

Trevor starts a celebratory jig. The American spins around without warning and for the first time in the whole conversation, attempts to lower his voice.

'Hey,' he says in a booming whisper, 'there's a guy up here doing some sort of weird dance.' He stares at Trevor, whose moves grind to a halt and we escape to the other side of the platform.

I can't believe we've never been here before – the view from the Arc de Triomphe is even better than from the Eiffel Tower and it is far less crowded. The sky is like an inky velvet cloak draped around the city's sparkling lights and the Champs Elysées carries a mesmerising stream of taillights that glow hot red against the black road. We stand gazing out across the city until a volley of blaring horns makes us look down. The massive round-about at the base of the arch is a hub for the12 wide boulevards that radiate off it and vehicles are charging around the huge circle in what looks like an out-of-control frenzy. Those waiting to join the melee zoom in from the feeder roads with suicidal desperation, motors roar and the smell of exhaust tinges the cool night air as we wince at yet another near miss. There won't be any of this at our next destination – only the soft swish of water, accompanied by an aria or two.

The next morning we check out, decline the concierge's offer of a taxi and instead ask for our luggage to be left at the front door. Then we make our way down the red carpet one last time. Something has changed for both of us during our time at the Hôtel Ritz Paris. The over-the-top service has made us realise how ridiculous it is allowing ourselves to be intimidated by something that is nothing more than smoke and mirrors.

Trevor and I stride over to our luggage, fiddle with the zippers until straps emerge from their hiding places and our soft suitcases are transformed into what they really are – backpacks. We sling them over our shoulders, buckling the large padded straps securely around our hips, and Trevor approaches one of the bellhops.

'Could you please take our photo before we leave?' he asks.

This is another thing I love about these luxurious hotels. None of the staff ever let on if they think you are doing something bizarre. If I strolled through the lobby wearing a lampshade on my head, the doorman would probably just nod and wish me a pleasant day. Rather than recoiling in horror at the sight of two backpackers standing on the hallowed steps of the Hôtel Ritz Paris, the bellboy smiles obligingly.

'Of course, sir. That's a very nice camera,' he adds in surprise, taking in Trevor's pride and joy. I can see a flicker of doubt cross his face – who are we and should he have paid us more attention while we were at the hotel? Trevor and I stand resplendent in our backpacks and hiking boots on the red carpet of the Hôtel Ritz Paris as the bemused bellhop struggles with the camera.

One click later, it is all over and we depart for the closest metro station. 'See you next time,' Trevor tells the hotel. It isn't a lie. He just neglects to mention we will probably be doing it from the seats outside with the rest of the tourists.

9

THAT ITALIAN THING

An 'it's-Tuesday-so-it-must-be-Paris-pass-me-another-beer' tour of Europe I did with Contiki in 1988 first introduced me to Venice and it was especially memorable. The visit was a complete disaster. A flu spread like wildfire through the bus and by the time we arrived at our hotel on one of the outer islands, I was a snotty, feverish mess. I spent most of the next two days in bed, snorting decongestants like a junkie and rubbing my nose raw with cheap Italian tissues, but, determined to see Venice at least once, I dragged myself around the narrow alleys, squares and hidden corners of the city on our last afternoon. Even through the haze created by a cocktail of flu drugs, I fell in love with Venice and vowed to return one day.

It is finally about to happen but as the plane touches down at Venice's Marco Polo airport I'm not feeling quite so confident about insisting that we come. Trevor only agreed to come here under extreme duress and he can't understand why I want to return to a place he's heard is nothing but a smelly tourist trap. He's also been vehemently against using our hotel credit in one of the most expensive cities in Europe. I've assured him that Venice is the perfect place to stay somewhere special and romantic but, even with the special rate we've been offered by the Leading Hotels of the World, our hotel still works out to be $1800 for three nights. There may be breakfast and afternoon tea thrown in each day, but it is a staggering sum for a couple of backpackers to come to terms with.

I haven't dared mention anything about my misgivings, but what if Venice isn't as wonderful as I remember? The last time I was here was a long time ago and I am not an impressionable teenage girl anymore. And I too am concerned about the price of our hotel. As we board the Alilaguna ferry – the Venetian equivalent of an airport bus – I decide it is too late to worry about it and watch the passing scenery instead. There are mansions covered in flowering vines, old wooden jetties and tumbledown houses with lush lawns leading down to the water. The wash from the passing boats slaps against the ancient retaining walls hugging the edge of the islands and everything sparkles in the sunshine. Trevor moves from one side of the boat to the other – sometimes taking photographs, but mostly just staring rapturously at the scenery sliding by. My misgivings melt away as I slip my arm around his waist, filled with joy and anticipation as the ferry docks near Piazza San Marco, also known as St Mark's Square.

It doesn't take long to find our hotel – it is in a fabulous location right near the square – but when Trevor and I approach reception, we are told they don't have our reservation. The young clerk goes to speak with her supervisor while Trevor rummages in his backpack for a copy of the letter confirming our booking, but just as he finds the documents, a senior staff member hurries over towards us. His elegant leather shoes look handmade and they make a soft swishing noise as he speeds across the highly polished marble floor.

'Mr and Mrs Templeman, please accept my apologies for the confusion. You may leave your bags here but, if you could follow me to the other side of the hotel, the staff there will be able to assist you. We cannot check you in here as Il Palazzo operates separately.'

Il Palazzo? Trevor and I exchange incredulous looks and try to look cool as we stroll along the corridor. Not an easy thing to do when you feel like punching the air like a crazed sports fan. This walk to the other part of the hotel can mean only one thing – we've been upgraded in the most spectacular fashion.

The Bauer Venezia has two sections – the Hotel Bauer and an exclusive private section of the hotel called Il Palazzo. Hotel Bauer, the hotel we booked, is spectacular enough, but Il Palazzo is something else again. The fully renovated 18th-century palace houses 75 individually decorated rooms, many of which afford stunning views of the Grand Canal, and the hotel's exclusive rooftop terrace is the highest in Venice. We drooled over

Il Palazzo when we were looking at the Bauer Venezia's web site, but have no idea why we've been upgraded.

Trevor and I are led through a series of corridors, before being proudly presented to Il Palazzo's senior concierge. The tall, imposing man with closely cropped steel-grey hair finishes his last bit of paperwork and looks up to study us with a pair of piercing blue eyes that have undoubtedly seen a lot of interesting things over the years.

'Welcome-a to Il-a Palazzo,' he says, throwing his arms wide as if he is embracing the hotel and us along with it. 'My name is-a Roberto and I am at-a your service.'

His heavily accented English is gorgeous – especially those long rolling consonants – and it feels like we've walked into an Italian version of 'Fantasy Island', especially when Roberto dispatches a handsome young Italian to escort us to our suite. It isn't especially large and the furniture is no fancier than what we've had before, but we can't stop staring. Not at what is inside, but straight out the window at a steady procession of gondolas sliding along the Grand Canal. They are sleek, black and silent except for the rise and fall of their gondoliers' voices singing.

Trevor staggers back from the window and flops down onto the bed.

'I have no idea how we scored this, but I'm sure they have the wrong idea about who we are. But you know what? I really don't care!'

After unpacking, we go down to the Bauer's restaurant and ponder his theory of mistaken identity. It is certainly a possibility. Our booking was organised by the personal assistant to the Vice President of the Leading Hotels of the World, so the staff may be wondering if we are writing an article on the hotel, personal guests of the management, or perhaps performing some sort of assessment. With Trevor's large camera bag and not a scrap of designer apparel between us, I have no doubt we are a mystery if nothing else.

We walk onto the sunlit terrace and are seated at a table right next to the Grand Canal by our waiter, who looks like a young Italian matinee idol. His good looks and hesitant English spoken with a heavy accent is a combination guaranteed to turn any red-blooded woman to warm jelly. Even Trevor admits our waiter certainly has 'it', even if his charms don't seem to extend to bringing us any food. We're practically faint from hunger after skipping lunch and our initial request for the afternoon tea included in our package is met with a cheery, '*Si, si*, afternoon tea. One moment please.'

Romeo returns promptly with a menu that includes not only tea, coffee and pastries, but various light snack options as well. Everything looks wonderful but it is also very expensive. Trevor returns the menus and explains we would like the afternoon tea included in our room rate.

'Ah, yes,' nods Romeo sagely, fluttering his eyelashes in a captivating fashion totally wasted on Trevor. 'Afternoon tea?'

'Yes, but not this one.'

Romeo nods again and disappears in the direction of the kitchen.

After waiting valiantly for almost an hour, there is still no sign of Romeo or our afternoon tea, so we get up and go to see the debonair concierge, Roberto. After a number of rapidfire phone calls and apologies for the confusion, he explains that as a set afternoon tea is no longer being offered, we can order off the standard menu. We return to the terrace, order coffee and sandwiches and try to concentrate on the view instead of our growling stomachs.

At least eating so late means we won't have to buy dinner, which is a blessing in Venice. The city's reputation for overpriced, underwhelming food is notorious and well-deserved, judging from what I experienced and overheard during my last visit. My fellow travellers all seemed to be talking about food and nearly every conversation involved a terrible dining experience. Indifferent service, poor quality food, exorbitant prices or, more often than not, a combination of all three. Trevor and I plan to do everything possible to avoid going out for dinner while we are here.

Il Palazzo isn't an establishment accustomed to hosting backpackers, yet at no time do we feel like we don't belong here. Considering our surroundings are an 18th-century palace and some of the artworks on the walls are worth more than our car back home, this is a strange sensation but thanks to our revelation at the Ritz it no longer bothers us.

Il Palazzo's other guests remind me of the couple we met at Huka Lodge who took off in the helicopter. Everyone except us has the same casual air of wealth. It is surreal being surrounded by incredibly rich people, whom we wouldn't normally mix with. This bizarre situation is most obvious when we go to breakfast the next morning. Wrought-iron chairs and dainty tables set with white linen and sparkling glasses dot Settimo Cielo, the restaurant on Il Palazzo's rooftop terrace, where we sit for hours, leafing through the wide selection of English language newspapers and enjoying the view. The canals are full of traffic and I never tire of looking at Dogana di Mare, the old customs house, located directly across from the hotel on the spit of land where Giudecca Canal meets the Grand Canal. The building's ornate tower is crowned by two identical statues of Atlas holding up a burnished sphere topped by a weathervane. The pointer of the weathervane is in the form of a female figure known as Fortuna and we admire her from a slightly different angle every morning of our stay. No matter what the day or the weather, Fortuna always looks impeccably groomed – just like the other female guests who join us on the terrace each morning. There is nothing flashy about their flowing trousers and matching linen shirts, but it is obvious even to my untrained eye that one of their outfits probably costs the same as the entire contents of my wardrobe at home. And that isn't including their shoes. When a waiter stops by to ask if he can get us anything, I am tempted to ask for a designer wardrobe and a pair of Salvatore Ferragamo sandals, but settle for more coffee.

After breakfast on our first morning, we leave Il Palazzo to explore Venice the way I did in 1988, with no map or particular destination in mind. I can tell Trevor feels uncomfortable without a map, which is his equivalent of a security blanket – he keeps looking out for street signs and trying to use landmarks to get his bearings – but he eventually relaxes and settles into a comfortable meander. At least he won't be able to tell me we're lost, I think with a smile. We walk towards the outskirts of the city, winding down tiny lanes and over bridges until the tacky gift shops thin out and the gondolas have all but disappeared. I hold his hand and point out things along the way, delighting in the fact I have someone special to share Venice with.

'This is so different to the last time I was here,' I say to Trevor, giving him an impulsive hug.

Sweet romance was the last thing on the minds of the party animals on my bus tour in 1988, but being in Venice with a lover is something I've always dreamed of doing.

Trevor and I keep going until the sound of children playing arouses our curiosity and we walk through narrow alleys to a small square where local kids have formed two teams and are kicking a soccer ball around. The World Cup competition may be in full swing, but no game we've seen so far is a match for this one. Local residents yell encouragement and the black and white ball bounces around the square with a ringing 'kaboing' as the children run from one end of the 'field' to the other. We smile at the mothers who are standing nearby and join in their cheering when one of the girls scores a goal.

To most people Venice is about gondolas and canals, but I love uncovering its hidden treasures like this soccer game, which is filled with the Venetians' passion and sense of community. Venice itself is beautiful, but the challenge of trying to see past its more obvious charms is even more alluring. When I was trying to convince Trevor to come here with me, I couldn't disagree with the bad things he'd heard – Venice *is* tacky and crowded and full of rip-off merchants. But this has been thrust upon Venice without its consent and it bears these things with stoic good grace. Nothing can hide its real charms, which are saved for those prepared to look past the tawdriness and into its heart. I am glad that now Trevor has seen them too and we've been able to share the beauty and mystery of '*La Serenissima*' (the most serenely beautiful one), as Venice is often known.

On the way back to Il Palazzo, we peer into small bars and cafés where locals are beginning to stake out the prime positions in front of televisions that have been set up for the World Cup match between Italy and Mexico. Tense excitement is building because if they lose this game Italy will be out of the competition. We are tempted to join the throng but with afternoon tea waiting for us back at the hotel, Trevor and I decide to keep walking.

This afternoon, we throw caution to the wind. 'If we can order afternoon tea using this menu,' Trevor rationalises, 'then we should be able to have anything.'

One coffee is followed by another and we both skip our usual sandwiches and enjoy the most exquisite pasta. It is only a simple bowl of spaghetti tossed with olive oil, fresh herbs and pancetta, but the fresh taste of the ingredients explodes on my palate. I twirl up the long strands and slip them into my mouth, trying not to moan with pleasure when I taste the garlic-infused sauce. Trevor has barely uttered a word since our food arrived – he is too busy eating – and is now using his spoon to scoop up the last drops of delicious sauce. Even though my attempts at spaghetti usually resemble overcooked worms, I vow to replicate the dish when we return to Australia.

As Trevor and I eat, we have fun watching the waiters take turns to disappear surreptitiously out the back, undoubtedly to watch a television that has been set up somewhere. We start making bets about which ones will sneak off next and laugh whenever they stop to check if the coast is clear before they disappear. When a waiter walks past our table Trevor inquires about the progress of the game.

'It is very close,' he advises gravely. 'If we do not score a goal soon, we are finished.'

After we eat, we linger for a while to watch the gondoliers. They play up shamelessly to everyone as they cruise past the restaurant and there's lots of good-natured competition to see who can sing the loudest and with the most overwrought emotion. The gondoliers in Las Vegas were far from authentic, but at least they got one thing right – 'O Sole Mio' is the song of choice in the real Venice as well.

'Look at him,' Trevor laughs, pointing at an elderly, and no doubt experienced, gondolier who is piloting his vessel while simultaneously holding the hand of one of his female passengers and serenading her. He pauses to raise his hat to us as he sails by, but most of the tourists in his gondola are spending so much time with video cameras pressed against their faces I wonder how much they are actually seeing. We are about to leave when the air is filled with a cacophony of tooting horns from the ferries and shouts of jubilation echo around the hotel. The staff race out the back en masse, before returning a few minutes later to confirm the good news – in the last few minutes of the game, Italy has scored.

'The whole of Venice was holding its breath until they kicked that goal,' Trevor yells above the noise.

I look out at the sudden increase in boating traffic on the Grand Canal now the game has ended. Italy has defended her honour on the soccer field so it's back to business as usual.

Il Palazzo is just as fancy as the Hôtel Ritz Paris, maybe even more so, but the hotel has a warm, casual feeling that is complemented perfectly by the Italians' natural style. Whenever an Italian baby is born, it must be someone's job to sprinkle 'debonair dust' over the child's soft, dark head. Even a mundane interaction with the most ordinary-looking Italian comes with a generous serving of cool and the women seem to glow with a vibrancy that makes even the plainest of them appear stunning. I am never tempted by the Venetian glass, lace or wooden gondolas for sale in the gift shops, but I'd pay almost anything for 'that Italian thing'.

Because we've had afternoon tea earlier than usual, or maybe it is all the walking, we are starving by early evening and realise we are going to have to eat out in Venice. I don't know if I can face the horror of such spectacularly ordinary yet expensive food, but Trevor comes to my rescue. When he promises we can have dinner for two in St Mark's Square, listen to a string quartet playing at a restaurant, and it will cost less than $15, I am sceptical but intrigued. He refuses to elaborate further but leads me around the streets, pretending to peer into bins to see what is in them to eat, before we arrive at his true destination. It is the local Burger King, where we pick up takeaway and return to St Mark's Square for our Venetian dining experience. We sit on the steps of a historic building and place our burgers on fine linen napkins from Il Palazzo before settling back to watch tourists wearing t-shirts with 'Venezia' embroidered in tacky gold thread ambling around the square or congregating in their tour groups. Most of them look exhausted and wear the slack-jawed expression of someone who is either awestruck or completely bored. It's probably a bit of both. I was in a similar situation on my Contiki tour but although I enjoyed it at the time I could never go back and do it again. I've come to relish the thrill of discovery that comes with planning our own itinerary and the freedom of travelling independently. Things don't always go to plan, but I enjoy taking things at my own pace and having time to watch the things going on around me. Even the disasters are fun – once I am safely home and can look back at them and laugh.

When a cheerful cleaner stops by to take our rubbish, Trevor comments we are probably enjoying better service than the people in the tourist-trap restaurants where our night's musical entertainment is about to begin. Two restaurants are located on opposite sides of the square and each has a four-piece string quartet, decked out in tails and crisp white shirts. The evening begins with an excerpt from Vivaldi's *The Four Seasons* from the restaurant on our right and, as the sound of soaring violins fills the air, we lean against a pillar and enjoy the music. Meanwhile, the quartet on our left chat while casting contemptuous glances at the other group of musicians. Before the last note has even faded, the second quartet jumps in and plays a well-known show tune. The first quartet laughs and huddles together for a quick consultation before firing back a string version of a popular jazz standard. The friendly competition becomes fiercer as the evening progresses and the volume of the two quartets increases as they try to outdo each other. After one group resorts to playing 'The Flight of the Bumble Bee' in double time, Trevor suggests we return to Il Palazzo. We link arms and walk through the streets of Venice, passing other couples doing the same. Most of them smile and nod as if to say, 'Can you believe we're here on such a perfect night?'. This day has been one of the best of our holiday, especially for me. I feel like a princess as we walk back through Il Palazzo's marble corridors, past the richly coloured paintings and towards the lifts at the far end of the hotel.

'Come outside,' Trevor says impulsively and leads me onto the terrace.

Gondoliers are still cruising past the hotel, but their singing is soft and romantic and the mood is very different from this afternoon. Venice is bathed in moonlight and she is silent, mysterious and achingly beautiful. Trevor puts his arms around me as we watch the lights from the boats cast flickering patterns on the surface of the Grand Canal and I can feel his warm breath on the back of my neck before he turns me around and kisses me.

After breakfast with Fortuna the next day, we go to see Roberto for some advice on which ferry we should catch to the outer islands.

'Oh no – you must let me organise a speedboat for you,' he declares, before adding hastily, 'and there is no need for it to be expensive. I can get you a special price.'

Perceptive as always, Roberto must have noticed our apprehensive expressions. We are sure he knows we don't have much money. While the ferry is certainly cheaper, he is right – the speedboat is an affordable extravagance, even for us. There will have to be some sort of hard-sell along the way for it to be this cheap, but we decide that the experience will make it worthwhile.

When we arrive at Il Palazzo's private jetty on the Grand Canal, the most stunning speedboat I've ever seen is waiting for us. Made of highly polished wood with sleek, sexy lines, it reminds me of the early James Bond movies.

I could be Tatiana in *From Russia With Love*, I think as we climb on board. Well, at least our name is almost the same, even if nothing else is.

With a jaunty wave to Roberto, our speedboat's handsome driver revs the engine, which rises to a throaty growl, and we pull out into the Grand Canal. As the boat picks up speed, we lounge on the bright red padded banquettes while tourists in the passing ferries point at us and wave. Trevor and I wave back and for 20 minutes I feel almost unbearably glamorous and sophisticated. For the first time, I am jealous of the people with money who can afford to live like this every day. It isn't so much the speedboat ride, but the little things I have become aware of since we started this trip that I've begun to yearn for. What would it be like to reach into the minibar for a mineral water or to ring for a $15 cup of coffee to be brought to our suite?

My reverie is interrupted by our driver's shout of 'Murano!'. I look past his outstretched finger to the small island we are approaching and a few moments later we pull up at a private jetty. Each white pylon is topped by a sculpture that glows from within as bright sunlight dances on its graceful curves. These are made of red, blue and green glass and resemble the parrots we saw darting through the trees at Iguazú and most of the sculptures are over a foot high. They remind me of the works of Picasso and look very expensive.

All the glass blowers of Venice were moved to Murano in the late 1500s after a terrible fire on the main island, although the glass blowing masters insist the move was made to keep their secrets safe from the rest of the world. Learning to be a glass blower takes a minimum of ten years and pieces of Murano glass are coveted by collectors for their beauty and historical tradition.

I am still gazing at the sculptures when a man in a sleek grey Italian suit walks out to meet our speedboat and invites us to see some pieces being made in the workshop. I take his outstretched hand and steady myself against the bobbing of the speedboat before stepping onto the wooden jetty, pausing to run my hand over the smooth glass contours of a nearby sculpture. I would love to take one home, but know they must cost an absolute fortune. We follow the man into a small shed to the right of the jetty and take a seat on a bench running along the back wall. It is hard and almost as uncomfortable as the seats at La Samaritaine's rooftop café – but not quite.

The workshop interior seems dark after the bright sunshine outside and is a complete contrast to the sleek jetty, with its decorative features and modern design, which has obviously been set up to receive tourists. There are no pretty sculptures lined up in here – just neatly arranged tools and an old glass blower who appears oblivious to the 15 or so people watching him. The white singlet covering his chest is smeared with grime and his cheeks are flushed bright red from the heat of the furnace. It looks like nothing could break his concentration as he teases the molten glass ball attached to the end of a metal rod into loops and curves that appear to defy gravity.

A handful of suave Italians wearing white open-necked shirts and charming smiles work the room, stopping to answer questions or give explanations of what is happening. We learn that the piece being created is one of a set of bowls commissioned by a 'prominent client' (we assume this means really rich) and that the old man usually only designs these days, but has been begged to return to the workshop as he is one of the few artisans in Venice with enough skill to fill the order. Our guide explains it takes at least 20 years to become recognised as a master craftsman of Murano glass. The old man pauses to wipe his sweaty face with a towel without giving the crowd on the benches a second glance.

When we've seen enough, our host makes what

sounds like well worn small-talk as he escorts us to the main showroom. I suspect Mr Smooth would be selling used cars instead of glass if Venice weren't closed to traffic. When Trevor gives him a smug smile and tells him where we are staying, I could kill him. Our host's eyes light up so brightly I expect to see dollar signs in them as he rushes past us to open a door. He is practically salivating.

'I can't believe you just said that!' I say under my breath.

'Why? It doesn't matter.'

'Yes it does! Now he knows we're staying at Il Palazzo, he'll think we've got money to burn. We'll never get out of here.'

Trevor doesn't get the chance to answer back as Mr Smooth returns clutching a set of keys.

'I have managed to get you access to our special showrooms – I think there are some things there you will like very much.'

The Murano glass we are shown in the locked room is remarkable. Gorgeous sculptures similar to those on the jetty are arranged on spotless perspex shelves and dazzling chandeliers are adorned with glass lilies so realistic I'm sure my nose will be filled with a heady perfume if I sniff them. Some of the statues are half my height and our host explains they take four strong men to lift. On our way to the next showroom, Trevor bends down and whispers triumphantly, 'See, we wouldn't have seen those if I hadn't said where we were staying.'

He has a point – being guests at a fancy five-star hotel entitles us to unique experiences.

We trudge dutifully through each showroom where rows of shelving hold so many bowls, sculptures, goblets, platters and paperweights, they begin blurring into one. Mr Smooth's hard sell isn't as pushy as it could be, but it is unrelenting and obviously aimed at wearing people down. If we say to each other that we like a certain piece (and it is impossible not to as some are truly beautiful), Mr Smooth latches onto this information like a pit bull and the item is explained and fawned over until his patter turns into white noise. By this stage, Trevor is taking particular care not to catch my eye.

It feels like we are caught in one of those nightmares where you're trapped in a building and every door you open is the wrong one – except in this case, they all lead to another showroom. I feel like grabbing Trevor's hand and making a run for it. We would have asked to leave ages ago, but the building didn't look big enough from the outside to house this many different showrooms so we are positive each one must be the last. In some ways it is like walking through an art gallery but, after nearly 40 minutes, we've had enough. Our polite insistence we have no money to spend and no room to carry anything extra in our bags is brushed aside by Mr Smooth, who is intent on showing us yet more tempting things, but it finally becomes too much. Through gritted teeth he is told we've seen enough and want to go and explore the island. The poor man looks shattered.

'But, but . . . I have more beautiful things to show you!'

One look at Trevor's thunderous expression confirms my suspicions – it is definitely time to go.

'Thanks, but I'm afraid we have to leave. Where is the exit to the street please?'

Mr Smooth's mission to make his supposedly rich clients buy up big hasn't been accomplished, yet how can he refuse to answer such a direct question? We can almost see the salesman and his inner conscience doing battle before he gestures reluctantly down the hallway in front of us.

'It is this way, please follow me.'

It feels like we've escaped from prison as we stumble into the small alley behind the factory. The tiny island of Murano takes all of ten minutes to explore, but along the way we have fun playing 'who can find the most hideous item' in the tourist shops cramming the main street. Trevor wins hands down, selecting a bracelet with glass animal charms resembling victims of a nuclear accident. It is priced at over $340.

We are on our way back towards to the glass factory when we come to a terrible realisation. As they have to summon the speedboat, we will not only have to re-enter the factory, but also walk back through the main showroom to reach the jetty. Trevor devises a strategy to take us as quickly as possible from one end to the other. We take a deep breath and stride confidently into the main showroom, greeting each salesperson with a cheery 'Good afternoon' without slowing our pace, until we emerge unscathed into the bright sunlight. Trevor and I are just about to congratulate ourselves when we hear a familiar voice.

'Hello there – you are back!'

We turn slowly to have our worst fears confirmed. It is the same salesman as before and he looks very pleased to see us.

'Did you have a look around the island?'

'Yes, thanks. We came back as we're ready for the speedboat to Burano. Could you please call it for us?'

We hold our breath and wait for Mr Smooth's answer.

'Yes, of course. In the factory I have . . .'

It appears this is about to turn into an unpleasant situation. If Mr Smooth insists we have a look at yet more works while we are waiting, we'll have to refuse in no uncertain terms.

'. . . some cold drinks. Would you like me to bring you a mineral water or lemonade to enjoy while you wait?'

He smiles and gestures to a table and chairs set up at the far end of the jetty and returns a few minutes later with a silver tray. Two crystal glasses filled with sparkling mineral water glitter in the bright sunshine.

'Here you are,' says Mr Smooth, placing our drinks on the small table. 'The boat will be here soon. Enjoy the rest of your time in Venice.' He shakes our hands warmly before walking back inside the factory. It is a kind gesture and as we sip our drinks I decide I've been too hard on the guy – he was only trying to earn a living. We watch the sun dancing on the water and revel in the experience of sitting on a jetty in Venice, surrounded by magnificent artwork, waiting for our speedboat.

The trip to Burano takes less than five minutes and its tiny village comes into view all too soon. The island is renowned for its lace-making industry, which dates back to the 16th century, and many visitors pay huge amounts for a piece of delicate handmade Burano lace. This holds no interest for either of us, but we are keen to soak up Burano's quiet fishing-village atmosphere and wave goodbye to the speedboat before walking down a labyrinth of tiny streets, half the size of the ones on Venice's main island. I feel like we're a million miles away from its crowded streets and canals.

The houses in Burano are modelled after ancient lagoon *casoni*, or fishing lodges, and they stand close together along the canal edges. Each is painted in a different colour, supposedly so the island's fishermen can find their way home in the dark of early morning. The little two-storey houses look bright and cheerful and are charmingly picturesque. Washing hangs on lines strung above the street and we walk along with our eyes turned skywards. Bright clothes flutter like prayer flags in the stiff breeze and provide a fascinating insight into who lives inside. On one line, tiny baby clothes share space with schoolgirl dresses that are crammed against the clothes of a fashion-conscious teenager. Voluminous housecoats swing off the clothesline on hangers and long apron strings dangle just out of reach. I want to run down the lane and leap high enough to tug on the cords.

Many residents sit in their doorways to escape the heat of the day and their melodic conversations are broken by companionable silences. Many are elderly and when we walk by each doorway our passage is greeted by a small nod, which we return. It feels like we are giving a secret password and therefore allowed to look into their lives, albeit just for a few minutes. Living here would be a simple and very different life from the one we know back in Australia.

A woman laden with bags full of fruit and vegetables walks past us and slips through her brightly coloured doorway. What is it like, I wonder, to live in a village like this, surrounded by such simple beauty and tourists in equal measure? Burano is a tiny island more than half an hour by boat from the mainland and it would provide an isolated existence. Did the woman grow up here? Did she move to Burano for love, a simple life or did her life somehow become so complicated that a small village held the respite she craved? I look up to see that the clothes on her washing line appear to be hers alone and wonder if she came to Burano to escape a broken heart.

We arrive back at the jetty just as a vaporetto is pulling in. These boats are Venice's public transport system and come in different sizes depending on where they are going. Vaporettos travelling to the outer islands are huge ferries, similar to those we saw racing on Sydney harbour, whereas the ones servicing the Grand Canal aren't much larger than a speedboat. To us, they seem far more exotic than taking a bus but locals see the vaporettos as nothing more than a means of getting from one place to another. I peer inside our boat's indoor seating area and see three Italian men dressed like waiters who are sitting in the corner, laying down playing cards on an adjacent seat. They stare at the vinyl cushion as their hands play out and talk quietly until we arrive back at St Mark's Square. The only time they look up is when the vaporetto begins docking at the jetty. One man scoops up the cards in a swift movement and they head towards a restaurant in the square while we walk in the opposite direction towards Il Palazzo.

Darkness is falling on Venice when we step onto the Number One vaporetto later that evening. The office workers have gone home and most of the tourists are still having dinner, so our small public ferry is nearly empty. Route Number One is the most popular in Venice as it goes from one end of the Grand Canal to the other, so we are lucky to have this vaporetto almost all to ourselves. We sit up the back of the boat, listening to the swish of the water and gazing up at the houses lining the canal. Women are cooking in their kitchens and high above us a young boy looks out the window of an apartment block. He hasn't seen us and appears lost in his own thoughts until he quickly turns away from the window.

'I bet his Mum just called him for dinner,' Trevor says.

It feels like we are watching a play without any

dialogue, with the drapes on either side of the windows making each backlit scene look like a theatre production. Trevor puts his arm around me as we round one of the Grand Canal's gentle curves. The beauty and romance of the evening are unaffected by the plastic seats and worn decking of our well-used vaporetto.

Amidst the debris of a renovation in progress, we watch through the window as a dashing man struggles to open a bottle of wine. His female companion leans towards him with a look of eager anticipation, her empty glass subconsciously outstretched in the direction of the bottle. The cork remains stubbornly wedged inside it and the woman's glass droops dejectedly by her side as our vaporetto slides slowly past their building.

'Look at the time!' Trevor exclaims a few minutes later.

I could have sworn we'd only just sat down, but it is well past ten o'clock.

We catch the next boat back up the Grand Canal to the jetty near Il Palazzo and tumble gratefully into bed. I listen to Trevor's rhythmic breathing and reflect on the potential this trip has to turn our lives upside down once we return home. Despite dwelling on almost nothing else but this holiday for the past year, the impact it could have in the future isn't something either of us has thought much about. How will we cope when we get back to Australia and have to deal with the reality of the everyday? There won't be any speedboats, champagne on arrival or room service. Instead Trevor and

I will return to the boring routine of paying bills and scooping out the kitty litter. Previously we were fairly content with our life, but how will we feel about it after what we've experienced and what is yet to come? We've talked about this a few times along the way, but more to joke about 'what the people in the real world are doing back home'. I don't think either of us has accepted that when this is over, that will be us too.

Trevor interrupts my thoughts by rolling over and snoring lustily in my ear, so I wedge both my hands under his shoulder and roll him back the other way before lying back to listen to the last few songs of the late-night gondoliers. Venice has outdone herself this time around.

10

DRINKING DONKEY WINE

THE HIGH SPEED catamaran from Venice pulls into Rovinj, a small coastal town at the top of Croatia, at eight o'clock in the evening and we struggle down the gangplank with our passports at the ready. We originally planned to do this trip by rail, which would have taken at least eight hours and involved numerous changes of train, but Roberto at Il Palazzo suggested taking a ferry direct from Venice to Rovinj instead. We didn't know such a thing existed and shared the smooth three-hour journey with a catamaran of predominantly Italian holidaymakers.

Croatia may be a popular holiday destination for Europeans, but finding information about it in Australia was difficult, especially as the only available guidebook I could get my hands on was out of date. Most of our friends didn't even know where the place was, except for Trevor's old school friend Johnno, who was born there. Croatia was part of the former Yugoslavia and we sat down one night with Johnno to look at photographs from a trip he took there in 1990. As we admired a shot of heavily laden grapevines obscuring an idyllic harbour dotted with vibrantly coloured fishing boats, Trevor turned to me with a raised eyebrow.

'Definitely,' I said and Croatia was included on our itinerary.

The staff at the Rovinj jetty are so casual that we begin to wonder if there will be any customs formalities at all, until a couple of guys in shabby uniforms wander over.

'Hmm . . . very nice photo,' one comments as he checks Trevor's documents.

We both grin, knowing exactly what he means. Trevor's passport photo makes him look like a startled rabbit. The customs officer hands back the passport with a wry smile, while the other man casts an experienced eye over our backpacks.

'You both have very big bags,' he says. 'Are there bad things in there?'

'No, no bad things. Just dirty clothes,' I tell him

'That is still very bad, but that is okay.'

My passport is returned and we are dismissed with a casual wave.

There are few people waiting at the jetty, and none seem to be hotel owners touting for customers.

'Doesn't the guidebook say pension owners come to meet the ferries?' Trevor asks.

He is right, but I prefer not to think about what it might mean that there are none here. We shoulder our heavy packs before setting off towards the lights of Rovinj, which are shimmering prettily about half a kilometre away. After years of travelling, we've worked out that not prebooking accommodation has numerous advantages – you can check out a room before you agree to take it, great places are often not listed in guidebooks and, most importantly, you can bargain for reduced rates when things aren't busy. Unfortunately, my worst fears are confirmed once we arrive in the town centre, which is anything but quiet. It is peak tourist season in Rovinj and we trudge up and down the cobbled streets, looking forlornly at 'pension full' signs written in up to six different languages. Tourists bustle past us in loud groups, talking and laughing, and restaurants have squeezed extra tables and chairs onto the footpaths to cope with the crowds of diners.

'This isn't looking good,' Trevor says, but we do eventually find a room in a ramshackle pension up an alley. It is run by a woman in her forties who looks exhausted, but she still has the energy to smile at our undisguised delight that she has a room. Trevor and I are willing to pay virtually anything for it – which I suspect she knows – but we are still only charged $30. As the previous guests have just left, the owner disappears upstairs to clean our room while we chat to her son, who is about to go out and hit the town.

'I'm going to drink at the bars tonight, but will be quiet when I come back,' he reassures us. It is nice of him to be considerate, but we are so tired I suspect nothing will wake us.

The humble pension is a far cry from the enormous

suites and marble bathrooms we've become accustomed to at the five-star hotels, but our small room feels comfortably familiar rather than disappointing. It is typical of the places we've stayed at on other holidays and I am surprised how easily we slip back into budget traveller mode after the splendour of Il Palazzo.

'It's just like a five-star hotel. We've even got a safe,' Trevor jokes, opening a small wooden cabinet with a piece of string instead of a handle. All our luxurious suites have had discreet notices advising guests to use the in-room safe for storage of precious jewellery and large sums of cash. The only time I've used one was at the Hôtel Ritz Paris, when I hid Trevor's hiking boots in there for a joke.

Trevor closes the door to our room as raucous laughter floats up through our window. Rather than inspiring us to venture downstairs, it reminds us how exhausted we are and Trevor and I take turns stumbling down three steep flights of stairs to the bathroom before falling gratefully into bed.

Croatia's fledgling tourism industry had just begun to take off when the Balkan wars broke out in 1991 and slowed it down, but now the conflict is over things appear to be moving ahead quickly – perhaps too quickly.

'Rovinj reminds me of Surfers Paradise on the Gold Coast minus the surf beach,' Trevor says.

The only locals appear to be those who work in the restaurants or hotels and Rovinj's narrow streets are crammed with ice-cream parlours, souvenir shops and restaurants advertising dinner specials in Italian, German and English. What was once a charming fishing village is now buried beneath the trappings of the tourist industry and it feels a bit like we've stumbled straight into holiday hell.

We quickly learn to do any shopping or chores early in the morning, so we can spend the rest of the day either in or near the water to escape the soaring temperatures. It is a humid 36 degrees most days and every swimming area around Rovinj is packed with holiday-makers floating in the calm water or lolling beside it on volcanic black rocks that plunge steeply into the sea. The rocks provide a stunning contrast to the electric blue Adriatic and the water is so clear we can see the bottom no matter how far out we swim.

The icy cold sea makes us gasp every time we get in, but I still love wearing the cheap bikini I pick up at one of Rovinj's tourist stores. Feeling the cool water wash over parts of my body that are usually covered with a modest one-piece feels so sensual it is almost wanton. I would be too self-conscious to wear a bikini back in Australia, but there is a certain freedom in being on the other side of the world where nobody knows who you are.

My alter-ego, who invariably makes an appearance whenever we travel, has finally arrived. She refuses to be sensible and go to bed early, even if there is a flight to catch in the morning, and is far more interested in having a good time than worrying about practicalities.

Then again, relaxing and not worrying about anything is easy to do when my biggest decision is whether to have red wine or white with dinner. Once we return home to the stress of commuting, deadlines and multiple projects, maintaining a carefree attitude is a lot harder and I invariably slip back into my old ways. It's something I find frustrating, but seem powerless to stop. Trevor takes a more proactive approach and always wears a loud Hawaiian shirt to work on his first day back, but aside from that, he doesn't do much better than me.

After two days in Rovinj, we take the bus to Rijeka, from where we take the overnight ferry to Hvar, a small island two-thirds of the way down Croatia's west coast.

We've splurged an extra $50 for a cabin on the ferry, but decide being close to the lifejacket lockers up on deck may be the better option once we arrive in Rijeka and see the boat. It is a cross between a container vessel and an ancient cruise ship and its rusted portholes are teamed with dirty white paint peeling off the hull in scabby flakes. The number on our ticket is preceded by a letter that comes a long way after A, which means our cabin is right at the bottom of the ship.

'This must have been a Russian cruise liner in the sixties,' Trevor says, when I point out faded signs in Russian and English directing us to locations like the disco (a cavernous room now filled with rows of stained seats) and the pool (crumbling and boarded over). Old black and white photos on the wall show the boat in its heyday: overweight men wearing tiny swimming trunks recline on banana lounges, proudly displaying their love handles and alarmingly hairy chests; pretty girls with demure smiles sitting beside them, not looking excited to be there. When we locate our cabin and squeeze through the door I know exactly how they felt.

Even in the ship's prime, our accommodation would have been one of the less desirable options. There is enough room between the narrow bunks and the wall for us to turn around so we can take off our backpacks, but only just, and I curse as I bash my elbow against the edge of an ancient metal bed frame. Fake wood panelling covers every surface except the walls, which are a sickly yellowish-green.

'Well, at least it will be better than the deck,' says Trevor, wrinkling his nose, 'although I hope the deck smells a bit better.'

The subtle yet unmistakable odour of ancient vomit teases our nostrils as we dump our bags and hurry back up to the deck where we sit on a rusting bench and look down at the bustling wharf below. There is no crowd throwing streamers and waving goodbye – just trucks, cranes and haphazard piles of wood and twisted metal. As our ship sounds its horn and pulls away from the pier, one of the dock workers undoes his fly and pisses into the oil-slicked harbour.

'Bon voyage to you too,' says Trevor.

Darkness falls and the huge ferry lumbers down the Croatian coast. The lights illuminating the deck area have been turned down low and the sea splashes against the hull. Even though it isn't cold, I snuggle up beside Trevor and watch the lights of small towns twinkling on the distant coastline. It's quite romantic if I ignore the rusted metal hanging off the handrails and the people lying on the deck in their sleeping bags. Trevor and I put it off as long as possible, but eventually we return to our cabin.

I take a deep breath before entering, hoping the smell isn't as bad as I remember. It isn't. It's even worse. Now the boat is moving, the drone of its ancient engines reverberates around the stuffy cabin and the vomit mingles with an overpowering scent of diesel fumes. The light of a single bare bulb makes the glossy wall paint glow with a sickly bilious sheen. I haul myself onto the top bunk, but the whole structure is so flimsy that the bed frame slams into the wall. I tumble onto the sheets and lie still, not game to even draw breath, until the shaking subsides. It takes a long time, but I eventually drift off to sleep and awake in the morning to find Trevor standing over my bunk.

'I can't believe you got some sleep – it was so noisy!'

'Didn't you use earplugs?'

'No. I wanted to be able to hear if there was an emergency and we had to abandon ship.' I get the impression he is only half joking.

When we wander back up onto the deck, which is bathed in bright sunlight, another traveller confirms the ferry is only a few hours from Hvar. We are still following Croatia's west coast but the closer the ship gets to

Hvar, the more small islands we begin seeing out in the distant sea. There are more than 1000 islands along Croatia's coast and it isn't long before we can see Hvar's secluded coves and inlets and the spectacular rocky mountain running down its centre like a backbone.

Our guidebook describes Hvar as an unspoiled medieval town, and we decide to stay at a family-run hotel in Podstine, an area 15 minutes' walk from Hvar's town centre. The cheap hotel has friendly staff and the view is just as spectacular as the one from our room at the Hôtel Ritz Paris, albeit a little different. There are no glamorous women walking across the Place Vendôme, but just like at the Ritz, there is always something to see. I love sitting on our tiny balcony and watching locals and tourists swimming off Podstine's rocky shore while boats of all shapes and sizes sail past in the distance. The sky is a brilliant blue, exactly the same colour as the glittering sea.

'Croatia's just like a fancy hotel,' Trevor jokes, 'even the sky and the ocean match.'

The cobblestones of Hvar's town square have been polished to a sheen by the footfalls of all those who've walked across them since it was built in the 1700s. Renaissance-style buildings made of caramel-coloured stone from the nearby islands of Korcula and Brac run around the square's edge and small cafés, with large umbrellas shading rickety tables, look cool and inviting. I hold Trevor's hand and concentrate on staying upright in my slippery-soled sports shoes as we walk along a

300-metre stone quay that was built in the 16th century. Tiny wooden fishing boats – just like the ones in Johnno's photographs – are anchored in the harbour. We stroll along the quay and sit near the end of it with our legs dangling over the water.

In the evening we walk down here to watch Hvar's sunset. I can smell the salt air as a large seabird circles lazily overhead and we wait for the light to fade. A few clouds always appear on cue during the afternoon and these turn a soft pink just before the sun disappears below the horizon. Trevor reaches for his camera bag but sees my crestfallen expression and puts his arm around me instead.

'It's beautiful, isn't it?' he says, gazing out to sea.

Hvar's town centre is so tiny that it only takes us a day to explore its narrow medieval streets, but we spend another week at Podstine, relaxing at the hotel.

'This is almost like a holiday from our holiday,' Trevor says as we lie on the hotel's deck chairs, which are set up on a concrete ledge above the sea.

After being away from home for so long, we enjoy the comfortable routine of making cheese and salami sandwiches for lunch and shopping at the tiny local supermarket near our hotel. Locals chat to the cashier, who greets everyone by name, while we pick up packets with Croatian labels and try to work out what is inside them. When people notice us struggling, they walk over to help or someone who can speak English will be dragged away from their shopping to come to our rescue.

But if buying groceries is difficult, choosing a decent bottle of wine from the huge selection at the supermarket is almost impossible. Croatia has a thriving wine industry and vineyards cover much of the country, but choosing a bottle when you can't read Croatian is a real challenge. Local grape varieties with names like *grk* don't help either. We've promised to bring back a bottle of local wine to share with John and Grainne but, after following a local's recommendation – which turned out to be dreadful – I decide to experiment and choose each bottle based on the picture on the label. It is a humbling experience for a wine aficionado, but my method is surprisingly accurate. I discover that fancy gold lettering seldom bodes well; pictures of grapes are generally reliable; buying the most expensive bottle is no guarantee of drinkability; an animal on the bottle is a sure bet and the more unlikely the animal, the better the wine.

I find my favourite Croatian wine at Podstine's tiny supermarket. It is a *plavac* produced on the nearby island of Brac and the label has a picture of a mule laden with baskets of grapes. The wine is similar in style to a cabernet merlot and is not only cheap, but extremely drinkable. We can't pronounce the wine's real name, so it becomes known as 'donkey wine' in honour of the label and we buy an extra bottle to take to London.

After a few days doing nothing but lying around on deck chairs, Trevor and I get restless and hire the hotel's boat to explore Hvar's surrounding islands. I am a bit nervous as we climb on board as Trevor has never driven a boat before but after he completes a few circuits of the small cove in front of the hotel and makes a polished first attempt at docking the boat, the manager declares my husband has passed his driving test with flying colours and executes a neat dive off the bow before swimming back to the hotel.

Trevor cranks up the outboard and we speed across the wide channel separating us from the outer islands, keeping an eye out for large ferries and tankers. We know this stretch of water is a major shipping route – a daunting prospect when you're in a tiny aluminium tinny with no safety gear – but it hasn't occurred to us to ask about lifejackets. In Australia I would never venture out on a boat without one, but we've discovered on previous holidays that safety standards in other parts of the world can be very different from those back home.

Many of the outer islands around Hvar are uninhabited, but all are ruggedly picturesque, with rocky edges dropping dramatically into the clear blue water and scrubby vegetation clinging to terracotta-coloured earth. Trevor navigates around a headland and noses our boat into a deserted inlet bounded on three sides by cliffs with small shrubs clinging doggedly to their steep shale sides. Just past the opening of the horseshoe-shaped cove, large white seabirds wheel against the blue sky and plunge into the sea. We toss the anchor into the water and dive straight off the boat. I gasp as the cool water surrounds me, then we strip off our togs and loop them over the tiller to dry. Swimming naked is liberating and the sea is extremely salty, which makes it easy to float. Other boats cruise past in the distance but when they see our cove is occupied they keep motoring up the coast. Everyone knows there is sure to be another secluded spot just around the corner.

We explore the coastline for a couple of hours, then decide to head back to Podstine because the wind is picking up, although we don't realise how much until our boat emerges from the shelter of the islands.

'It's at least a two-mile trip back to the mainland,' Trevor says anxiously as savage gusts of wind whip at our clothes, 'and I don't like the look of those waves.'

Small whitecaps are cresting the shipping channel but we don't have much choice. Our boat is due back at the hotel and we are out of drinking water. 'Don't worry, we'll be fine,' I tell him.

Trevor's face is a study in grim determination as he points our boat towards Podstine and the engine burbles into life. As we shoot out into the channel I wish we'd at least asked about the lifejackets. The boat's flimsy hull slams into each whitecap, bucking wildly as the outboard struggles valiantly against the pull of the tide and a strong headwind. We cling to the tinny's sides, keeping our feet clamped down on the hotel's beach towels so they don't blow into the water. This is far scarier than the wild ride at Iguazú Falls.

No large vessels were in sight when we left the islands but when I look to my left I can see a large ferry in the distance. It is travelling a lot faster than we are. Trevor notices it too and looks horrified.

'Can't we go any faster?' I yell.

'No!' he shouts back, but his words are snatched away by the wind.

Except for the bone-jarring jolts whenever we hit a whitecap, it feels like our tiny boat isn't moving and the huge ferry looms steadily closer as Trevor pushes the outboard to capacity and concentrates on Hvar's coast-line, trying to keep us on the shortest possible route. As we lean towards the bow of the tiny boat, urging it to go faster, I think about our friends and family back home and wonder if we'll ever see them again. Panic is begin-ning to close around my chest as I ask if we should flag down a passing boat.

'No,' Trevor says, his eyes never leaving the shoreline. 'I think we're going to make it.'

I look back towards the ferry, which is so close I can make out the people standing on its decks, and hope he is right. The wind is now partially blocked by the island of Hvar and our progress is faster than out in the middle of the channel. A few minutes later I tap him on the shoulder.

'We're clear,' I say, pointing back towards the ferry, which is still some distance away. 'I think it looked closer than it was.'

'Which was still too close,' Trevor says emphatically.

There is barely a ripple on Podstine's sheltered harbour when we pull into the hotel's jetty a few minutes later. We strip down to our swimsuits and dive back into the sea. I love Australian beaches but know I'll miss Croatia's clear waters when we return home.

The next day, we travel by ferry to Dubrovnik, the medieval city at the bottom of Croatia which is enclosed by ancient walls rumoured to be the finest of their kind in Europe. We spend the seven-hour trip looking through our guidebook, trying to decide where to stay. The hotels in Dubrovnik are more expensive than in Hvar but, after our wonderful stay in Podstine, we are keen for another similar experience.

When the ferry docks, Trevor and I stride purposefully past the locals offering rooms and towards a phone booth, where our hopes of a hotel room are dashed. After the third phone call, it becomes obvious that the prices in our guidebook are hopelessly out of date, with most of the hotels in Dubrovnik costing more per night than the budget for our entire stay. We turn back towards the dock to discover that the initial throng of locals renting out rooms has dwindled to a small handful. Not only will we be staying in another pension, rather than our eagerly anticipated hotel, but it looks like being one that nobody else wants.

I turn around as a man taps me on the shoulder and asks in French, German, English and Italian if we want a room. The same phrase in four different languages slips silkily off his tongue as he waves a map in my face and places his hand on my arm.

'Very nice,' he says with a creepy wink. I'm not sure if

he is referring to me or the picture of a room that he's obviously cut out of a magazine, but we don't hang around to find out.

'No thank you,' Trevor says firmly and whisks me away as a woman wearing a concerned expression appears by our side.

'Good idea, he is trouble,' she says in German, gesturing discreetly towards the man who was hassling me. 'Would you like a room or are you okay?'

What she has to offer sounds wonderful, but the cheap price seems too good to be true. We take the room anyway, although I am sure the pension owner and I are experiencing a communication breakdown caused by having to speak German, a second language for both of us.

'A double room with our own bathroom?' I reiterate. 'Not to share?'

'That's right, and 15 minutes to the Old Town,' she explains. 'My son is at university, but will be here to take us soon. He speaks beautiful English,' she adds proudly.

We sit on a park bench with her in companionable silence until a small red hatchback screeches to a halt in front of us.

'How does he fit in there?' whispers Trevor as a burly Croatian with jet black hair unfolds himself from the front seat and waves us over towards the car.

'Zdravo,' he says, extending a beefy hand. 'Pleased to meet you. Let me help with your bags.'

Our host's son squeezes the three of us plus our luggage into his car and explains that his mother manages the rental of the rooms he's added to their family home.

'Is it hard to get approval from the government to add on rooms?' Trevor inquires.

'Approval?' Our driver lets out an incredulous laugh. 'We just do it – no problem! If we run out of money for building, we stop and wait until there is more.'

This bit of information goes some way to explain why most of Croatia's houses look like works in progress. Our accommodation is no exception, but the guest rooms are semi-detached from the main house and far more private and well-maintained than those at the pension in Rovinj.

In the afternoon, we make our way to the area known as the Old Town, wondering what we'll find. The city of Dubrovnik was founded in the 7th century by Roman settlers and thanks to its location on a major sea trading route it developed into one of the most powerful economic entities in the southern Adriatic. The wealthy republic built nearly 2000 metres of heavily fortified walls to enclose the city and spent large sums of money on architectural gems that were safely housed inside. But even these impenetrable walls couldn't protect Dubrovnik from the ravages of the Balkan wars.

The city was held under siege for more than six months and I can remember watching the shocking news footage. It started when Slovenia and Croatia, two of Yugoslavia's most prosperous republics, decided to leave the Yugoslav Federation. Before Croatia had even officially declared its independence, one of its northern towns close to the Serbian border was attacked by the Yugoslav Army and on 1 October 1991 the first bombs were dropped on Dubrovnik. No one believed the Yugoslav Army would shell a UNESCO-listed city hundreds of miles from the front line, but that was exactly what they did. The war turned the Croats and Serbs, who formed a huge portion of Croatia's population, against each other and more than 200 people died and over 600 were injured during the Dubrovnik siege alone.

Dubrovnik's two distinct parts – a modern city with over 56,000 inhabitants and the ancient area enclosed by the fortified walls – did their best to put the war behind them, but more than 70 per cent of the buildings took direct hits.

Trevor reaches for my hand as we come within sight of the Old Town. It seems impossible that such damage could have been undone.

'This bit seems okay,' Trevor says hopefully, looking up at Pile Gate.

A statue of Saint Blaise, Dubrovnik's patron saint, stares down from the huge stone arch as we cross a drawbridge that looks like something out of a medieval movie. It turns out that evidence of the damage suffered by the Old Town is almost non-existent, but we notice small things that bring memories of the news footage flooding back. Marble cobblestones are pitted with jagged craters caused by flying shrapnel and numerous build-ings have neat lines of small holes where they were strafed by bullets. I try to imagine what it would be like to sit in my lounge room at home, listening to gunfire and the sounds of fighting on the streets outside, but I can't even begin to understand what it must have been like for the people of Dubrovnik.

I am captivated by the Old Town's ancient architec-ture as we walk along narrow alleys, past other small groups of tourists and up and down the steep stairs following the town's fortifications until we see a small hand-lettered sign with the word 'Bar' pointing to a hole in the wall. We duck our heads and walk through the thick archway, emerging on the opposite side of the metre-thick castle walls where winding concrete steps cascade down to the water. About halfway down the stairs a bar clings to the side of the cliff – past its red and white umbrellas I can see people swimming in the bright blue sea far below.

Coming closer, it is obvious that the bar is nothing fancy, but the view is breathtaking. We wave to the guy behind the trestle table being used as a counter and take a seat at a table near the railing. I look down the length of the fortifications, which are broken by towers, bastions, angular fortifications and one large fortress. Several of the 17 towers are visible from where we are sitting and I marvel at how many disparate things we've experienced during the last few months. The natural beauty of Iguazú Falls is a marked contrast to the brashness of Las Vegas, which was completely different from the French capital's refined class, and the romantic fantasy of Venice was the exact opposite of Washington's dry political history. And now we are in Dubrovnik, drinking red wine in the shadow of ancient fortifications silhouetted dramatically against electric blue sky.

The next morning, we walk down to the Old Town after breakfast, and return to the bar, but not for a drink – it is time for a swim. Trevor and I climb to the bottom of the long flight of stairs until we reach the sea, where black rocks form natural platforms and a few locals have laid out their brightly coloured beach towels. We negotiate the slippery rocks carefully and let out joyous whoops as we jump in to join them. I kick out into the deep water before rolling over to float on my back. The towers I saw yesterday loom directly above us like castle battlements in a children's story book, but the city's walls are anything but whimsical. Viewed from the water, it is easy to imagine how intimidating they must have appeared to anyone who approached by sea, hoping to capture Dubrovnik. It isn't something many have been foolish enough to attempt.

After swimming for nearly an hour, it is time to get out, but this popular local spot has no steps or similar conveniences installed for the benefit of tourists. The only way back to shore involves clambering up the rocks using the swell. The locals make it look easy, but something tells me we're going to struggle. Some areas are easy to climb up, but you have to be tall to negotiate the large gaps between the natural steps in the rock face. This is okay for Trevor but I have to wait for a wave with enough power to lift me high onto the rocks without smashing me against them. It feels like a suicide mission.

'Are you okay?' asks Trevor, peering down into the water.

I give him what I hope is a confident grin and swim back out for another attempt, sure that this will be the one. Feeling the gentle push of the swell signalling an approaching wave, I swim towards the rocks, aiming for the wave to catch me at the perfect spot about one metre back from them. As Trevor paces backwards and forwards above me, I decide that if I'm not successful this time, I will have to ask him to sit down. He is making me more nervous by the minute.

When it comes, the wave is larger than the others, but I am determined to ride it all the way in. Just before hitting the rocks, I lift up my legs and wedge my feet into a crevice before grabbing a rocky outcrop and hauling myself up at the same time. Now the wave has receded, it is a long drop back into the ocean. The muscles in my arms tremble as I hang suspended over the water before starting to climb up the rocks like a drunken crab. I am extremely relieved no one is still in the water to watch my wobbly thighs and bikini-clad bum make their clumsy ascent.

* * *

We stop by the tourist office to organise a walking tour of the city for the next day, but the staff's antics are mystifying. They're almost jumping up and down in triumph when they inform us 'We have got you Vesna!'. I have no idea why this should excite us, until I meet Vesna the next morning. It is like someone has turned on a bright light in the tiny tourist office. Vesna is vibrant and intelligent, with wavy brown hair tumbling over her shoulders, and she laughs easily and often. A simple olive sundress skims her athletic figure as she strides confidently down the street towards the Old Town and, although she must be close to 50, every man between the ages of 20 and 80 turns to watch her pass.

We walk through Pile Gate and she explains that the moat below us was once filled with water and the drawbridge was raised every night. Then we walk along Placa, the wide pedestrian promenade that is nearly 300 metres long and paved with limestone.

'Dubrovnik passed the Regulations of Hygienic Measures back in the 13th century,' Vesna explains. 'Placa was designed as a decorative thoroughfare, but it also provided a paved covering for the main sewer.'

Vesna also tells us about Dubrovnik's water supply system, which was built in the early 1400s. 'A masterpiece for its time and still operational,' she explains, pointing to the fountain where we are refilling our drink bottles. 'That water comes from a well 20 kilometres away.'

The fountain has a panel on each of its 16 sides with

carved stone heads that remind me of Zeus. The brass water spouts coming out of each figure's mouth are covered in verdigris and the fountain has been worn so smooth from people sitting on its edges that it feels like glass.

This is the thing I love most about Dubrovnik – the extraordinary history that is embraced as a part of everyday life, not locked away in a museum. We come from a country that celebrated its bicentenary not that long ago, where anything more than 100 years old is considered ancient, so being surrounded by all this history is remarkable.

Seeing Dubrovnik through Vesna's eyes is a revelation and we spend over two hours exploring the Old Town, continually impressed by our guide's staggering knowledge of the city's history and the way she makes it come alive. Vesna smiles when Trevor asks how long she's been working as a guide.

'For years now, even though there's no money in it,' she shrugs. 'I love it and that is enough.'

As we walk through Luza Square, Vesna fills our heads with the sounds of vendors spruiking their wares and ancient scales clanking as exotic spices from across the sea are weighed and measured.

'The marketplace is the heart of any city,' Vesna explains, before pointing out the 'ell', the Dubrovnik Republic's ancient unit of length, which was the distance between the fingertips and elbow of the statue of a knight standing on a pedestal in the middle of Luza Square.

Vesna takes us far away from the well-worn paths mentioned in our guidebook and into tiny laneways high above the city, where we glimpse local residents sitting in secluded gardens and inhale the spicy aroma of somebody's home-cooked lunch. It is about halfway through the tour when our guide excuses herself and hurries to catch up with a grey-haired gentleman walking ahead of us. It seems to be a friendly conversation, but Vesna is making him blush furiously and the man holds up his hands as if to deny whatever she's saying. After a few minutes, Vesna returns and apologises for interrupting our tour.

'I'm so sorry to rush away, but that is our maestro,' she informs us proudly. 'He performed at a concert last night and I just had to tell him how wonderful it was. They beg him to conduct throughout Europe – he is world famous.'

I watch the maestro disappearing into the distance. His skinny white legs are sticking out comically from a lurid pair of purple boardshorts and the huge Technicolor beach towel draped around his shoulders is covered with goofy-looking fish. The outfit is topped off by a floppy red towelling hat. It is hard to equate 'world famous conductor' with the man I'm seeing on his way to the beach. In many ways, the maestro typifies Croatia: for a country with so many cultural riches, its lack of pretension is endearing.

When our tour ends, Trevor and I say goodbye to Vesna and the old city of Dubrovnik, as we are flying to London the next day. Croatia is the first country on this trip where we haven't stayed at a Leading Hotel of the World but when I think back to the discussions we had about this before leaving home it is hard not to laugh. Trevor and I had worried about backpacking for an extended period after the luxury of our five-star hotels but we've settled back into budget travel without a hitch. Rather than pining for the five-star lifestyle, we've enjoyed the comfortable familiarity of being backpackers again. It's switching back to five-star mode that is the challenge: what looks high class in the surroundings of a budget hotel just doesn't cut it once you hit the red carpet.

11

TIME TO CONFESS

TREVOR AND I are on our way to the Dorchester, our next five-star hotel, but I am beginning to wonder if we'll make it there in one piece.

'Look at those idiots with their backpacks,' someone behind us mutters as we struggle towards the Underground while trying to ignore everybody's dirty looks. Nothing is going to stop us checking into the Dorchester as early as possible – even if it means catching a peak-hour train.

'It'll be worth it once we get there,' Trevor reassures me as another commuter shoves us aside.

Looking at everyone around us – with their uncomfortable suits and resigned expressions – makes me glad we are off to a hotel instead of the office. The platform is packed and when the train pulls in, the carriages are so full we decide to wait for the next one. And the next one. And the next one.

'No more waiting,' Trevor says decisively.

When the next train arrives he grabs my arm and we

squeeze on board. Someone jabs me in the ribs on the way through – either accidentally or on purpose – and I rub the sore spot gingerly as fluorescent lights flash by outside. The carriage sways from side to side but we are wedged by so many people there is no danger of falling over. The carriage is hot and stuffy and I can smell the stale coffee breath of the two men standing beside me. When the train pulls into Marble Arch station, we ride the wave of commuters as it surges forward and follow them up the escalator and onto the street.

The sky is a dismal slate grey and peak-hour traffic crawls past us as we stand at the kerb, waiting to cross the road. Trevor gets out the *London A to Z* and stares at the map, his eyes screwed up in concentration, which is a sure sign he has no idea where we are going. Hyde Park must be over to our left as I can see the bright green tops of large trees but, aside from that, we are surrounded by traffic-clogged arterial roads. It isn't very picturesque and a light rain is beginning to fall.

'I'll ask for directions,' I say, spotting two familiar-looking figures up ahead.

'Excuse me.' I brush a bedraggled strand of hair off my face and shift my backpack into a more comfortable position as the two bobbies turn around to face me. 'Could you direct us to the Dorchester please?'

A smile tugs at the corners of their mouths.

'We have a suite booked,' Trevor adds, 'but we're a bit lost.'

The bobbies look us up and down before one of

them points towards a nearby street. 'Walk down Park Lane and keep a lookout for the Rolls-Royces. You can't miss it.'

Their laughter floats back towards us as the two policemen continue on their way and it starts raining in earnest. We glance enviously at the people snug and dry inside their cars as we trudge past historic buildings and expensive looking shops, until Trevor drags me into a doorway just around the corner from the hotel.

'We're wringing wet,' he sighs, looking at my outfit. My pale blue cotton blouse is a crumpled mess and it looks like two bedraggled black cats are clinging to my legs instead of the smart velvet jeans I put on this morning. We are about to check into one of the best hotels in London and I look like a drowned rat. I fuss with my collar and tuck in my shirt, but we eventually give up trying to make ourselves presentable – after all, they can't turn us away – and walk towards the hotel. A group of paparazzi hover discreetly near the entrance, their eyes darting hungrily towards it like vultures each time the doors open, but they don't give us a second glance. We walk past gleaming Jaguars and the promised Rolls-Royces and through the front doors.

'Good morning – welcome to the Dorchester,' the doorman says, without giving our backpacks or wet clothes a second glance. Instead of the fussy interior I've been expecting, full of overstuffed couches and stiff-upper-lipped staff who say 'ma'am' a lot, the Dorchester's lobby is light and airy, with butter-coloured walls and a plain black reception desk. There are no towers of modern lilies and spiky greenery – just enormous bowls of plump roses and pretty spring blooms that look like they're fresh from somebody's garden.

The check-in staff greet us with genuine smiles and an Australian twang lurks under the English accent of the guy showing us to our room, making him sound like a cross between a jackeroo and a character from 'The Bill'. I bet he is wondering how we can afford to stay here – our room is one of the original Dorchester Suites. It would take a mountain of Aussie dollars to stay in it for just one night, let alone three.

The bedhead is draped with romantic swathes of fabric fixed at ceiling level so they cascade over the wall behind it and an internal corridor leads from the enormous bedroom to a separate living area with a formal dining table topped by a vase of dusty pink roses. I've seen so much mahogany furniture and plush uphol- stery it has begun to blur into one, but little touches like fresh flowers that perfectly match the curtains still impress me.

The sitting area has enough couches and armchairs for eight people and an imposing cabinet houses a large television perfect for watching the Wimbledon final, which is taking place this afternoon. There are chandeliers throughout the suite and a massive bank of windows with breathtaking views of Hyde Park runs along one whole wall, revealing large expanses of green grass and gracious old trees surrounded by traffic-choked streets.

Our accommodation also has something we've never come across at any other hotel: Trevor and I each have our own huge bathroom with the longest, deepest bathtubs I've ever seen. I can't wait to try mine out and turn the taps on full, adding a generous squirt of bubble bath which mingles with the hot water to fill the suite with the delicate scent of jasmine vines in flower as steam billows softly out the bathroom door. Trevor comes in a few minutes later to find me kneeling over the tub like an old washerwoman, scrubbing away furiously at a pair of jeans.

'I'm out of clothes,' I offer by way of explanation, dumping each sodden but clean piece of clothing onto a pristine white bath sheet. Water oozes out of the clothes, soaking through the towels and creating a rapidly spreading puddle on the white tiles. I drape the remaining few dry towels over the soggy mountain and jump up and down on it to squeeze out the last of the water. I am just finishing up when Trevor says something that makes me stop mid leap.

'Where are you going to hang it all?'

Damn – I didn't think of that. The smooth walls of our luxurious suite don't offer the old nails and broken fittings I use as anchor points in our usual hotels. I fetch our black elastic travelling clothesline, only to discover its two suction caps won't stick to the Italian marble walls of the bathroom. There is no shower curtain, so I can't use the rail to hang things on, and the couple of tiny towel racks aren't going to do a thing. This isn't looking good. After tripping over the wet clothes on the floor and flicking myself in the head with the clothesline a few times, I manage to stretch it between the hot tap on the basin and the cold tap in the bathtub. I unroll the bundle of limp clothes and drape saggy t-shirts, faded cargo pants and tatty underwear around the makeshift laundry, completely ruining the splendour of my bathroom. The maids who service our room later can't resist straightening each item so it hangs more neatly on the washing line.

In the afternoon we watch Lleyton Hewitt win Wimbledon and spend the following day in Hyde Park. Trevor makes us a picnic lunch and we pass a lazy afternoon dodging the rain and watching squirrels scampering around the huge old trees. The grass smells fresh after each shower and tiny white flowers I don't recognise push their heads up through its thick green carpet.

Thankfully my laundry is dry and put away by the time John and Grainne arrive on our last evening at the Dorchester. The coffee table in our lounge holds a silver tray displaying fine glassware, an ice bucket with ornate tongs, slices of lemon in a crystal dish and an artfully presented cheese board.

We are looking forward to seeing John and Grainne again, but have no intention of telling them about our win straight away. Trevor has come up with the perfect way to get back at John for all his Steve Irwin jokes at

Huka Lodge. When they arrive, Trevor gives a tour of the suite while I make everyone a gin and tonic.

'I can't believe you're still on holidays,' Grainne says.

It has been over two months since we last saw John and Grainne but while they've been rushing to and from work, cooking dinner after a hard day at the office and squeezing in housework on the weekends, Trevor and I have been doing nothing but enjoying ourselves. When I hear their contented sighs at the thought of not having to go to work for so long, it dawns on me how far removed from reality we've become.

'This really is very nice,' comments John, in typically low-key fashion. 'Have you stayed at the Dorchester before?'

I get the feeling he is fishing for information. A room like ours would cost more than $4000 per night so he must suspect something funny is going on.

'No, we've always stayed with friends in the past,' Trevor says honestly. I notice he doesn't mention that this involves sleeping on someone's floor, not living it up in the luxurious surroundings of a rich chum's country estate. John and Grainne are trying to be discreet, but they keep looking surreptitiously around the room. I know they're wondering how we can afford to stay in one of the Dorchester's top suites, but doubt they'd ever be so crass as to ask. Then again, John and Grainne have already surprised us once tonight.

We were amazed when they told us about getting engaged on the night we met them at Huka Lodge. We are delighted for them and also incredibly touched when we think back to our time at Huka Lodge. They were staying somewhere very romantic (not to mention expensive) and the proposal was something John had been planning for ages, yet they'd been more than willing to share such a special time with us. Travel provides the opportunity to experience deep connections, not just with places but with the people you meet along the way, and this certainly happened with John and Grainne. I am still thinking about it when John raises the question of where we should go for dinner.

'Well, we're keen to try the restaurant at the Ritz London,' Trevor replies.

There is no way we could ever afford to do this, but John and Grainne don't know that.

Grainne gives John's knee a firm squeeze – the couples' universal signal for 'Do something, for goodness sake!'.

'Well, um, it's a bit pricey – even by London standards,' he says. 'But I know a few nice restaurants around here we could go to instead.'

I look over with what I hope is a convincing frown and murmur a disappointed 'oh'.

Trevor sighs heavily. 'I suppose we could go somewhere cheaper if you like,' he says, trying to keep a straight face.

When John and Grainne nod enthusiastically, we decide it is time to confess that a cheap restaurant was always going to be the only option and we tell them about our prize.

'We won our three nights here in a competition,' I explain, 'which also included three nights at Huka Lodge, the Alvear Palace Hotel, the Hôtel Ritz Paris, the Windsor in Melbourne . . .'

Trevor helps me reel off the names of all the hotels. John and Grainne's eyes get bigger and bigger.

'Does it make sense now?' Trevor asks.

'Yes, that does,' says John. 'But how can you afford tonight's drinks and that cheese plate? They must have cost a fortune. Are they included in your prize as well?'

'If only! No, we organised it ourselves.' Trevor explains that we've worked out room service doesn't charge for things like linen, plates and ice.

'The gin is duty free and the tonic and everything else is from the supermarket down the road. We used my penknife to cut up the cheese and the cheese knife and fancy plate came up with the things on the silver tray. We've got the routine down to a fine art now.'

John and Grainne start laughing and admire our handiwork. Over the course of the trip we've slowly become adept at working things to our advantage. It would make things easier if we had money, but you don't need to be rich to have a good time at hotels like this. Cutting up cheese in our plastic breakfast bowl may lack the cachet of a white gloved delivery from room service, but I guess you can't have everything.

After sharing the bottle of Croatian 'donkey wine', we

go out for dinner at a small bistro around the corner. It's not the Ritz London, but none of us care. I am sorry that London is one of the few places where we've been able to share our prize: we often find ourselves thinking of our friends back home and have started naming which couple we'd invite to stay with us at each hotel. It's fun even though it makes us miss everyone.

By the time John and Grainne come back to our suite and we finish having coffee, it is well past midnight. It was much easier when we said our goodbyes at Huka Lodge as I knew we'd be seeing each other again soon, but this time it is different. They live in London and soon we'll be back on the other side of the world. There is always the phone and email but it isn't the same.

John and Grainne mean as much to us as our friends in Australia and I wish we'd met them there instead of while we are on holidays. John shakes Trevor's hand and gives me a hug, then puts his arm around Grainne's shoulders.

'There's a couch at our place with your name on it,' she says with a watery smile, giving us one last hug and beating a rapid retreat before she starts to cry.

Trevor closes the door softly behind them. Meeting John and Grainne may have been wonderful, but it has also been a bittersweet experience. I would love to see more of them but know this is unlikely, at least in the short term. We can't afford a return journey to London for their wedding and it is a long and expensive trip for them to visit Australia.

* * *

Our excursions in London don't amount to much more than strolling around Hyde Park underneath two Dorchester umbrellas. We've been here on previous trips and have already visited the popular tourist sights, plus the weather isn't great. I feel like a movie star in our huge suite and I'm happy to sleep in late then spend the day lounging around.

Now that Trevor and I are no longer so intimidated by our five-star surroundings, there is nothing for it but to surrender ourselves to the luxury, relax and enjoy every moment – something I wish we'd worked out earlier.

And the more relaxed and at home we appear, the better we are treated. It certainly isn't because of the way we look. All of our clothes have given up and, in many ways, so have we. I no longer go to the trouble of applying make-up every morning and don't worry too much about what I am wearing either, provided it's clean. On our last day at the Dorchester, we walk down for our complimentary breakfast in the Grill Room, the hotel's signature restaurant, where our waitress from the day before stops by for a friendly chat as we spread out the newspaper and start reading. Or at least Trevor does. I sit back and watch what is going on around us.

The restaurant has a pleasant buzz and the staff walk between the tables with a reassuring and brisk efficiency. Everyone looks like they belong there, including – much to my surprise – Trevor and me. The Dorchester is more formal than many of our previous hotels, yet we are completely at ease in our lavish surroundings and, what's more, we are truly enjoying them. I wish we could turn back time and revisit some of our earlier prize hotels. Things always look different with the benefit of hindsight, but I still can't help wishing we'd left Australia knowing what we do now.

It is hard to believe we'll be back there in just over six weeks. My earlier bouts of homesickness are forgotten when I think about returning home and the harsh reality of the mundane – work, commitment, responsibility – overshadows my joy at the thought of seeing friends and family again. Paying our bills, scrubbing the kitchen floor, answering hundreds of work emails and cleaning the toilet will all be there waiting for me when we get home. I know the life we've been leading isn't real, but that doesn't mean I am ready for it to end. Just knowing we are about to leave London is bad enough, especially when I think about our next destination.

Syria has so few ties with the western world that it's one of the few places without a single McDonald's. Not that this is necessarily a bad thing, but it does make me suspect we're in for a huge culture shock. 'Why?' was always the response whenever we told people about our impending visit, closely followed by 'Where's that again?' My reply – 'on the border of Iraq, Jordan, Israel and Turkey' – was usually met with ill-disguised horror and an anxious request to take care. Not even Trevor's enthusiasm for Syria's largely untourished mosques, markets and ancient ruins has managed to convince people we are doing the right thing.

'Mate, I hate to break this to you, but did you ever stop to think *why* there might be no other tourists? Do the words "military dictatorship" ring a bell?' said one concerned friend.

Syria isn't a destination often written up in glossy magazines or newspaper travel sections and the only time most people hear about it is on the news. After September 11, the United States accused Syria of supporting terrorism and relations between the two countries are still strained. Syria is officially a republic, but it operates more like an authoritarian regime and political opposition to the President is treated with zero tolerance.

Trevor pleaded with me to visit Syria and I agreed, but suspect his second destination of choice has people wondering whether we are incredibly adventurous or just stupid. I can see why a photographer would be itching to go there but, as for me, I don't know what to think. As we take off from Heathrow for the six-hour flight to Damascus, my apprehension starts to grow.

12

WHAT SEAN CONNERY SAID

SYRIA'S DESOLATE LANDSCAPE is bathed in the eerie orange glow of sunrise and rusting hulks of old aeroplanes litter the sides of the runway. Trevor and I walk across the tarmac and take a seat in the bus waiting to ferry passengers to Damascus' airport terminal. Arabic music wails over a crackling sound system and it feels like the searing heat outside is pushing against the vehicle's ancient doors, trying to get in. Everything around me is already completely alien and we haven't even left the airport. The events of September 11 created a lot of tension between Syria and the western world, but we appear to be attracting curious rather than hostile gazes from the locals who are on board the bus. They watch us discreetly as we avoid eye contact with the machine-gun-toting guards posted around the arrivals area and collect our bags, scanning the crowd for our driver.

Our hotel in Damascus is the Leading Hotel of the World Trevor selected to add on to our prize as he thought some decadent Western luxury would help us deal with any initial culture shock. We are looking forward to some sleep and are relieved to find our driver waiting in the arrivals hall. I've always scoffed at travellers who organise things like airport transfers when public transport is readily available, but now I can appreciate the comfort of knowing someone will be there to meet you. He spots us straight away but doesn't say much more than good morning during the entire trip, despite our attempts to initiate conversation. The 1980s sedan pulls onto a highway lined on either side by billboards covered in Arabic script, and posters of Syria's President, resplendent in full military dress, are everywhere. The billboards eventually thin out and are replaced by crumbling cement apartment blocks with metal reinforcing sticking out of them at odd angles, like broken bones emerging from damaged flesh. The tumbledown buildings are crammed together and look like they're about to collapse, yet all of them are heavily populated.

The urban landscape whizzing past the window is like nothing I've seen before. In Australia, most of the country is made up of bright colours – vibrant green leaves, deep blue ocean, golden fields of wheat. Even the sand in the desert is a rich terracotta. However, in Syria it looks like everything is muted. The harsh sunlight seems to suck colour out of the landscape like a child slurping greedily on a snow cone.

'I wonder how much further it is?' Trevor says.

Our hotel is in the heart of the CBD, so judging by what is outside I figure we are miles away, but our car screeches to a stop before I get the chance to say so. As a uniformed man approaches the car, I notice the embroidery on his lapel and look out incredulously at the dusty streets and battered buildings.

'Welcome to Cham Palace,' he says formally, reaching down to open the door. 'I will get someone to assist with your baggage.'

It isn't as if the streets are choked with beggars or roaming animals. There are plenty of well-dressed people walking up and down outside the hotel, but it still feels like we are in a country town. There are no shopping malls or glossy shopfronts. The stores aren't much more than holes in the walls and nearly all of them have a shopkeeper standing outside, leaning on the door frame and looking up and down the street with casual disinterest. Damascus' bitumen roads are coated with a thick layer of sandy dust and the cars make it feel like we've stepped back into the 1970s. The battered boxy sedans are ancient and nearly all of them belch copious amounts of smoke. Trevor has said he wants to experience the past in Syria, but I doubt seventies motoring greats are what he has in mind.

Once in the foyer I am hit with a sense of déjà vu. I could swear we were back at a Las Vegas theme hotel. The Cham Palace's reception area has an atrium filled with tiers of cascading green creepers in planter boxes, giving it the ambience of a jungle inhabited by light brown couches. We check in and stare out our suite's window at tightly packed buildings straggling up the hill behind the hotel. They are either square or rectangular which makes it look like some greater being has scattered handfuls of brown blocks over the steep slope.

It is a relief to climb into bed for some much needed sleep. My senses are being bombarded by so many unfamiliar things that the only escape is to close my eyes. When we awake, Trevor and I have a shower and cast cautious glances down at the street.

'Do you feel ready to go outside?' he asks.

Even viewed from a distance, the streets are like nothing we've ever seen before, but I take a deep breath and together we head downstairs to brave the most foreign place I've ever been.

The men in suits appear out of place on Damascus' dusty streets and the spicy smells wafting out of hole-in-the-wall kebab shops tempt and terrify us in equal measure. I wonder how long it will take before we are game enough (or foolish enough) to venture inside one of them. Either way, it will be sooner than we learn to read Arabic. There is no way the ornate dashes and squiggles will ever make sense to us and I wonder if our plans to travel around the country independently may be a bit ambitious. We have no phrasebook so are relying on the basic information in the back of our guidebook, which is better than nothing, but not much.

We have sewn cloth patches of the Australian flag onto our backpacks in case people mistake us for Americans and I read up on cultural considerations before we leave home. I am wearing ankle-length pants, one of

Trevor's baggy long-sleeved shirts and a bandana to cover my short blonde hair, but we still attract lots of attention. Heads turn constantly as we walk past and many people stop what they are doing to smile, nod or simply stare.

Two boys run up to us on a dare to say 'hello, hello' before scampering back towards their friends. We are a curiosity and a novelty, yet I feel safer here than the last time I went to Sydney. Far from Syria being the slightly hostile place I was expecting, I am struck by its innocence which has been swallowed up long ago in other parts of the world. Where else would it be considered daring for teenage boys to approach a couple of tourists?

The language barrier certainly doesn't stop people coming up to us. When we are waiting with a group of locals to cross the road, an elderly woman dressed from head to toe in black reaches out and touches my arm.

'Hello,' she says and smiles.

I try to start a conversation but discover this is the only English word she knows, so I say hello back in Arabic, which is the only word I know as well. She is delighted and clasps my hands in hers for the most touching welcome I've ever received. A few men shake Trevor's hand and some of them shake mine too, but no male makes direct eye contact with me. It is more like a glance from beneath lowered lids and reminds me of the coy smile Lady Di became so well known for.

We return to Cham Palace and eat an early dinner of *shwarma* – spiced lamb wrapped in soft flat bread – in the hotel restaurant before asking the concierge to find us a local guide for a walking tour the next day. While we may be able to find our way around on the streets outside, we need someone to help us make sense of it all.

Our guide, Aymon, arrives promptly the next morning in a neatly pressed short-sleeved shirt, slacks and shoes polished to a high shine. He is a lecturer at the University of Damascus, but does guiding on the weekends to earn extra money. He doesn't tell us what he lectures in, but I suspect it is history as he takes us straight to Syria's National Museum and explains its exhibits in great detail. The artefacts are impressive, with many dating back to the second millennium BC, but after several hours I am wondering how to break it to Aymon that if we have to marvel at another crumbling statue, I'll scream. Just before I reach breaking point, he announces we've finished at the Museum and our next stop will be Souk al-Hamidiyya.

This will be our first visit to one of the ancient middle eastern marketplaces known as 'souks' and despite our guidebook's warning that the one in Damascus is the closest thing Syria has to a tourist trap, 18 months of anticipation is bubbling inside me. Syria was part of the Roman Empire and thanks to its prosperous trade routes was once regarded as a prime province. Souk al-Hamidiyya was constructed on Roman streets similar to those we saw in Dubrovnik and its cool, dimly lit interior is a relief after the harsh light outside. The wide cobbled walkways are covered by a soaring roof and my eyes dart from one side to the other, checking out stores where goods have been arranged carefully in the windows. Souk al-Hamidiyya is different from other Syrian souks as it is comprised of permanent shops rented by local merchants rather than the more traditional collection of market stalls. This makes it feel a bit like a shopping centre and the air smells of dirt, spices and a sweet honey-like aroma I can't identify. We look through the shop windows at cushions, sweets, bridal wear and fabrics, but the traders stay inside so we never feel hassled to buy. I am amazed how clean everything is, especially compared to the grimy streets outside.

It seems everyone comes to shop at Souk al-Hamidiyya and the walkways are packed with locals who stare at us discreetly. Most of the shops on the main thoroughfare sell clothes, gifts and furnishings but there is one with so many people crammed inside, we can't see what it is selling.

'What's in there?'

'That's Bekdach. The best ice-cream in Damascus – perhaps even all of Syria,' Aymon explains. 'Would you like one?'

'What about the milk?'

'It's okay, all the ingredients are boiled.'

Trevor and Aymon aren't tempted but ice-cream is my favourite food, so I decide to try it and venture into the melee with Aymon. People jostle for position with a good-natured determination but, rather than being rude, there is order to the chaos and we are propelled by the crush to the cash register. Aymon exchanges a few coins for a brightly coloured plastic token and points through the crowd.

'Take this, go to that counter where the men are scooping ice-cream and point to what you want. I'll wait outside the shop.'

I feel like a child on the first day of school and have to fight the urge to grab Aymon's hand and ask him to come with me, but I needn't worry. Several locals shuffle me cheerfully to the front of the queue where I point to what looks like vanilla. My cone is piled extra high, with a dollop of strawberry and chocolate added so I can try them too, before the creamy tower is rolled in crushed pistachio nuts and handed over with a smile. The ice-cream is delicious and reminds me of a cross between creamy gelato and sorbet.

We appear to be the only tourists in a city of eight million people, which is strange enough, but it is even harder to adjust to the treatment we are receiving. For Trevor and me, checking to ensure we haven't been short-changed, fending for ourselves when it comes to getting places and asking for assistance only as a last resort has become second nature when travelling. However, tourists in Syria are seen as guests of the country and we discover that the matter of hospitality is taken very seriously here. The kindness I experience in Bekdach is the first of many similar incidents and something we come to rely on during our visit.

After a quick look around the souk, Aymon leads us towards Umayyad Mosque. We've been looking forward to seeing this too, but Trevor and I are both apprehensive. Neither of us has been inside a mosque before, and the first one we are going to see is only slightly less spiritually significant than the mosque at Mecca and one of the most important buildings in the whole of Islam, as Damascus was considered the capital of the Islamic world back in the first century BC when the Umayyad Mosque was built.

'Over one thousand artists and stonemasons were employed in its creation,' Aymon says.

He explains the mosque's religious importance – a green-domed structure in the middle of its prayer hall is said to contain the head of John the Baptist – but it is hard to concentrate on what he is saying. I can't help but feel this visit has the makings of one huge cultural blunder. Despite reading up on etiquette and local customs and dressing with the utmost care, I am terrified of disgracing myself.

Aymon enters an office around the corner from the mosque and emerges with a voluminous black garment for me to put on over my trousers and long-sleeved shirt. 'You must wear a robe before we can go in,' he explains. It feels like I am wearing a horse blanket and the sweat begins trickling down my back almost immediately. I am so uncomfortable that I don't notice Aymon is talking to someone.

'This man and his son would like to have their photo

taken with you,' Aymon tells me. Trevor and I look at each other in surprise.

'Of us? Why?'

'Tourists, especially Westerners, have become an unusual sight, but it is probably because they are Bedouin – desert nomads. You seem very exotic.'

I smile at the boy and his father encouragingly, amused to be considered exotic when I feel so hot and grotty. Aymon takes the man's battered camera and he and his son stand rigidly beside each other as the four of us shuffle closer together. When the young boy jumps with surprise as I place a friendly hand on his shoulder, I am positive my fears of committing a terrible social gaffe are being realised before I've even reached the mosque. I only work out everything must be okay when I look down and see the boy staring at me with undisguised delight. If only I had that effect on every man! After Aymon takes the photo, the boy's father thanks us in Arabic and they disappear in the same direction as the mosque. I wonder what the folks back home will make of his happy snap.

The three of us walk towards Umayyad Mosque, squinting against the sunlight reflecting off the mosaics in its large courtyard. The mosque's outer walls are covered with gilded designs of palaces, fruits and trees and people hurry through its doorways, eager to escape the heat of the day. I leave my head covered but we remove our shoes as we enter. I am shocked by what I see. The beauty of the building is as I imagined, but nothing else is as I expected.

I thought people would be kneeling in silence or walking reverentially through the mosque as they went about their spiritual business, but it is nothing like that at all. The mosque is as much a meeting place as a place of worship and there are groups of women relaxing on the intricately patterned carpets as their children tumble around them like kittens and men stand in small groups talking. It is cool and welcoming and the people kneeling in prayer seem almost secondary to the other activity taking place around them. I forget about my uncomfortable cloak and exchange smiles with the women, wishing I had the confidence say hello. It is strange feeling so shy and awkward – I am usually very outgoing.

Our tour ends after we visit the mosque, but Aymon offers to walk us back to the hotel even though Trevor has already paid him. I've enjoyed hearing Aymon talk about his wife and two young children who live in a house on the hill we can see from our room. How they spend their time – seeing friends, going for walks, visiting relatives – sounds very similar to the life Trevor and I live back in Australia.

We are just around the corner from Cham Palace when we almost collide with three teenage girls who are walking in the opposite direction. They apologise and keep going but I can't take my eyes off what they are wearing – clingy little tops and skirts that leave almost nothing to the imagination. When Aymon notices my expression, he starts to laugh and explains how common it is to see two sisters walking down the street – one in a chador covering her whole body and the other in an outfit straight from the Britney Spears school of style.

'I thought it was compulsory for all women to take the veil,' Trevor remarks.

Aymon explains some Syrian women feel more comfortable in traditional clothing as it helps to safe-guard their reputations, but it is up to the individual. But women in Syrian society are quite restricted in other ways. The husband or his family is automatically awarded custody of sons older than nine and daughters older than eleven if a couple divorces and women are under a lot of pressure to behave modestly to ensure their family's good reputation remains intact. Not an easy feat when a man can damage a woman's character simply by addressing her disrespectfully.

Much of what I've seen has been very different from what I imagined Syria would be like. The dirt-covered streets in the middle of the city, the inquisitive looks, the myriad shades of brown forming both the urban and natural landscape – I am exhausted from trying to take it all in.

By the time Aymon shakes our hands and says goodbye, I am feeling more at ease, but the more I learn about Syria, the more obvious my ignorance becomes. The only way to approach the next few weeks is to push aside my preconceived ideas and start afresh.

The next morning, after managing to convince our bemused hotel receptionist that we really do want to catch a bus to Palmyra, not take a chauffeur-driven car, we head to the bus station clutching a note with our destination written on it in Arabic. It is unnerving to realise we are unable to read the local language enough to even discern the destination on the front of a bus.

When we arrive at the bus station, I debate the wisdom of having said no to the car. We breathe through our mouths in a futile attempt to avoid the acrid black exhaust from the ancient vehicles and approach two rickety tables set up beside the entry gates. Apart from the heavily armed guards, it looks more like a stall at the local fete than a security checkpoint. The two men gesture roughly for Trevor to remove his pack and they make a half-hearted inspection of the contents, but my hands are shaking so much I can't undo the buckles on mine. It takes me so long to extricate myself that they give up and wave us both through.

Westerners must be an unusual sight at the bus station because we attract even more attention than usual. Local travellers point us out to their friends and have animated discussions about our arrival. Trevor hands our note to a porter who dismisses ticket touts like he's swatting flies and leads us to the official ticket counter and then to the correct bus. It looks like one of the long-suffering vehicles I remember from primary school excursions – faded paintwork, a musty interior and an engine that wheezes like a weary old man – and it's filled with locals going about their daily business. Everyone stares when Trevor and I get on board, but we are almost used to it by now.

As the bus makes its way through a vast sandy desert

towards Palmyra, I open our guidebook to a well-thumbed page and read again about Palmyra's rise and fall, a tale that reads like a children's fable about the dangers of greed. The ruins themselves date from the second century AD, but the city of Tadmor (as Palmyra was originally known) is mentioned in historical texts as far back as the 19th century BC and has long been a regular stop on a popular trade route. It prospered until 267, when Odenathus, Palmyra's brilliant leader, was assassinated. His second wife, Zenobia, took control of the city in the name of her young son, but there were rumours regarding her possible role in her husband's death so Rome sent an army to deal with her. Zenobia defeated them and, after successfully invading Egypt, she declared her independence from Rome and minted coins bearing her own image along with that of her son. It was too much for the Roman emperor Aurelian, who then defeated Zenobia's forces in battle before laying siege to Palmyra itself. Zenobia made a dramatic dash for Persia on the back of a camel but was taken prisoner by the Roman cavalry. No one found out for sure what happened to Zenobia after Aurelian paraded her through the streets shackled in gold chains, although many claim she starved herself to death rather than remain a prisoner. Less than a year later, after Palmyra's inhabitants killed 600 Roman archers stationed there, Aurelian's troops retaliated, killing Palmyra's residents and torching the city. It became a Roman outpost and slowly lost its wealth, before falling to the Muslims in 634 and dwindling to nothing more than a small village.

The four-hour trip passes quickly and when we get off the bus in the centre of town it appears that Palmyra's economic situation hasn't improved. Nearly all the streets are still dirt and Palmyra has the grubby, down-trodden air of a place fallen on hard times. Every shop we see is filthy and even the food in packets looks dubious. Resigning ourselves to eating nothing but flatbread and honey, we walk to the Heliopolis Hotel, where our arrival provokes such excitement I wonder how long it has been since they've had a guest. The manager sweeps out from behind the front desk and pumps Trevor's hand up and down enthusiastically.

'Let me show you our best room,' he says grandly and, without waiting for a response, leads the way up two dingy flights of stairs.

The room itself isn't a patch on the Dorchester – it has rusty taps, a sagging double bed and smelly brown carpet – but the view is better than five-star. Trevor stands beside me at the window and we look out over a lush green oasis, full of date palms, towards the spectacular ruins of Palmyra. It looks like every Roman ruin I've ever seen has been picked up and dropped in the middle of the Syrian dessert. The ancient colonnaded road in the centre of the site is at least a kilometre long and surrounded by a mind-boggling number of temples and tumbledown antiquities.

We are anxious to begin exploring but the harsh

desert conditions mean we have to wait until 4 pm, and even then the temperature is still close to 40 degrees. When we leave the hotel we walk along dusty streets, past listless traders sitting on upturned crates outside their shops and towards the archaeological site less than half a kilometre away. Even though the ruins cover 50 hectares, they remained largely unknown until the 1600s and the first archaeological survey wasn't carried out until the 20th century.

Trevor and I are drenched in perspiration by the time we reach the ruins so we decide to visit the amphitheatre first to get out of the heat. The structure itself is not particularly remarkable, but the sun has dipped just far enough behind the amphitheatre's walls to cast shade over the tiers of stone seating wrapping around its edge. We climb up to the back row and are engrossed in the guidebook when we hear a voice booming in the distance. It continues getting louder until its owner emerges through the theatre's stone entrance, accompanied by two wilting ladies who sink onto a stone bench at the front of the theatre. The large and rather portly Syrian man strides into the middle of the amphitheatre like a ringmaster, making grand gestures with his arms and telling the ladies stories from Palmyra's history. Although I've read most of it in my guidebook, he makes it so exciting that I find myself listening to it all over again. It is probably rude to eavesdrop when we haven't paid for the tour, but it is impossible not to lean forward and hang on his every word.

'Come down, come down – there's no need for you to stay up there.' It is more of a command than an invitation. I am embarrassed we've been found out, but secretly delighted and we trot down obediently to join the party of three.

'Do you mind?' I whisper to one of the ladies as the guide chats to Trevor.

'No, truly, we don't mind at all, do we, Mummy?' the younger woman says in a posh British accent that makes me feel like we've stepped straight into a BBC costume drama.

'Of course not,' agrees Mummy. 'It's a bit lonely doing the tour with only Mohammed and Sarah.'

I think Mohammed is like ten people rolled into one, but he is an excellent guide. He helps Mummy climb onto a low stone platform where there was once an ancient marketplace.

'How much for this beautiful woman?' he crows, throwing his arms out wide.

Mohammed is exhausting but he is a lot of fun. After we've walked through the ruins, stepping over broken antiquities like they are bits of litter, Mohammed finishes the tour with a quick overview of an ancient toilet block that comes complete with plumbing, then escorts the ladies to their chauffeur-driven car.

We are still marvelling at the channels in the ground which we assumed were simply decoration when I realise Mohammed is talking to us.

'Since you missed the early part of the tour, I'll walk

you back through the ruins,' he offers as the ladies' car speeds off in a cloud of sandy dust.

As we walk along the colonnaded streets, Mohammed's stories of what went on there in days gone by makes for fascinating listening, but they aren't as interesting as the man himself. September 11 came as a particularly cruel blow for Syria as the country had just started opening up to tourists. America accused Syria of harbouring terrorists and denying its citizens basic civil rights and this generated a lot of negative media coverage around the world. There are so few visitors to Syria these days that it is almost impossible for local guides to make a living, but Mohammed hasn't been sitting around feeling sorry for himself: he used the spare time to learn a couple of extra languages in addition to the French, English and Arabic he already spoke.

'Now I can do tours in Italian and German as well,' he says. 'People will come back, I am sure of it.'

I hope he is right. Although I doubt I'll ever get used to being constantly stared at, I never feel unsafe or even vaguely threatened here. Locals often stop Trevor and me to thank us for visiting Syria and we've been made to feel welcome everywhere. We are completely out of our depth culturally, but Syria is far from the dangerous and sinister place suggested by the media.

Mohammed is as curious about our lives as we are about his and his standard tourist patter is gradually replaced by an animated conversation about all sorts of things. Trevor pulls out a photograph of our house in

Australia and we discuss our daily lives, what food we enjoy and a little about our friends. Just as we reach the road leading back into town, Mohammed stops abruptly.

'Come with me,' he commands and begins striding in the opposite direction. I look at Trevor, who shrugs helplessly, and we set off after Mohammed who leads us back through the ruins until we arrive at a small, non-descript building that isn't much more than a hut. Mohammed knocks loudly until the door is opened by a wiry man in his mid-fifties, who is still dragging on a shirt. Trevor and I are introduced and ushered inside, but the man's name is lost in a jumble of Arabic sounds

'My friend has lived here for many years as the custo-dian of the graveyard,' Mohammed says proudly. I press my face to the window, expecting to see tombstones, but instead I am looking into a wire enclosure filled with archaeological treasures. There are broken columns, carved plinths and elaborate statues piled randomly on top of one another and many of the pieces are even more stunning than those we saw outside.

'These things will eventually be restored to their correct place in the ruins, but until then they must be protected,' explains Mohammed, before speaking to his friend in Arabic.

As the man sighs and disappears behind a curtain, I can't help feeling sorry for him – being Mohammed's friend must be rewarding and exhausting in equal measure. The single room we are sitting in has a few wooden chairs and a small table, but it feels warm and homey and, despite the sand outside, the bare wooden floor is spotless. Our host emerges with a battered silver pot and four glasses which he fills with steaming tea. He hands one to each of us in turn, holding the glass with two hands and presenting it with a formality that wouldn't be out of place at the Ritz. But here it means so much more. While we are still guests, this time it is in somebody's home – it is a privilege and by invitation only.

I raise the glass to my lips and take a sip of the hot sweet liquid. It is strong, but not bitter. Sugar must have been added to the pot to bring out the intense flavour of the leaves and although I am a regular tea drinker it is like nothing I've tasted before.

'This is the best tea I've ever had!' I tell Mohammed.

'Sean Connery said the same thing,' he replies proudly. 'I was his guide when he visited Palmyra.'

I look around the spartan room and try to imagine the actor perched on one of the battered chairs. Trevor and I had thought that one of the five-star hotels would provide the best chance of a brush with fame, but it looks like we were wrong.

The sun sinks lower in the sky and eerie shadows play on the ancient pieces in the graveyard outside as our host slips away to wash up the tea things. He returns silently with a rug which he kneels down on. I look out at the low red glow on the horizon and realise it is time for *Salatu-I-Isha*, the Muslim sunset prayer.

'Should we leave?'

Mohammed smiles at me and shakes his head. 'There is no need. Praying is such a part of his life, it is like breathing,' he says.

The reds and purples of the woven fabric glow richly against the floor and the rhythmic incantations of his murmured prayers are almost musical. Mohammed continues talking quietly while he waits for his friend to finish praying.

Trevor and I eventually say our goodbyes and walk outside where a full moon is bathing the ruins in a soft glow. Unexpected highlights like this are something I love about travelling. No matter how much planning you do, each trip always seems to contain at least one truly magical moment, so perfect you couldn't have dreamed it, let alone organised for it to happen.

By the time we visit Hama a few days later, the novelty of being Western tourists in Syria is beginning to wear thin. We are finding it increasingly difficult to buy food that won't make us ill and are feeling tired and run down. The constant heat is exhausting and travelling from one spot to another means going through the stressful rigmarole of working out which bus to catch and finding suitable accommodation once we arrive. Being tourists in such an alien environment is a struggle and being unable to understand the local language can make simple tasks almost impossible. Buying tickets to Hama took us so long that we missed the bus and had to wait hours for the next one. I am tired of being stared at and, despite our best efforts, we are both suffering from food poisoning. We have little energy and Hama, which we've taken so much trouble to get to, is a disappointment. Trevor wanted to see the town's famous *norias* – large water wheels – which have been used for irrigation since ancient times, but there is so little water in the river that none of them are turning. The *norias* are overgrown with weeds and the river is stagnant and clogged with rubbish. Though we are anxious to move on, we are forced to stay at a dingy hotel for three days until our food poisoning settles down enough for us to travel.

By the time we arrive in Aleppo, Syria's second-largest city, all Trevor and I are interested in is getting to our accommodation. Since leaving Damascus we've stayed in some of Syria's more expensive hotels, but they have still been rough and ready – there is seldom hot water, rooms are basic and fine desert dust coats every surface.

As we walk through the narrow alleyways of the Aleppo suburb of Al-Jdeida, tall stone buildings with largely blank façades block out the harsh sunlight, making the alley feel like a cool, cobblestone haven. Al-Jdeida's buildings open inwards onto elaborate courtyards that can't be seen from the street, so at first our hotel, Beit al-Wakil, appears to be little more than a door. But as we enter and approach reception, I can see a stone fountain splashing gently in an intricately tiled courtyard and plump satin cushions scattered artfully around the boutique hotel's common area. The 450-year-old Ottoman house has been carefully restored and

I decide that, even though we plan to haggle, I don't care how much they charge for a room. Perhaps I wouldn't feel the same if we were on one of our usual backpacking adventures, but our prize hotels have shown us how wonderful being pampered can feel and right now a bit of luxury is just what we need.

The wooden furniture in our room is covered with carvings of fruits and vines, the stone bathroom has a font salvaged from an ancient *hammam* (traditional bathhouse) and intricately woven kilims cover the floor. There are 19 rooms at Beit al-Wakil but today we are the only guests. The staff of five do their best to keep busy but spend most of their time hovering around reception talking amongst themselves to help pass the time. Whenever we ask for anything, they almost fight over whose turn it is to help us. Beit al-Wakil doesn't have the polish of some of the Leading Hotels of the World but, with a bit of tweaking here and there, it would make a worthy addition to their portfolio.

After a good night's sleep, we brave Aleppo's souk, which is completely different from Al-Hamidiyya in Damascus. There are no fancy shopfronts, just the hustle and bustle of a real marketplace and stall-lined alleyways filled with donkeys carrying goods. The souk is divided up like a supermarket – gold down one aisle, fabrics down another. And then there are the butchers: Trevor and I smell them before we stumble into their alley, although I really wish we hadn't. Huge sides of beef drip blood onto the dusty floor and slabs of meat are piled high on solid wooden tables. Everything is covered in flies and there is no refrigeration. I try not to think about our dinner last night at one of Aleppo's best restaurants. The food was delicious, but the meat came from here. My stomach clenches involuntarily as I breathe through my mouth to avoid the pungent stench of raw flesh.

After leaving the souk, we are walking back towards Beit al-Wakil when two policemen hurry towards Trevor and point to his chest.

'Camera, camera!' they shout.

Trevor holds onto the strap around his neck defensively but the young policemen loop their arms around each other's shoulders and point to the camera while striking their best pose. No matter what country we are in, it is always the same story: women are reluctant to be photographed because Trevor usually asks to do it when they are going about their everyday life. He may be after a charming shot of a local sweeping her doorstep, but I could tell him no woman wants to be photographed wearing her 'around the house' clothes. The men, however, straighten up and preen discreetly, before assuming a suitably noble pose. Having their photo taken feeds their egos and the size of Trevor's camera never fails to impress.

Lying down to escape the heat after lunch, we discuss our next move.

'I don't know if I can handle another Middle Eastern

destination straight after Syria,' Trevor says seriously. 'Do you still want to go to Turkey?'

I haven't thought about it until now, but he has a point. Istanbul, one of our most anticipated destinations of the trip, no longer holds the same appeal. We still aren't well and the bus trip from Aleppo to Istanbul will take more than 24 hours. Trevor and I don't want to stay in Syria any longer, but we don't want to go straight to another destination with similar food and its associated problems either. Turkey's Middle Eastern culture seemed so exciting and exotic back in Australia, but now it is the last thing we want to experience.

'Perhaps we could fly back to Paris?' I suggest. The seductive promise of our favourite city's familiar comforts sees us poring frantically over our Syrian guidebook for the location of Aleppo's airline offices. We are consumed with the idea of rerouting our flights and literally run out of the hotel, but it is to no avail. Going to Paris would cost a fortune, as well as creating severe logistical problems later in the trip, and flying to Istanbul instead of taking the bus is impossible too. Although the flight is less than an hour and a half long, the airfares cost around $380 each.

We spend our last night in Syria enjoying Beit al-Wakil and steeling ourselves for the long bus trip. But when we arrive at the Aleppo bus station the next morning, we discover an accident on the main highway has stopped all traffic getting through. We sit in the bus company's stifling waiting room for hours, watching the fan in the corner turning listlessly as the manager makes frequent and increasingly more irate telephone calls to try to find out what is going on. We pass the time by taking turns to use the filthy squat toilet out the back.

We each have enough time for several visits before our bus finally pulls up and we climb aboard, desperately wishing we were going anywhere but Turkey. We are physically and mentally exhausted by what we've been exposed to during the past ten days. Syria's cultural challenges, strange food, difficult language and the constant attention we attract have been overwhelming. We slump back into our tattered seats and drift in and out of sleep as the bus speeds through the night.

'We must be in Turkey,' Trevor says early the next morning.

I look out of the window to see a brightly lit billboard advertising burgers and Coke and know he is right. After experiencing Syria's culinary challenges, just the sight of some western-style junk food – which I usually avoid – makes my mouth water. Perhaps Istanbul won't be so bad after all.

13

IS IT MY CARPET'S TURN?

IF YOU'RE EVER wondering what to bring back as a memento of your time in Turkey, the best piece of advice I can offer is this: a filling from the local dentist is not what you want.

Friends have told us how 'Middle Eastern', 'exotic' and 'different' Turkey is but after spending time in Syria the place seems so westernised it feels like we're back in the States. But that is before I go to the dentist.

Istanbul held the promise of exotic delights before we left home but, aside from the mosques and minarets, it looks very similar to any large European city. It isn't quite Paris, but it also isn't the strange, stressful destination we've been dreading. We have no trouble getting a good deal at a budget hotel right near the Blue Mosque which takes its name from the colour of the 17th-century Iznik tiles lining its interior and is one of the most visited sites in Turkey.

Being able to have a long, hot shower feels like the height of luxury and, after wolfing down a burger and chips at a fast food joint down the road, we go up to the hotel's rooftop bar for a drink.

As we sit down at a wobbly plastic table for two on the plain concrete terrace, it's obvious this rooftop terrace is a world away from the one at Il Palazzo in Venice, although it is just as good in its own way. The sun is hot, but a gentle breeze dissipates much of its heat. I pull my hat further down over my eyes and look out at the six evenly-spaced minarets forming part of the Blue Mosque. I didn't realise how close it was when we agreed to take the room. In fact, Sultanahmet, the area where our hotel is located, is also known as 'Old Istanbul' and has been listed by UNESCO as a World Heritage site because it contains so many buildings from the Ottoman Empire. Although a lot of the cheap accommodation is located here, there aren't many tourists around at the moment. Throughout our trip, we can't help but notice what a devastating effect the events of September 11 have had on tourism around the world.

The hotel's other guests are mainly young people wearing cargo pants, battered joggers and faded t-shirts, who lounge around drinking ice-cold beers straight from the bottle. Trevor may ask for a glass, but apart from that we fit in perfectly. I listen to the other back-packers' familiar Australian, Canadian and New Zealand accents and gaze out at the view, amazed at how lucky we've been to stumble on such a great spot. Mosque domes rise out of the urban sprawl like mushrooms and old trees with enormous canopies scatter splotches of dark green across the landscape. The sky is a washed-out pale blue and, just behind the cream-coloured domes of the Blue Mosque, the Bosporus sparkles in the sun.

The waiter brings our drinks and a small bowl of nuts, and I continue staring into the distance. The 32-kilometre-long stretch of water connecting the Black Sea with the Sea of Marmara separates Europe and Asia and was reputedly once crossed by Ulysses. For us it marks the beginning of the last part of our trip. I am glad we've come to Turkey. Watching the large container ships and assorted ferries travel slowly up and down is relaxing and I smile to myself and pop another nut into my mouth.

Craaaack! I've been so busy looking at the view I didn't notice the unshelled pistachio nuts. I extract the remains of one from my mouth and probe my jaw experimentally with my tongue. It isn't hurting, but one of my back teeth has split right down the middle and there is now a gaping hole where a filling used to be. Trevor asks anxiously if it can wait until we reach Hong Kong, but there is no chance of that. I will probably develop a raging infection if I don't get my tooth seen to immediately and Hong Kong, our next destination, is over a week away. We finish our drinks and walk down to reception for some help finding a reputable dentist.

Turkey isn't the ideal place to require medical attention. While it seems very western compared to Syria, our guidebook recommends exercising caution when it comes to choosing where to undergo medical treatment. But the guy on the front desk recommends a private hospital with a dental surgery attached – one of the best in the city, he assures me.

This certainly isn't how we planned to spend our first day in Istanbul, I think ruefully as we leave the hotel early the next morning clutching a piece of paper with scribbled directions. Stepping onto a tram ferrying commuters to the other end of the city, it seems strange to come across people going to work while we are swanning around on holidays. 'That will be you in less than a month,' Trevor says, glancing at a woman in a tailored black suit.

His comment does nothing to improve my mood. When we get off the tram, I am sure we have made a mistake. This doesn't look like an area where a quality private hospital would be located. Rundown office buildings are crammed against discount shops and most of the people walking past us are wearing clothes that have seen better days. I clutch my small daypack protectively as we walk up the street and turn a few corners until we reach a dilapidated old building in a back alley, where I check the official looking sign against the name written on our piece of paper. With a sense of impending doom I watch the procession of sickly-looking people going in and out of a set of large swinging double doors. It looks like this is it. The place isn't like any private hospital I've seen before. It looks grimy and uncared for and my first impressions don't improve once we walk through the door.

A waiting area is filled with patients who droop

dejectedly on mismatched folding metal chairs and the stale air reeks with a mixture of heavy duty antiseptic and vomit. I stop a harried-looking woman in a stained white uniform and, thumbing through my phrasebook, ask where the dentist is. Following where she points, we head up a flight of stairs, down a long grey corridor and finally to a reception desk. This area is slightly better, but not much. There are no sick patients but there doesn't appear to be anyone waiting either. Perhaps the dentists are so bad that no one else is crazy enough to come here. Trevor squeezes my hand reassuringly as I attempt to explain my predicament to the receptionist, offering a silent prayer of thanks to my colleague Nicola, who gave me the Turkish phrasebook as a going away present. I mangle the phrase *'Dolgum düştü'* (I've lost a filling), wishing the book had the Turkish for 'Can you please recommend somewhere else?', and the receptionist gestures for me to sit and wait. I can feel the cold metal through my cargo pants as I perch on the edge of the chair, listening tensely for any muffled cries of pain emanating from behind the closed door to the surgery. Everything is silent except for the soft rustle of papers at reception.

Suddenly the door opens and a swarthy man with heavy black eyebrows, who looks like he's stepped straight off a 'Turkey's Most Wanted' poster, strides out into the waiting room. He has a quick chat with one of the women on reception, then looks in my direction and says 'You next' in a guttural growl. Without looking to see if I am following he disappears back into the surgery. As I stand up and walk reluctantly towards the half-open door, Trevor gets up to join me.

'I'm coming in with you,' he says.

I try to convince him that watching me undergo dental surgery isn't a good idea, but he won't be swayed. Inside, Trevor sits on a stool and I slide onto an ancient dentist's chair with vinyl upholstery so old it crackles when I sit down. Then I look around. There are no calming fish tanks or jaunty posters of happy teeth and smiling toothbrushes – it is spartan in the extreme. The off-white walls look like they've been stained with pollution and cigarette smoke and a wide yellowy-brown mark forms a ragged band near the ceiling like the tide mark left behind by falling floodwaters.

I look up at the dentist nervously as he motions for me to lie back and open my mouth. His white coat is fraying at the collar and a black mole with two strands of long curly hair growing out of it lurks just under his left nostril. The stale, slightly rancid odour of smoker's breath hovers above me as I watch his hand reaching towards a nearby trolley. Trevor and I notice what is on it at the same time and with eyes like saucers we stare at the contents of the metal tray. The neatly arranged instruments are so old that their once shiny exteriors are a worn tarnished silver and they look like they've been stolen from a museum. I am wondering if they've been sterilised when the dentist picks up a spray bottle and gives the long silver torture device he is about to put into my mouth a perfunctory spritz with what smells like Dettol. He might as well have wiped it on the sleeve of his jacket. Trevor's face is the same colour as the surgery walls as the dentist begins probing with zealous enthusiasm. Each time the metal touches the area near my broken tooth, I grab the edge of the chair so hard my knuckles turn white.

Having the filling replaced turns out to be a fairly major procedure. This is no surprise as I can still recall how long it took when I first had it done, but reliving the experience in Istanbul is even more memorable. I really wish Trevor had stayed outside. Although I can't turn my head, I can see him out of the corner of my eye and he is beginning to look extremely ill. In addition to worrying about the assortment of diseases I am probably being exposed to, it looks like I am going to have to scrape my husband off the floor too.

When something that sounds suspiciously like a 50 cc motorbike begins chugging away under my chair, I don't know what it is powering until the dentist re-emerges brandishing a clunky drill. I try not to think about where else it might have been as he puts it in my mouth and begins grinding away the rough edges of my broken tooth. When I let out a strangled squeal, the dentist stops and looks at me with kindly concern.

'Pain?'

I nod but as he reaches down to pick something up Trevor leaps out of his chair and shouts 'No!'. The dentist almost drops the large needle in surprise and turns to me for guidance, but I suddenly decide it isn't hurting quite so much anymore. There is no way that needle, with its crusty handle and spray-on antiseptic, is going anywhere near my mouth. I shake my head and smile weakly before pointing back to my mouth and motioning for him to keep going. He finally agrees, but only after shooting Trevor a malevolent glare and getting him to move his chair as far away as possible. Three-quarters of an hour has passed from the time I sat in the chair until the time we pay the bill and leave. The dentist did all he could to be gentle, but the nerves in my jaw are jangling as we walk down the stairs and back onto the street. What cost nearly $300 in Australia has come to less than $40 at a private dental hospital in Istanbul – which just goes to show you get what you pay for.

'Glad that's over,' Trevor says fervently.

I couldn't agree more. My mouth is hurting and Trevor's face is still a pasty white, but we are keen to put the dentist's visit behind us and get out and see the sights. I pop some pain killers and we head off to explore the city.

But over the next four days, something happens which I never would have thought possible: Trevor and I find we are missing our previous destination. Not the dusty streets or the dubious food, but Syria's people, who made our stay memorable for all the right reasons. Istanbul's locals have none of their innocence or guile-less charm and we discover Turkey has enthusiastically embraced the opportunity to make a buck from the tourists.

Although I can empathise with the shopkeepers who stand outside all day trying to tempt passers-by to come in for a cup of apple tea and a sales pitch, we still get tired of being hassled. Occasionally it's funny – how can I resist the line 'Is it my carpet's turn yet?' – but I am less comfortable with the more underhanded tactics. The 'friendly locals' who fall into step beside us and begin chatting, invariably suggest we pop into their shop, which we always just happen to be walking past. It is very unlike the genuine hospitality we experienced in Syria and I hope our three-night cruise will show us a different side of Turkey.

The phrase 'cruising up the Turkish coast' sounds akin to our glamorous speedboat trip in Venice, but the boats known as *gûlets* are more popular with backpackers than wealthy travellers. The wooden yachts usually have six small double cabins with showers and toilets and food is included in the cost of the cruise. While we are in Istanbul, we get a last-minute deal on a cruise that visits the seaside towns running along the bottom of Turkey's coastline. The boat is leaving from Kale, so we take a bus down the coast, stopping to spend some time in a small harbour town along the way.

On the day of the cruise we arrive at a small marina where two yachts are bobbing in the bright blue sea. One is a black-hulled beauty with royal blue tarpaulins strung invitingly over matching mattresses laid out on a polished wooden deck; the other is a battered old hulk that looks like it is about to sink. To my delight, it is the first boat, not the second, which turns out to be ours. We are first on board and, after exchanging a few jokes with the Australian cook, Sharon, we sit back to watch our fellow cruisers arrive.

When a Dutch couple turn up with their two little boys just after we do, Trevor and I resign ourselves to doing the cruise with a couple of kids – something we aren't overjoyed about. Ina and Jeroen seem nice but we have visions of their no doubt hyperactive boys running riot for the next three days. We chat to the parents before walking over to check out 'the enemy', who appear remarkably subdued for kids under ten. I decide they must be saving their energy for maximum effect once we set sail, and am so preoccupied with the children that I don't notice someone else has boarded until he is standing right in front of us.

'Hi, I'm Rick.'

Trevor introduces us and asks Rick what part of Canada he is from: Rick's accent is so strong, there is no need to ask where home is. He is softly spoken and comes across as a bit of a sensitive-new-age-guy, especially with the ponytail he is sporting. Turkey is his last stop on a six-week holiday and he isn't keen on returning to Canada's cold temperatures.

Next come Gabrielle and Marie, two students from Paris, who are at least ten years younger than us. They stop by to say hello before going off to dump their bags.

An Australian called Dave ambles up the gangplank about ten minutes later, offering a casual 'G'day everyone' before slipping his powerful frame as quietly as possible into a corner. Dave's shyness is at odds with his imposing appearance – he stares down at his hands and can hardly get a word out when the pretty French girls start talking to him – but it doesn't take him long to loosen up. I overhear him explaining he flew to London for a wedding and decided to visit Turkey on his way back home.

When the last two cruisers get on board, I wish we'd sailed off without them. Jon ('without the "h"' he informed everyone) has a grating American accent and gives a contrived little wink whenever he introduces himself. I am embarrassed to discover that Fabio, his opinionated travelling buddy, is from Australia. Okay, so the guy's name isn't really Fabio, but it should be. He tosses his mane of glossy black hair like a vain teenage girl and struts up the gangplank like the love god he obviously thinks he is. As soon as he's made it on board, Fabio strips off his t-shirt and flexes his (tiny) biceps. I can hear Ina and Jeroen trying not to laugh.

'I know where I'm sitting,' he says to Jon, and swaggers over to the French girls without giving the rest of us a second glance.

Jon goes to join him, but only after handing his bag to Sharon. 'Will you see this goes to my cabin, love?' he says and walks off. Sharon looks like she's thinking about throwing Jon's bag overboard.

As Fabio and Jon treat everyone to their frequently ill-informed opinions on Turkish culture – they think everyone drinks apple tea because it is an aphrodisiac – Trevor shoots me a knowing glance. It's no secret I've been looking forward to this cruise since before we left Australia. My daydreams about cleaving through azure waters on a glamorous yacht were so vivid I'd forget the wind in my hair was from the erratic air-conditioning vent above my desk rather than a stiff ocean breeze.

As we motor out of the harbour, Sharon joins us on the top deck. Everyone else is stumbling about like drunks, but she clambers over the mattresses with the ease of an experienced sailor and sits down beside me. The wrinkles around the corners of her eyes deepen whenever she smiles and her dark brown skin has a leathery texture which speaks of hours in the sun. This is Sharon's fourth season working on the *gûlet* charters and, during the course of the cruise, we discover her 'work uniform' consists of a variety of bikinis with a singlet worn over the top, plus two pairs of Billabong board shorts that she rotates each day. Sharon has a sunny personality but she strikes me as someone who is searching for something and I often notice her staring out to sea with a melancholy expression that she banishes when someone approaches.

Once we leave the shelter of Kale's harbour, Seval, the young Turkish deck hand who has a ready smile but doesn't speak much English, picks his way around the lounging passengers and unfurls the yacht's large white sails. They billow in the stiff breeze as the yacht turns so we are sailing parallel to the Turkish coast. Despite the heat of the day, a cool wind whips my hair into a wild bird's nest, and I can see low mountains covered in shrubby vegetation on one side and open sea on the other. The water and sky are impossibly blue and the scenery reminds me of Croatia.

Everyone is lying on the mattresses up on deck, except for Jeroen and Ina's boys, who are sitting in the downstairs dining area quietly playing chess. They appear to be the only single males who aren't trying to seduce Marie and Gabrielle, except for Dave, who is sitting at the front of the boat reading.

The other guys are busy with their own unique approaches to 'getting the girl'. Jon is doing his best to be funny, but reminds me of a try-hard comedian bombing out in front of a live audience, and Fabio is playing the suave man-about-town, while taking every opportunity to subtly ridicule his mate's efforts.

Rick's approach seems to be getting the best response, although he is probably laying the sensitive-new-age-guy thing on a bit thick. Gabrielle and Marie look uncomfortable about the attention they are attracting and eventually excuse themselves to go downstairs. I feel a bit sorry for them – it doesn't look like their cruise is going to be very relaxing.

We drop anchor for the night at a secluded cove near Üçağiz, a small fishing village. Everyone strips off their clothes to reveal bikinis and boardshorts and jumps off the edge of the boat into the clear blue water. The coast-line shimmers in the distance as we swim out into deeper water, splashing, diving and laughing with the sheer delight of such a perfect afternoon. We stay in the water until the sun sinks towards the horizon and people gradually begin clambering up the ladder on the side of the boat. We take turns standing under the deck-mounted hose to wash off the salty water before going down to our cabins for proper showers.

The cabins are too hot and stuffy to sleep in, but they are fitted out with ensuites and clever areas to stow luggage. When I see myself reflected in the bathroom mirror, it is like looking at a stranger. After four months of travelling, my hair resembles straw-coloured raffia and my previously pale skin is a deep honey brown. I've never seen myself with such a deep tan before and find it alters the planes of my face, making me look fitter and younger than I am. My eyes are bright and the worry lines that usually radiate from their edges are all but gone. I give the girl in the mirror one last glance before joining Trevor upstairs where Sharon is squeezed into the galley preparing a meal for 15 people in an area the size of a five-star hotel's wardrobe.

A huge pot of vegetarian casserole bubbles on the stove and she is chopping up mountains of tomatoes, zucchini and eggplant to stir through a wild rice mixture. I think the ocean is incredibly calm but, as I walk through the small dining area, it looks like Dave disagrees. He is sitting just outside the door on a box of lifejackets, his face an alarming greenish-grey. I don't even get time to say hello before he springs up like a jack-in-the-box and races back down to his cabin.

After dinner, the crew are kept busy getting things prepared for the next day, but the rest of us sit up on deck drinking and talking. Every time I look at Jon and Fabio, I am reminded of two sheepdogs. They've herded Gabrielle and Marie into a corner of the deck where they are trying their hardest to impress the girls. Fabio's tone of voice hints at manly tales of derring-do in the wilds of Australia and he is carrying on like a weedy Steve Irwin. When we notice Ina and Jeroen smirking at what is going on, Trevor and I go over to join them.

'I think your boys are the best behaved on the boat,' I tell them.

Ina laughs so hard that Rick looks up from writing his postcards to see what she's found so funny. When Fabio disappears into the kitchen to get another beer, we go to the two French girls' rescue. Unlike Jon, they look very glad to see us and we discover Marie and Gabrielle are both in their final year of law at the Sorbonne. They're certainly smart: I notice they have set up their beds for the night next to the children.

The distant thump of bass floating across the water from an on-shore disco lures Jon and Fabio away for a night of dancing to bad 1980s music, but the rest of us are content to enjoy the relative peace of our surroundings.

Trevor and I lie on our mattresses and stare up at the

sky. The prospect of sleeping on thin mattresses out in the elements would horrify us back in Australia but at this moment I can't think of anywhere I'd rather be – not even a five-star hotel. The air is warm and we've chosen a spot near the mast which extends for what seems like miles up into the sky. The boat's gentle swaying makes it look like a pendulum keeping a silent beat for the thousands of stars above us. One large star, brighter than all the rest, is hidden as the boat bobs to the left, only to re-emerge coyly from behind the mast when the boat moves back the other way. I have no idea which one it is as I am completely lost when it comes to the constellations of the Northern Hemisphere and as we drift off to sleep, I remind myself to ask one of the other travellers about it the following night.

The next morning we all awake to the rising sun. Gabrielle and Marie have already changed into their bikinis and are relaxing near the bow and everyone else starts packing up their bedding. In less than half an hour, the top deck has been cleared and is occupied by Jon, Fabio and Rick, who are wearing their best board-shorts and getting ready to put on a show. Ina gives me a conspiratorial glance as Jon's loud American twang floats towards us.

'Well, guys, 50 is no problem for me.'

If he is talking IQ points, I suspect Jon is being rather generous. He is keen to continue boasting about his physical prowess but Fabio drops to the deck and begins doing push-ups like a man possessed. Pity he ruins the effect by panting like a porn star after he's done less than ten. Jon crouches down to join him and Rick looks on with a slightly embarrassed expression before sinking reluctantly to the deck on his hands and knees. After the push-ups, they take a few moments to catch their breath before switching to sit ups, pausing occasionally to check if Marie and Gabrielle are watching. They are – but with amusement rather than awe.

Dave – the quiet achiever – walks over and starts talking to the girls instead. As the other lads pump and preen, we can hear Gabrielle and Marie laughing.

After breakfast, we continue sailing towards the seaside town of Kaş as more towns appear along the coastline. Some are small seaside resorts with people and beach umbrellas covering the pebbly shore, but the volcanic coastline is back by the time we approach our destination. There are quite a few tourists in town, but their numbers are matched by locals who also appear content to while away time in the teahouses and cafés surrounding the central square. We decide to join them and stop for a cup of coffee and a small sticky biscuit. Most of the tiny stores surrounding the square are devoted to souvenirs, but it is easy to imagine what Kaş used to be like, with fresh produce and hand-baked breads taking the place of overpriced sarongs. Retaining a town's charm and making money is a delicate balancing act and so far Kaş is succeeding, although I suspect the tourist shops' inflatable crocodile li-los are hatching a plot to take over the town in the next year or so.

When we get back on board, Sharon says we'll be able to get to our next destination under sail thanks to the stiff breeze that has picked up while we've been exploring Kaş. Seval unfurls the sails and Sharon comes to sit with us on the blue banquettes at the rear of the boat.

The captain steers out of the harbour and into open water as Seval raises the bright blue spinnaker and the yacht springs forwards like a headstrong racehorse. Fat white clouds float in the sky and the coastline is populated by villages with buildings rambling down gentle hills towards the sea. This cruise is turning out to be everything I hoped for and more, and we sit back to soak up the sun.

'Do you ever get tired of seeing the same section of coastline again and again?' Trevor asks Sharon.

'I guess it's like asking someone if they get sick of seeing the same thing out their office window – it's just part of coming to work,' she says, flicking a strand of blonde hair out of her eyes. 'Although this is probably much better than what your average office worker looks at every day.'

I can vouch for that. The pigeon-poo-streaked walls of the buildings surrounding my office in Brisbane don't even come close to the Turkish coastline, with its small beaches and sharp cliffs plunging into the sea. I can imagine how jealous Sharon's Australian friends are of what they perceive her life to be, but there's no way I'd swap jobs with her. Despite the lousy view, at least I get to go home at the end of each day. Sharon works 24/7 in cramped conditions and is frequently surrounded by people she wouldn't normally choose to keep company with. When I ask if she plans to do another season on the boats, Sharon shrugs and gives me a crooked smile.

'Maybe – if something better doesn't turn up. I'm still waiting for Prince Charming to come walking up the gangplank, but he's taking his time.'

The last day of the cruise is spent sailing and watching the lads make their final plays for Gabrielle and Marie's affections. We're dying to know if any of them has been successful but, despite Trevor's pleading, I can't bring myself to ask the girls something so personal. The question remains unanswered until later that evening, after we've docked at Fethiye, our final destination. From our hotel window I spy two familiar people walking into town. There is no sign of Gabrielle, but Dave has his arm looped around Marie's shoulders – something both of them look very happy about. Jon and Fabio's flashy approach was designed for maximum effect, but it was the quiet achiever who ultimately got the girl.

'I told you Marie was smart,' Trevor says with a smile.

The cruise has been even better than we'd expected, but we are glad it's over. We've become so accustomed to only having each other for company that being surrounded by other people in such a confined space felt a little overwhelming. I enjoyed their company but by the end of the cruise I felt like retreating to my cabin for a bit of time out.

We stay in Fethiye for two days before making our way back to Istanbul in time for our flight to Hong Kong. Istanbul is fascinating and I enjoyed the cruise, but Turkey hasn't captured me the way I anticipated. In hindsight, our expectations were probably unrealistic. I had spent plenty of time daydreaming about charming locals, lively bazaars and bright blue seas while conveniently sidestepping the cold, hard facts. Turkey is a relatively poor country relying on tourism to survive and it has been doing so for some time. I should have realised it wasn't going to be the unspoiled Middle Eastern destination the glossy travel brochures promised.

I know from prior experience that our time in Turkey will take on a rosy glow once Trevor and I get home and things that annoyed us will turn into funny stories we enjoy remembering and retelling. I've even begun to see the humorous side of my visit to the dentist – although I'm not keen to repeat the experience any time soon.

14

TYPHOONS AND TELESCOPES

STANDING UNDER THE bus shelter across the road from the Peninsula Hotel, Trevor and I look hopefully up at the sky, wondering if the driving rain is going to ease off long enough for us to make it to the hotel's front door. We wait a few minutes but the rain seems to be getting harder, so Trevor dashes out, pushes the button to activate the 'walk' signal and runs back to join me. When the little green man flashes up, we stumble across the road, past a fleet of Rolls-Royces angle-parked in a gleaming row and through the Peninsula's front doors.

Not counting the eight hours we spent trying to sleep on a bench at Hong Kong's Kai Tak Airport a few years ago, this is the first time Trevor or I have been to Asia. Though it's much closer to Australia than all the European destinations we've been to, we wanted to see places like France, Hungary and the Czech Republic more. Asian destinations, with their similar climate to Australia and close proximity, haven't held the same exotic allure.

Our visit to Hong Kong will be brief but we'll be spending the three nights at one of our most anticipated prize hotels – the Peninsula. All the articles I've read have extolled the virtues of the Peninsula's impeccable service and luxurious rooms decked out with gadgets like remote-controlled curtains. The Peninsula is just across the road from Victoria Harbour and everything about it, from the pale stone façade to the polished brass door handles, oozes class.

I expected a lobby dripping with rich Chinese reds and golds but in fact it's as English as the Dorchester, with delicate cornices and a colour scheme of creams and browns. It isn't hard to believe that Hong Kong was a British colony until it was handed back to the Chinese in the late 1990s. Elegant ladies clink fine bone-china cups as they enjoy high tea in the lobby lounge and the muted hush of conversation fills the air with genteel background noise. We take a few moments to straighten ourselves up and walk across the lobby towards reception.

The Peninsula really is no ordinary hotel and none of the usual formalities of checking in apply here. A charming young receptionist walks out from behind the desk to greet us, holding a smart black leather folder prepared in advance of our arrival. A porter spirits our bags away and we are led past a towering arrangement of orchids and into a lift. When we get out, we are standing before a door bearing an ornate plaque with the words 'Silver Glitter Suite'. The name sounds beautiful and exotic, but it is nothing compared to the room itself. Our suite is similar in size to our room at the Dorchester, but there is one major difference – it wraps around the end of the hotel and offers a 180-degree view of Victoria Harbour. I shudder to think how much it would cost if we were paying for it.

The receptionist shows us around, before sitting us down and checking us in. We've just finalised the paperwork when there is a knock on the door. A woman in a tailored uniform enters our suite and introduces herself as the floor hostess, graciously offering her services should we require anything from housekeeping. Not long afterwards, a young valet knocks on the door and bows deeply before also offering his assistance.

I assume the procession of staff has come to an end, but a young man in a white uniform with a high collar enters next, carrying a traditional Chinese tea set on a lacquer tray, which he places on the table in front of us. With a nod to his colleague and a small bow to us, he disappears as silently as he arrived.

'Would you care for some tea?' the receptionist asks, reaching for the fine china pot.

Trevor and I nod, but I am finding it hard to tear my eyes away from the view outside. I've never seen so many buildings crammed into such a small area. She pours two cups of tea and stands up, presenting one to each of us with a small bow.

'Welcome to the Peninsula Hotel. We hope you have a wonderful and memorable stay.' And with that, she leaves.

Now I understand what all the articles were raving about. The formality of the tea ritual and the seamlessness of the check-in process were flawless. Out of all the hotels we've visited so far, this is the first time we've experienced such polished service.

We finish our tea and go for another walk through the suite. A silver bowl filled with exotic Asian fruits sits in the centre of the dining table, accompanied by a glossy brochure with exquisite botanical sketches and a detailed description of each fruit's taste and texture. Two white plates, linen napkins and small silver paring knives have been placed beside the bowl.

The bedroom has a king-sized bed with a shining gold coverlet, red and gold silk cushions and heavy floor to ceiling curtains – plus something else that we would never have expected: a fully operational telescope on a wooden stand is set up in the corner of the room.

Trevor stops to check it out while I continue through a dressing area which is the size of a standard bedroom and into the bathroom which has wrap around windows with venetian blinds that can be raised and lowered with the touch of a button. All the controls are waterproof and within easy reach of the two-person spa bath. I spend a pathetically enjoyable few minutes playing with the blinds, making the bedroom curtains open and close and turning the lights on and off. I don't think things can get much better until I see our bathroom goodies.

Instead of the usual cake of soap sitting on the side of

the bathtub, there is a blue box from Tiffany's. It contains a felt pouch holding a pure white cake of soap with the store's name embossed on one side. I pick it up and cradle the box lovingly in my hands, unable to believe it is mine to keep. How could someone actually use it? The rest of the soaps are fancy too – each cake is wrapped in crinkly paper and presented in a dark green oval tin with 'The Peninsula' written on the lid in gold letters – but they pale in comparison to my precious blue box. The Tiffany soap is a one-off, but each time we souvenir a tin, another appears magically in its place.

Less welcome is the laminated piece of A4 paper we find placed neatly in the centre of the dining table.

'I've just discovered why it's raining so hard,' Trevor says, handing it to me. The notice advises that a typhoon is heading for Hong Kong, although at this stage it is only a Category One, which means lots of rain and wind. Trevor returns to his telescope and I go into the bathroom where I fill the enormous tub and sink into it before pressing the button to raise the venetian blinds. Victoria Harbour is huge – much larger than I expected – and seems to have ten times more boats than Sydney Harbour. Traditional Chinese junks share the water with large passenger ferries and container ships, and miscellaneous other craft lumber backwards and forwards between them. I even see a submarine on its way out to sea. The harbour looks so crowded and dis-organised I can't believe the boats aren't smashing into one other. I watch them zipping around until the bubbles in the tub dissipate and the water is cold, then, wrapped in a fluffy bathrobe, I walk into the bedroom to discover Trevor still standing at the telescope.

'This is amazing,' he says, looking down towards the harbour. 'It feels like I'm right there!'

And that is the problem with staying at the Peninsula. We love our accommodation so much that we hardly leave the hotel and aside from one brief look around the streets, we are content to view Hong Kong from afar. We could blame it on the typhoon but I think the same thing would have happened if it had been sunny. We have spent so many months moving from place to place that the opportunity to simply stay put is irresistible. I know we are missing out on the chance to experience the people, the culture and the excitement of the city – for our first trip to Asia, we aren't seeing much of it – but we succumb to travel fatigue without putting up a fight.

I'd be appalled if someone else told me they'd gone to Hong Kong and hardly left the hotel and, during the four days we are at the Peninsula, Trevor and I do feel a bit guilty about what we're doing – but it isn't enough to tear us away from the Silver Glitter Suite. At the beginning of the trip it felt like our holiday would last forever, but now the end is not only in sight, but getting closer every day. Very soon the luxurious life we've been leading will be nothing but a memory and we are desperate to squeeze every ounce of enjoyment out of our last few hotels.

It is because of this that we decide to treat ourselves

to a Chinese meal from Spring Moon – one of the Peninsula's renowned restaurants. The food is expensive but it arrives on a white-cloth-covered trolley that has been set up like a formal dining table which two staff members wheel into the suite and set up by the window. We look out at high-rise buildings covered in so many lights that their reflections in the harbour make it look like a shimmering Impressionist painting. The area across from our hotel seems like the central business district of any large city during the day, but at night the skyline transforms into a glittering curtain.

The staff drape fine napkins over our laps and pour our supermarket wine without batting an eyelid. Having room service delivered feels like the ultimate indulgence and I am cursing the fact that we didn't do something similar at our earlier five-star hotels until I remember we would have been too uptight to enjoy it. Much to our surprise, we feel completely comfortable being served so formally when we are wearing bathrobes and matching Peninsula slippers. It is amazing how much we've changed since the beginning of our trip. Back then, we were permanently ill at ease and so obsessed with trying not to stand out that it probably had the opposite effect, but now we are having a ball.

After ensuring everything is to our liking, the young men bow in perfect unison and slip out the door, closing it behind them so the latch engages with a gentle click. This meal is nothing like the thickly battered sweet and sour pork from the local takeaway that I ate as a child when Mum and Dad ordered their 'Shandy Special' every Friday night. What essentially read as 'chicken with ginger and shallots' on the menu is one of the best things I've ever tasted and when the staff return to remove the plates there isn't a scrap of food left.

Despite the fact we hardly leave the hotel, time goes surprisingly quickly, passing in a haze of bubble baths, gazing through the telescope in our bedroom and swimming at the Peninsula's pool, where staff bring us tumblers of lemon-flavoured ice water on small silver trays. The pool is in the perfect spot on a covered outdoor terrace overlooking the harbour and has been enclosed by folding glass walls due to the typhoon. Trevor and I watch the rain pouring down them as we swim.

In the past I've never understood how people can treat a hotel as a destination in itself and hardly step outside, but winning this prize has opened my mind to the pleasures that places like the Leading Hotels of the World can bring. I wouldn't want this type of holiday all the time, but I can see its appeal. Getting out on the streets and exploring a destination was once our only aim, but we now understand there is nothing wrong with sitting back and soaking up the uniqueness of *any* special place – even if it happens to be a luxurious hotel.

When Trevor and I check out of the Peninsula, we feel rested and refreshed and more than ready to continue with our adventure, although the typhoon looks like it is planning to hang around. It is raining so heavily that the

Rolls-Royces in the driveway are almost completely obscured from view, making me wish we were taking one of them to the airport instead of the bus. Just as we are preparing to walk outside and get soaked, one of the staff from the foyer approaches.

'Sir, madam – please, where are you going in this rain?'

When we tell him, he is aghast and insists someone will be along to help us at once. Less than a minute later, a bellboy with a luggage trolley and three umbrellas appears and loads up our bags before walking us to the rear entrance of the hotel and handing us an umbrella each. Once he is sure we will remain dry and comfortable, he takes the last umbrella and manages to shield both himself and our bags as we begin our slow trundle to the bus stop. Trevor and I have dressed with comfort in mind for our flight to Thailand – which means we look about as glamorous as two sacks of potatoes – yet we are walking up the street accompanied by a shiny gold luggage trolley and a bellboy from the Peninsula. People step aside as we swan past, glancing at us with bemused expressions as Trevor and I amble along behind our luggage. When we finally reach the bus stop, the people already waiting there gawk as we hand back the umbrellas to the bellboy, who bows deeply before wheeling the empty trolley back towards the hotel.

I feel like I'm in a bizarre dream, although I am brought back to reality with a resounding thud when the bus arrives. It is packed and we are forced to hang on to whatever we can get our hands on so we don't tumble over during the two-hour trip to the airport. The rain plays havoc with the peak-hour traffic and by the time we arrive at the check-in counter, sweaty, anxious and late, the luxury of the Peninsula seems a million miles away.

15

SATIN ELEPHANTS

AFTER COMING TO terms with Syria's dirty streets and shopping at its souks, with their raw meat and strange smells, Bangkok doesn't provide the culture shock we've been anticipating. The Thai capital's confusing signage and chaotic markets are nothing compared to what we experienced in Syria. Our time there toughened me up and in a classic case of 'absence makes the heart grow fonder', Trevor and I are only just beginning to appreciate the time we spent there now that it is behind us.

After Syria, the cacophony of beeping horns and the crush of people on Bangkok's streets doesn't faze us, although we marvel at the strange mixture of expensive fashion boutiques and food stalls set up shanty-like on every corner. Hot, spicy smells rise out of their simmering pots of noodles while glamorous Thai women wearing impossibly high heels walk past us, chatting on their mobile phones.

For a change of pace, we visit historical sites like the

Royal Palace, which has been Thailand's religious centre since the early 1700s.

Each Thai king was permitted to add buildings in his own preferred style – be it Western, Chinese or Thai – so now, after more than two centuries, the Grand Palace had been transformed into an eclectic collection of magnificent buildings surrounded by statues of monkey-gods and demon-guards made from gold inlay, glass mosaics and porcelain tiles. Hundreds of them shimmer in the humid air as they stand to attention outside the different temples and watch the passers-by.

We explore a different part of Bangkok every day, before returning to our hotel, the Sukhothai, which is a haven of silk, granite and teak with acres of landscaped gardens. Instead of the ubiquitous chocolate, a small satin elephant appears on our pillows every night – yet one more thing for me to attempt to cram into my bag. I have no idea what I'll do with all of these things when we get home, but the Sukhothai's brochures, match-books and pretty soaps somehow seem too special to leave behind. The closer we come to the end of the trip, the more obsessed I become with collecting them.

It is as if I've decided that gathering tangible evidence of what we've done, where we've been and what we've experienced, will help me hang onto the magic of it once we get home. I know our memories of the four days we spend in Bangkok, haggling at local markets and dicing with death every time we cross the busy roads, will remain, regardless of whether I take that extra miniature bottle of shampoo or not, but it doesn't stop me squirrelling things away. By the time we take the shuttle bus to our second-last prize hotel, the Dusit Resort and Polo Club at Hua Hin, a small coastal town three hours drive south of Thailand's capital, I've had to buy an extra bag from one of Bangkok's markets to carry it all.

Trevor and I have started trying to convince ourselves we are ready to go home, but so far we aren't having much success. Although I can feel faint stirrings of excitement at the prospect of seeing our friends and families again, they are being overshadowed by thoughts of the everyday drudgery that awaits on our return to Australia. When it comes to housework, I haven't done much more than wipe down a bench in the past five months and that was with a towel I knew the maid would replace with a clean one the moment my back was turned.

There is no comparison to sitting on a sun-kissed balcony, looking out at the Gulf of Siam and watching Thai children playing in the Dusit's pool. It is the size of a football field and surrounded by towering frangipanis which drop their fragrant flowers into the water. This prize hotel is very different from the others we've stayed in because even though it is a Leading Hotel of the World, the room rates are surprisingly affordable. This makes it just as popular with the locals as it is for overseas guests, and while our room is fairly basic, the staff are delightful and we never want for anything.

We were initially unsure whether to put the Asian hotels at the beginning or the end of our trip, but I am glad we left them until last. By the Dusit Resort and Polo Club (which, for some reason, doesn't have anywhere to play polo), we are so relaxed we don't do much more than lie around the pool and choose which restaurant to dine at each night.

Being relaxed has changed both of us for the better and I find it hard to remember why some things once seemed so important. The time I wasted scrubbing the underarms of t-shirts with tiny guest soaps could have been better spent soaking up the sights, smells and sounds of the world outside. How could I have thought that having a backpack full of clean clothes was more important than listening to an Argentinean busker singing love songs or watching kamikaze pigeons divebomb hapless tourists in St Mark's Square? Over the past four months, I've come to understand the importance of taking time to appreciate the wonders of everyday life. I hope I'll remember this when we get home.

Our stay at Hua Hin coincides with a Thai long weekend and the Dusit is filled with family groups enjoying the resort's facilities. Slick, wet little bodies with skin the colour of strong milky coffee run between the pool and its surrounding deckchairs, laughing and shouting with excitement. One thing has remained constant throughout our trip: no matter where we have been – a Parisian park, the Sydney Harbour foreshore or a dusty village in the Middle East – the interaction between children and their parents is the same. The parents protest they want to be left in peace, but invariably get caught up in their children's enthusiasm for whatever new and exciting wonder they've discovered. Over the next four days, in between lying by the pool and eating far too much Thai food, I watch families interacting and feel my yearning to be back home slowly grow stronger.

After taking the shuttle bus back to Bangkok, Trevor and I fly to Hong Kong, where we've booked one night at an airport hotel in preparation for the next day's flight to Denpasar in Bali. We are so busy talking that we don't even notice the airline employee until he begins speaking.

'Are you still waiting for luggage?' he asks.

'Just my wife's bag – it looks exactly like this one,' Trevor says, indicating his backpack sitting on our trolley. It is then that we notice there are hardly any suitcases left on the baggage carousel and mine isn't among them. So close to the end of the trip, my bag has gone missing, albeit only temporarily. The guy takes my ticket and baggage receipt and goes off to investigate, before returning to explain the situation.

'Your bag's still here in the airport, but they've taken it down to load on tomorrow's flight,' he tells me. 'It was checked right through by mistake.'

He explains my backpack will be delivered to the hotel as soon as possible, but this will probably take hours by the time it has been located, cleared customs and the relevant paperwork has been completed. Sure enough, it doesn't make an appearance until the early hours of the morning, although there is no danger of its arrival waking us up. Whoever built our hotel spent all their money making it look like a five-star paradise (with prices to match) and neglected to insulate the place against noise. The walls are so thin we are able to tell the person next door is a man by the sound of the seat being flicked up whenever he goes to the toilet. By the time we front up to check in for our flight to Denpasar, the inconvenience of the day before combined with a lack of sleep has made me decidedly cranky.

'I see there was a problem with your baggage yesterday,' the girl says, scanning her computer screen. 'It was returned?'

'Yes, although not until early this morning.'

I catch myself just before I launch into a full-scale whinge and muster a brave smile. 'It was difficult to manage without it, but everyone did their best to help.'

I'm desperate to vent my bad mood, but know it is unfair to take it out on the girl checking us in. It wouldn't achieve anything – unlike my polite response, which ends up achieving a lot. After tapping away at her keyboard, the woman looks up and smiles.

'On behalf of the airline, I'm deeply sorry for any inconvenience you may have suffered,' she says sincerely, handing over our boarding passes. 'I've upgraded you both to business class and hope you have an enjoyable flight.'

We stare in disbelief at the seat numbers on our passes – 1A and 1B – and thank her, just managing to stop ourselves before we say 'that really wasn't necessary'. What if she puts us back down in cattle class where we belong? As we prepare ourselves for five hours of French champagne and personalised service, Trevor looks over at me and smiles. Months ago, when we were sitting on our balcony at Iguazú Falls, Trevor said that sometimes he felt like pinching himself because he couldn't believe we were really experiencing all these amazing things. We clink glasses and exchange glances, knowing exactly what the other is thinking – what a perfect way to travel to our last five-star hotel of the trip.

I'm about to mention that I am a bit worried about our final hotel experience, but the mood doesn't seem right, so I keep it to myself. For the past few weeks, I've become increasingly concerned about the Oberoi Hotel on the island of Lombok. My fears have no real basis – I've heard nothing negative about it and the brochure looked lovely – but I am hoping desperately that this hotel will see us finishing our trip on a high. It would be a pity to have another lacklustre Cham Palace experience at our last prize hotel. We hold hands as the plane takes off, knowing our trip is nearly over and this time next week we'll be on our way back to Australia.

After so many economy class flights, what follows is such a revelation, I am (almost) glad we didn't get upgraded earlier in the trip. Until now, it has been a case of not missing what we've never had but Trevor and I discover the pointy end is a whole new world – and one we are desperate to return to. I'm not trying to be mean, but I do feel a bit smug watching everyone else walk through the business class section on their way to economy. I know exactly what they are in for and am ecstatic that, for once, the two of us aren't back there with them.

We are full of food and wine when we touch down in Denpasar and organising somewhere to stay seems far too boring to waste time worrying about. When I suggest one of the cheap places in our guidebook, Trevor nods enthusiastically and propels me towards the phone so we can make arrangements.

'Any old flea pit will do,' he says, with a bonhomie brought on by one too many champagnes. 'It's only for a night.'

16

BACK WHERE WE BELONG

THERE'S NOTHING LIKE a 'No Prostitutes in Rooms' sign above reception when it comes to giving a place that homey touch. Although it is a bit rundown, the hotel in Kuta doesn't look too bad from the outside. It doesn't look too good either – but we are still tipsy enough not to care. However, once I notice the sign and the guy mentions paying a deposit if we want to use the television's remote control, I feel a sense of unease and realise I must have been drunker than I thought when we made the booking. Why else would I have agreed to pay in advance? After walking down a cracked concrete path flanked by garden beds littered with empty beer bottles, it is no surprise to discover our room resembles a mildew-stained dosshouse. We could ask for another one, but something tells me they're all the same. I am glad we are spending less than 12 hours here, especially when the thin sliver of moonlight shining into the room reveals a long tail hanging out of the air-conditioner's filthy vent. I spend most of the night awake, anticipating the dull plop of well-fed rat landing on the bed and scuttling over my face on its way out the door.

When we arrive at the airport in the morning, I am still preoccupied with my concerns about our last five-star hotel, but they soon disappear once I catch sight of the plane. My worries about the hotel can wait – we have to make it there alive first. Trevor takes one look at the ancient aircraft waiting on the tarmac and grabs my arm.

'Please tell me that's not ours,' he says.

There is no point telling him the plane is fine, because even to my untrained eye it obviously isn't. What look like wide brown snail trails, either from oil leaks or rust (or both) run down the sides of the plane, which is in desperate need of a clean and a fresh coat of paint. As we walk towards it, I expect to see bright pink chewing gum holding on the wings.

'Don't worry – it's only a short flight,' is the best I can do.

As we walk up the rickety stairs and into the nicotine-stained cabin, I notice several other passengers looking around apprehensively and after Trevor and I take our seats – right near the emergency exit, much to his relief – we both reach straight for the safety cards and start reading.

'Put your head on your knees, brace for impact and repeat after me: "We're all going to die,"' Trevor says with a wry smile, replacing the card in the sagging vinyl pouch in front of his seat and reaching for his seatbelt.

His expression makes me think he's put his hand into something unspeakable. Has someone thrown up on the previous flight? No, but I think Trevor would prefer that to what he's just discovered – a seatbelt with a buckle straight out of the seventies and a strap so frayed there are more threads than belt. He looks around the plane, but the other seats are all taken and I only get halfway through my offer to swap before discovering my seatbelt is even worse. We buckle up regardless and focus our full attention on the safety demonstration. When the pretty Balinese hostess mentions where to find the lifejackets, we aren't the only ones who check discreetly to make sure they are there. As she finishes, the plane's engines splutter into action and we taxi to the end of the runway where things improve slightly. The ancient aircraft surges forwards with surprising speed and takes off towards Lombok, one of Indonesia's eastern islands off the coast of Bali.

Despite the fact it appears the airline can't afford to maintain the aircraft and it is only a 40-minute flight, we are still served a light meal. The hostess is almost running around the plane in her haste to meet the tight deadline and I bet we aren't the only passengers who would gladly exchange their neatly boxed snack for something more substantial in the seatbelt department.

'The plane may be a joke, but it's got a good pilot,' Trevor says after our impressively smooth landing. We collect our backpacks, and Trevor organises a taxi to take us to the Oberoi.

Lombok is a world away from the bars and tourist strip of Bali's Kuta. Not much is known about Lombok's history before the 17th century, and it still has the feeling of being untouched by modern civilisation. The taxi speeds through partially cleared farmland surrounded by leafy palm trees and dense tropical vegetation, and I can see cows grazing contentedly in people's front yards. Most of the houses are fibro and remind me of the holiday shacks my family rented at the beach when I was a child. They have the same ramshackle air and I remember charging up the stairs to tell Mum about the latest treasure I'd found on the beach. Lombok's children seem to be doing much the same thing. There is lots of squealing, shouting and laughter and each ragtag group looks up as the taxi passes, pausing to give us wide grins and friendly waves before returning to their game.

After winding through villages and jungle-covered hills, the taxi pulls up at the entrance to the Oberoi where a porter greets the driver by name and unloads our bags while Trevor and I walk into the foyer. So far it doesn't look like the resort is going to be a disappointment, although the mixture of traditional Balinese architecture and five-star opulence is a bit strange – the Oberoi has the first thatched hut I've ever seen with a marble floor. After checking in, we are escorted along frangipani-lined paths to our accommodation. The pungent flowers impregnate the air with a heady scent that screams 'tropical holiday'.

Although we've been told the resort is quite full, the only other people we see on the way to our accommodation are cleaning staff zooming along in golf buggies laden with mops, buckets and piles of fresh towels. Trevor and I are so busy returning their cheery greetings, we are taken by surprise when our host stops in front of a walled enclosure with a solid wooden gate. It is impossible to see inside until she flicks the latch and we walk into a shaded courtyard.

'This is your private villa,' she says.

It isn't just private – our accommodation is like a mini resort for two. Inside its high surrounding walls is a spacious terrace surrounded by immaculate garden beds filled with tropical plants and, as we come in the door, I notice a tiny rock pond with pink flowers nestling against fat lily pads. I can't believe I've wasted time worrying about whether the Oberoi would be a fitting end to our trip! At the back of the terrace is a raised dining pavilion that looks like something straight out of *Vogue* magazine, but we hardly give it a second glance. We only have eyes for what dominates the paved sandstone terrace – Trevor and I have our own, impressively large, private swimming pool.

'Just loop this over here,' our hostess says, indicating the handle of our wooden entry door and the intricately carved 'Do Not Disturb' sign she is holding, 'and no one will enter until it is removed.'

Visions of romantic midnight swims fill my head as we go inside to unpack. Our suite's cream soft furnishings contrast perfectly with the carved Balinese furniture and the four-poster bed is draped with swathes of fine muslin. In the bathroom, I place the rubber ducky I bought for Trevor earlier in the trip as a joke on the side of the sunken marble bathtub. The duck's chubby yellow body sticks out like a beacon. At the beginning of our trip I wouldn't have dared to sully the polished perfection of our suite with something so tacky, but a lot has changed since then.

Before Trevor and I left home, we imagined the five-star hotels would all be much the same, but we couldn't have been more mistaken. There are some similarities – king-sized beds are de rigueur and earthy naturals appear to be the colours of choice – but the different atmospheres really stand out. When some society princess was quoted as saying 'I'll *only* ever stay at such and such a hotel', I'd written it off as pretentious drivel but I now understand what she was talking about. Nearly all our prize hotels have been elegant, opulent and populated by endlessly polite, highly trained staff, but there are only a handful where I've felt truly at home. Earlier in the trip I put this down to feeling intimidated, but in hindsight this isn't entirely true: the difference has been the style of service.

I expected to relish the formal service at hotels like the Ritz but, in reality, it was often tedious and frustrating. Such fawning attention somehow never seemed sincere.

I much preferred the individual attention we experienced at some of the hotels. In Hua Hin, for example, our allocation of complimentary bottled water automatically increased when the housekeepers noticed we sometimes ran low and at the Windsor in Melbourne, Trevor got extra handmade chocolates on his pillow each night because one of the maids overheard him saying how much he liked them. These things, which were done especially for Trevor and me just to make us happy, meant far more than any amount of bowing and scraping.

During our trip, we've never failed to appreciate the beauty of our suites, the history of the hotels or their tradition of excellence, but I am happy we've experienced both types of hotel – the five-star and the most definitely *not* five-star – as what we've discovered has been a revelation. We've found out that what makes a hotel special to us isn't necessarily the luxury of our surroundings – it is the memories we take away at the end of our stay. While being ensconced in a magnificent room at a grand hotel can certainly up the odds of having a great time, it is by no means a guarantee.

At the Oberoi freshly picked tropical flowers are scattered around our room every day. The resort has a stunning view of the Gili Islands, just off the coast, and we can see their golden beaches flanked by large, green trees shimmering in the hot sun. Frangipani flowers bathe us in their sweet fragrance as we stretch out by the pool and gaze at the blue ocean. Trevor and I divide our time between the main swimming area, with its charming thatched huts with large cushions and fluffy beach towels, and our own private paradise. The only set part of our daily routine is turning up for the complimentary afternoon tea which is served in a pavilion adjacent to reception. People start milling around it just before 3 pm, with some couples going to great pains to pretend they just happen to be there – the equivalent of having 'new arrival' tattooed on your forehead. Guests who've been at the Oberoi for a few days walk confidently towards the low table laid with traditional teacups and white platters of dainty Indonesian pastries and help themselves.

The afternoon teas are a great opportunity to chat to the other guests, who are predominantly from Europe and the United Kingdom and each afternoon without fail, one of them asks why we are at the Oberoi. Is it a special occasion perhaps? I am glad we haven't been faced with this earlier in the trip, as the prospect of being 'found out' would have seen us grabbing something to eat and getting out of there as fast as possible. Back then, we would have been mortified to admit the truth, but these days we couldn't care less who finds out we are staying at the Oberoi for nothing.

After Trevor and I explain the story behind how we've come to be here, the conversation invariably turns to the rest of our trip. It is only in the retelling that we begin to realise the scale of what we've been doing. As we describe things like the view from our suite in New York, our escapades at Iguazú Falls, drinking champagne in the Peninsula's bathtub, watching fake volcanoes explode in Vegas, eating croissants at the Hôtel Ritz Paris and cruising on a Turkish yacht, I begin to understand that our prize, which was billed on the entry form as 'the trip of a lifetime', was exactly that. We've become so self-conscious about appearing like we are showing off that we tend to downplay what we've been up to, especially when there are people present who've heard it all before. One afternoon, one of the other guests decides to tell Trevor and me exactly what he thinks of us.

'That big prize and all the stuff you've done,' he begins, making us put down our teacups with an anxious clatter, 'should make me jealous as hell – and to tell you the truth, it does.'

I wish everyone hadn't decided to pick this exact moment to stop chatting. The pavilion seems oddly silent and I notice that Trevor has shifted his feet, ready to make a quick getaway if things start getting unpleasant.

'But you guys obviously had such a ball that I've got to say it couldn't have happened to a better couple.' He gives us a wide grin and pops another pastry into his mouth, completely oblivious to the anxiety he's just caused.

After a week of swimming, sunsets and lying by the pool, we allow ourselves one last luxurious treat. Trying not to think about how much it is costing, which is more than enough to undo any feelings of relaxation, we book into the Oberoi's health spa before our flight home. Traditional Balinese music plays softly in the background as we slip on frangipani-scented bathrobes and walk into an open-air massage pavilion. White walls prevent people from looking in and two tiny Balinese women stand side by side on a raised wooden platform, waiting patiently for us to walk up the marble stairs. Blue sky and palm trees peek through the gap between the pavilion's roof and the top of the wall and the women step aside in unison as we slip off our robes and lie face down on the massage tables.

Once they begin kneading our shoulders, there is no sound but the water splashing from a fountain and massage oils being rubbed into our skin. With so little to distract me, there is no escaping the reality that this time tomorrow, our trip will be over and we will be heading home.

Over the past few weeks, my longing to see friends and family again has been growing steadily every day until it has become so overpowering, I feel like the sheer force of it alone will propel me back to Australia. I am surprised to discover my excitement at seeing everyone is exactly the same as how I felt before we departed for the trip. How I've felt about things that happened during this trip has often come as a surprise as well. It is still hard to believe how emotional I became during our crazy Elvis wedding and what a profound experience it was to sip tea in a desert shack.

* * *

After leaving the Oberoi and surviving our return journey to Denpasar on Rustbucket Airlines, we board our second-last flight of the trip. Provided we don't think too much about returning to work, we are both happy to be going home. I love the spirit of adventure and not knowing what each day will bring while we are overseas, but I can also appreciate the comfortable routine of our everyday life. Going for coffee at our favourite café, cooking dinner together and being able to speak to friends whenever we like for the price of a local call are things I previously took for granted, but now I appreciate how important they are.

We are probably destined to be budget travellers for the rest of our lives, but Trevor and I still feel rich, albeit in a different way from regular guests at five-star hotels. We'll never have to worry if our friends like us for ourselves or our money and travelling will always be fun because it is a world away from our everyday life. After so many flights, we are content not to see the inside of another aeroplane for a month or two, but as the plane begins its descent into Darwin, we are already planning our next trip.

Just like on our flight over the Grand Canyon, Trevor leans over me to catch a glimpse of the vibrant blues and greens of the Australian coast, but this time I don't offer to give up my seat. Instead I look down and drink in the colours greedily. The plane touches down with a couple of skipping bumps.

'We're back,' Trevor says quietly.

Everything in the airport feels completely familiar yet foreign at the same time. The Australian twang of the immigration officer's accent is so pronounced it sounds like he is speaking a different language, scrubby Australian bush surrounds the runways and even the inside of the airport seems unusually bright and colourful. Perhaps it is just the comfort of the familiar, but being away from Australia always makes us appreciate the place even more when we return.

The physical and emotional challenges we faced on our journey allowed Trevor and me to experience things we'd never even contemplated and my eyes were opened to a world of possibilities. After riding the rapids at Iguazú and surviving my trip to the dentist in Istanbul, things which felt so daunting before we left home don't seem worth worrying about. Even how my career is progressing is no longer the huge concern it once was. Our trip has shown me that almost any obstacle can be overcome – including sneaking pizza into the Hôtel Ritz Paris – if you have the courage to try. Now we are back, I am determined to remain as open to new experiences as I was while we were away. The five-star hotels may have come to an end, but discovering new things about myself and the world around me doesn't have to stop just because we are home.

Our flight to Brisbane doesn't leave for another five hours so Trevor and I walk to the departure gate and choose a quiet corner near the rows of plastic seats.

I lie down, using my daypack as a pillow, slip on my eyemask, put in earplugs and curl up on the scratchy carpet for a couple of hours' sleep that couldn't be further removed from the relaxing slumber I've enjoyed in all the five-star hotels' king-sized beds.

We are definitely back where we belong.

ACKNOWLEDGEMENTS

Thanks to the following people for their invaluable support and assistance while I was writing this book: Faith Bradley, Jo Butler, Susan Currie, Jessica Dettmann, Karen Hudson, David Iliffe, Damian Kelleher, Jude McGee, Kirsten Moore, Jared Morgan, Leone Morgan, Barry O'Sullivan and Rob Wiggan.

Thanks also to Trevor Templeman – this wouldn't have happened without him.